Shooting Digital Video

DVCAM, Mini DV and DVCPRO

Also by the same author:

Arriflex 16SR Book (Focal Press)
Arriflex 35 Book (Focal Press)
Arriflex 16 SR3: The Book
Arriflex 435 Book
ARRI 16SR Book
ARRI 35 Book

Shooting Digital Video

DVCAM, Mini DV and DVCPRO

Jon Fauer, ASC

Focal Press

Boston Oxford Auckland Johannesburg Melbourne New Delhi

Focal Press is an imprint of Butterworth–Heinemann.

 A member of the Reed Elsevier group

 Recognizing the importance of preserving what has been written, Butterworth–Heinemann prints its books on acid-free paper whenever possible.

The publisher and author have made every effort to ensure the accuracy of all information in this book at the time of publication. But the sale, use or other handling of this book is without warranty or liability even if damage or loss is caused by technical misinformation, printing errors or other fault. There are no warranties, expressed or implied, in the use of this book. We encourage all users of the book to test and verify all technical information taken from this book prior to production.

ISBN: 0-240-80464-3

The publisher offers special discounts on bulk orders of this book.
For information, please contact:
Manager of Special Sales
Butterworth–Heinemann
225 Wildwood Avenue
Woburn, MA 01801-2041
Tel: 781-904-2500
Fax: 781-904-2620

For information on all Focal Press publications available, contact our World Wide Web home page at: http://www.focalpress.com

10 9 8 7 6 5 4 3 2 1

Printed in the United States of America

"When I started out as a cameraman in 1896 the Biograph camera weighed close to a ton. These were the days before movies were ready to be projected on the screen. They could be seen only when the viewer turned a crank and looked into a peep-show machine at the penny arcades."

G. W. Bitzer
Billy Bitzer, His Story
Farrar, Strauss and Giroux
1973

"A new machine is now ready to be exhibited to the public, which is probably the most remarkable and startling in its results of any that the world has ever seen.

Several marvels of inventive genius have, in past years, gone forth from the Edison Works, located at Orange, New Jersey.

"The Wizard of Menlo Park" has conceived and in due course perfected the Phonograph, the Kinetoscope and the Kinetophone, each of which in turn, has excited the wonder and amazement of the public and, from a practdical stand-point, opened up opportunities for exhibition enterprises, many of which are paying handsomely to this day."

—from the Vitascope Company's promotional brochure, 1897

"Everything must start with an idea. Ater the idea comes the plan, more or less complete but gradually perfected as the the work progresses. So with motion pictures; there must be an idea or plot for a film story, followed by a more or less complete set of plans for the actual production."

Austin C. Lescarboura
Behind the Motion Picture Screen
Scientific American Publishing Co.
1919

Table of Contents

How to Use a DV Camcorder

Appendix

Introduction to Digital Video

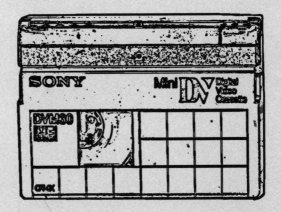

Introduction
to Digital
Video

Introduction

What's this? How could Jon Fauer be writing a book on video?

I shoot film for a living. Along the way, I have written a few books on cinematography and how to use professional motion picture cameras. So, imagine my surprise at being asked to write a book on digital video.

Most of my previous film books began by accident, as a self-help series of notes on how to use equipment that costs more than most houses, but comes with less instructional enlightenment than the average VCR. Digital video camcorders are certainly cheaper than houses and most film cameras. However, their instruction manuals are often just as baffling, and just as easy to lose.

"Shooting Digital Video" is something of a chronicle of my own indoctrination into the exciting, new format of DV. I hope it will be useful not only for beginners using it for the first time, but also for die-hard film fanatics like myself who would like to know what digital video is all about, how we can use it, how it compares with film, and where it's going to take us.

This book is a more deliberate attempt, instigated by the intrepid Marie Lee, editor of Focal Press, to reach a more diverse audience than just the ranks of professional cinematographers and their assistants, to include the whole panoply of potential shooters from amateurs to students, home users, prosumers, video professionals and even cinematographers like me who are making the first wobbly steps into terra incognita.

I began shooting DV for fun when it first came out and my daughter first began walking and talking. DV and daughter have both been evolving at a rapid rate, and now we are using DV on some of our jobs.

Almost all of our commercial, feature and television film work has been shot on 35mm motion picture film. I began in the corporate and documentary world, went on to do movies, television and most recently, have been directing and shooting commercials. Along this journey, we have used mostly 35mm motion picture cameras, but also 16mm, video, and lately, DV. I usually wound up buying the latest cameras, only to find out that there were better instruction books on how to fly the space shuttle. User-friendly manuals were rare, and rarely traveled with the intended equipment. I became an accidental tourist in the world of writing manuals, starting with a few of notes scribbled for camera assistants who would be working with my equipment. The notes soon grew into six textbooks on cinematography and, most recently, this book.

Movies have traditionally been shot on 35mm motion picture film, which has the same width and square sprockets as the film in your still camera, although the picture area is slightly smaller. This size was determined over a hundred years ago, when Thomas Edison first asked George Eastman to supply film for his prototype Kinetoscope. The result became a worldwide standard, and emerged to define the prominent art form of the twentieth century.

Recently, a new standard has emerged with such vigor that it can only be called revolutionary. Welcome to DV. It already appears to be an art form defining the beginning of the twenty-first century.

Digital video has become a universal medium. It is shared equally by both amateurs and professionals, film students and independent feature crews. It is used by new parents to record baby's first steps at home and by news crews to broadcast first speeches of new presidents in far-off lands.

This book is for anyone planning to use a DV, DVCAM or mini DV video camera: student, amateur, consumer, prosumer, or professional.

The book took shape after four different people asked me the same question: what kind of video camera to buy.

> When a top broadcast executive asked me what kind of video camera to buy for his wife, I realized there were overwhelming choices of equipment.

> When a colleague's son asked whether his high school film class should use DV, the accessibility of this new medium became clear.

> When I started using DV to shoot cutaway scenes in a national commercial, I began to learn about the potential of digital video.

> And when a chemist friend asked about editing DV on her computer to document an experiment for a grant, I saw how quickly the worlds of computers and imaging were rapidly merging.

So here it is—a book simple enough for even professionals to understand, with hopefully enough theory and explanation for the home hobbyist and film student, along with sufficient pictures and tables for corporate and educational users.

I will mostly discuss mini DV camcorders, because they are smaller and lighter than their Big Gun cousins that accept both Standard and mini DV cassettes.

What Is DV?

Let's pretend that you have just returned to civilization from a 5 year expedition tracking and filming the rare red rhinoceros with your workhorse 16mm camera. While you were away, a revolution happened in the world of moving pictures. The highly technical, complex process with which you acquired images, edited and distributed them was transformed by a digital video format called DV, and popularized by the computer.

What makes DV so special and so exciting is that it is truly the first moving picture format that is really easy to use. A mini DV cassette is less than 1/12 the size of a standard VHS tape, and records up to an hour of material. The DV standard was the result of a consortium of 50 companies (including Sony, Matsushita, Philips, Thomson, Toshiba, Hitachi, JVC, Sanyo, Sharp and Mitsubishi).

Easy in--easy out. VHS and Hi-8 Video Cassettes were just as easy to use. But not so easy to get out. You usually edited the tape on a linear tape-to-tape system, and the quality got so degraded each time it was copied that by the time you went down a couple of generations, it looked like it was shot through Scotch Tape. The other alternative was a non-linear editing system requiring you to digitize the picture (convert it from analog to digital) with expensive hardware.

DV is already compressed (5:1). It is a digital signal. You just plug a Firewire cable into your computer, click a couple of buttons, and the entire digital stream is copied to the hard drive in real time. No loss of quality. Distribution can be as simple as uploading a file to the web, for all to see.

Digital video's universal appeal is its use of the computer and cheap editing software. Not since the personal computer replaced typewriters has there been such a democratization of a creative process. DV editing software will become as widely used as word processing software, with similar paradigms of cut and paste.

Five years ago, a high-end AVID or Media 100 computerized editing system cost anywhere from $20 to $100 thousand dollars, requiring special circuit boards to convert analog NTSC or PAL video signals into digital files, which were compressed into manageable sizes. Recent offerings of editing software, while admittedly not as powerful, come free with various new computers, or can be downloaded from the web, while popular packages like Final Cut Pro can be bought for $990.

DV is a 1/4" digital video format, originally designed for the consumer market. Like many previous tape formats, the consumer version has been adapted for professional use by speeding up the tape along with some other refinements. The slightly faster, slightly more professional version of consumer mini DV is called DVCAM by Sony and DVCPRO by Panasonic.

The term "DV" is sometimes a bit vague and too all-encompassing. It is often used to label anything digital, whether consumer, prosumer, or professional. DV is not DigiBeta, nor is it Quicktime, MPEG, HDTV or any of the other video formats stored as bits of zeroes and ones.

Fifty different video formats have come and gone in the past 30 years: 2", 1", 3/4", Beta, VHS, S-VHS, D1, D2, 8, Hi-8, and so on. A cynic once wondered whether the manufacturers decided to come out with a new format every 3 years just to pay for their R&D. There is no doubt that DV will evolve into another format, probably supplanted by a recordable DVD or other random access storage device.

As with many new technologies, this one is accompanied by hype and evangelical proclamations heralding this latest format as the end of film. We have heard this for over thirty years now. Don't scrap your film cameras yet. Remember that every advance in video over the last 30 years has been met by an astounding leap in film technology: reduced grain, increased sharpness, speed, latitude, contrast, color. Film has been around for over a hundred years. As the sage said, all you need to see film is a lens and a light. It is a universal medium, future-proof and archival. I don't think DV is the killer-app to kill off film. However, I do see DV as the killer-app to popularize visual expression in ways we haven't even dreamed of yet.

Digital video is not the end of film. It's an exciting part of the evolution of image capture and exhibition. We all know the same thing happened to words just a few years earlier. Writing or typing was a linear process. Major changes meant retyping the page. A non-linear approach was to cut the page up and re-paste the paragraphs--but someone still had to retype it. Computer programs changed all that with simple shortcuts for cutting, copying and pasting.

At first, there was much regret that all this would lead to a proliferation of unprofessional writing. Critics were quick to counter that few things are more democratic than a ballpoint pen, nor is any other technology easier to master. Yet the invention of the ballpoint pen did not spell the demise of great writing, nor will digital video be the end of great filmmaking.

Although video tape had been around for half a century, and consumer video gave us VHS, Video8 and Hi8, the force that has led to billions of dollars of sales of a new format was not only the format itself, but the computer and the wires that connected computers to cameras.

Shooting DV with style is as elusive as pounding out the next great novel on your laptop. Just as there are books and courses on how to improve your writing skills, here is a book on how to improve your DV filmmaking skills, with emphasis on how to shoot it well, and with style.

What DV Is (and Isn't)

DV (Mini DV and DVCAM) Is

- Small, light, fast, portable, cheap
- Great for film schools
- Perfect for home movies (videos)
- Wonderful for news, documentaries, events, corporate video
- OK for low-budget features, but cost of blow-up is huge
- Digital, component, 5:1 compressed video format
- DCT (Discrete Cosine Transform) Compression method
- 1/4" (6.35mm) wide magnetic tape
- 60 minutes (DV), 40 minutes (DVCAM) recording time on mini cassette
- 270 minutes (DV), 184 min (DVCAM) recording time on large cassette
- 18.812mm/sec (DV), 28.193mm/sec (DVCAM) NTSC tape speed
- Also called DV25 (compared to DV50, which is higher resolution, same tape)
- 25 Mbps (Million bits per second) video data throughput per second
- 29.97 NTSC or 25 PAL video frames per second

DV Is Not

- Future-proof. It will be replaced by something better.
- A universal standard. You still have to choose between NTSC and PAL.
- Archival. Fewer dropouts than analog video, but life is still about 5-10 years.
- HDTV. But most certainly the next generation will be.
- Film. It has about 1/10th the picture information of 35mm film.
- Film. Exposure range is about 9 stops compared to film's 13.
- Film. Contrast is limited. Highlights will burn out.
- 35mm film blowups will look like video blown up, not like film.

Acronyms

Just as motion picture camera companies love to name their cameras and accessories with indecipherable acronyms (WLCC or FITZAC), video manufacturers must have an entire staff of copywriters who dream up weird names for otherwise self-explanatory functions. InfoLithium is a battery that can display its status. SuperSteadyShot is image stabilization. Stamina Power Management System is just an extra-large battery. Therefore, I have tried to weed out all weird names and trademarked obfuscations, and call things by what they really are. My apologies to the copywriters.

Disclaimer

Since these are litigious times, the inevitable disclaimer must be made. Some of the recommendations, specifications, modifications, accessories and procedures described in this book may not be accurate, nor have they necessarily been tested or approved by the manufacturers. As such, following my advice may void the warranty on the camera, the service contract, or the rental house agreement. It worked for me, but there always lurks the potential for misprints and errors.

When I was a kid, my best friend, Jim Pfeiffer, and I built amateur radios from plans in *Popular Electronics* magazine. Turning the home-made device on for the first time was often a spectacular event. Sometimes sparks would fly and the room would fill with acrid smoke from molten components. Inevitably, we would read about the mistake or typo in the next month's issue of the magazine, where they apologized for showing a resistor instead of a capacitor, or the accidental line in the schematic that depicted soldering a plus to a minus wire.

The kids have grown up. Jim Pfeiffer became an English teacher, screenwriter, producer, cameraman, video production company owner, high-tech consultant and dot-com executive. But I still remember him as partner in sparking electronic projects, which, along with all his other qualifications, should make him ideally qualified and compassionate as proofreader and editor of this book—a veritable burn-prevention, quality-control unit.

However, typos and errors still may lurk within these pages. Shooting tests is recommended whenever there is ever any doubt. Although we have made every attempt to check the facts and techniques described in this text, there still is the possibility of error, for which we apologize, but are not responsible or liable. Please let us know for future editions or update notices by going to www.fauer.tv and contacting us.

The Future

There is a video facility in New York with a twelve-foot long display case tracing the history of video tape and technology. Starting at the left, you begin with 2" video tape. A little plaque below notes the date invented and the company involved. As you walk along, you pass 1", 3/4" Umatic, Betamax, VHS, S-VHS, 3/4" SP, D1, D2, BetaSP, Video8, 3/4" Umatic SP, Hi8, DigiBeta, mini DV, DVCAM, DVCPRO, HD, Digital8, and so on. It is remarkable that as each of the 50 different formats was introduced, the time between each innovation became shorter.

The future of technology is not easy to predict. If it were, the world's richest man would have anticipated the Internet earlier, Betamax would be the standard instead of VHS, and arguably, 95% of the world would be using Macs instead of PC's. TV was supposed to put film out of business, and VCRs were supposed to be the end of theatres.

Who would have predicted 100 years ago, when film was viewed as a flickering, postage-stamp size image on a Kinetoscope, that 100 years later we would still be viewing a flickering, postage-stamp image—but this time delivered to us at home, on the Internet, and very often shot on digital video?

How do I see the future of imaging technology? Resolution independent, on-demand delivery of any film ever made, piped directly anywhere in the world, wirelessly. Home-viewing on large, hybrid, flat-panel computer/TV displays. Portable viewing on small pop-out screens.

One thing is certain. The mini DV we're shooting on today will be replaced within a couple of years by a smaller, lighter, faster and probably cheaper format that renders even better image quality.

I would guess that within a year or two we'll have consumer and prosumer mini DV and mini DVCAM with HD resolution. We are already seeing DVCPRO HD in professional cameras. The tape will run faster, so you'll change cassettes more often. The improved resolution will make 35mm blowup and electronic projection even more compelling. These cameras will also probably output to standard NTSC and PAL, known as "down-converting."

On the professional level, we'll see 1 inch high-resolution single chips in cameras within a year, offering the advantage of using ANY high quality 35mm motion picture camera lens without beam splitters. In two years, the resolution of camera imaging chips should be up to 2,040 horizontal lines. In four years, resolution should be doubled to 4,000 lines: the holy grail known as "4K" that approaches current film resolution.

Although video technology has not quite kept apace of Moore's law of computers, which speculates that processor speed doubles every 18 months, along with reduction in size and price, I think the ever-growing consumer demand will accelerate research and development of interesting innovations. Gordon Moore just retired, but digital video technology has really just begun.

In five to six years, the chips will have expanded light sensitivity, offering an exposure and contrast range similar to the 11 to 13 stop latitude of most contemporary negative color film stocks.

Of course, film technology advances in the same rapid steps. For the last twenty years, every time we heard that video was going to render film obsolete, along came a faster film stock, or films with exciting new characteristics or better film to tape telecine machines.

As digital video evolves, with higher resolutions, it will be ever more demanding of storage space. Currently, one single frame of 35mm motion picture film requires almost 35 Megabytes of uncompressed space when scanned from film to digital. A single frame of DV is currently about 900Kb. So, instead of recording on a moving tape, in a few years we'll be recording on DVD, disk or some form of cheap flash memory instead of tape. It will offer instant random access and higher storage potential than tape.

But wait. Stop the presses. The future is gaining faster than we're predicting. I wrote the previous paragraph two months ago. Today, Hitachi has just announced a mini camcorder that records 1.9 Mega-pixel still images and 720k video onto an 8 cm (3 1/8") diameter DVD-RAM disc that is rewritable up to 100,000 times. For some reason, they neglected to include a FireWire connection. That will surely show up in the next model. Sort of like the weather in Wyoming. If you don't like it, wait a few minutes.

A Short History of Film and How It Relates to DV

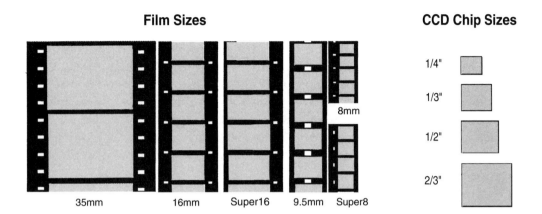

Film Sizes

35mm   16mm   Super16   9.5mm   Super8   8mm

CCD Chip Sizes

1/4"
1/3"
1/2"
2/3"

35mm

Most film historians agree that George Eastman and Thomas Edison met in 1889 to discuss the specifications of film for Edison's Kinetoscope. George Eastman is said to have asked "how wide?" Thomas Edison held up his thumb and forefinger. George Eastman took a ruler out of his pocket and measured the distance. It was 35 millimeters wide (1 3/8 inches), exactly half the width of the film Eastman was making for his original Kodak still camera. The film was made by slitting the roll of still film down the center, and splicing the two ends together to yield a length of motion picture film about 50 feet. It had four rectangular perforations on each side of each frame—almost the same dimensions and specifications still in use today.

9.5mm

Format wars are not a new phenomenon. In 1922, Pathé of France introduced the first amateur format motion picture camera: 9.5mm. A year later, Kodak came out with 16mm film and cameras. The Pathé 9.5mm format is virtually unknown in the United States. But every few years, someone "rediscovers" it as the latest great new film size. It has almost as much picture as 16mm in a gauge half the width. The reason it never gained widespread popularity was probably the marketing muscle of Kodak, not to mention the fear of a sprocket tooth, positioned in the midst of the image area, poking out your precious picture. Even today, there are passionate 9.5mm film clubs in France, the UK and US.

16mm

Eastman (by then Eastman Kodak) released the first amateur motion picture film, along with cameras to use the new 16mm format, in 1923. The Kodak Cine Special camera and other 16mm cameras were used by a few amateurs, but mostly by documentary and industrial filmmakers, who loved the new format for its speed, light weight and ease of use. Schools bought 16mm projectors for educational films and for analyzing football games.

Super16

Super16 uses the same size film as regular 16mm, with perforations along one edge instead of two. The aspect ratio is 1.66 instead of 1.33:1 (4:3).

In fact, Super16 has become so popular, that most 16mm sold today is single-perf.

Very few cameras have sprockets on both sides, with the exception of a few high-speed Photosonics and other specialty cameras.

8mm

In 1932, Kodak slit its 16mm film in half, lengthwise, and came out with 8mm. It had twice as many perforations, which were also smaller. Suddenly, film was accessible to almost everyone. Its low cost and ease of use gave 8mm equipment an entry into many American homes. Its small image size required large magnification by a projector, which of course, magnified the film's grain. It was mainly relegated to home movie use until the late 1950's, when improvements in technology gave it a boost as an avant-garde medium. Grain suddenly was good.

Super8

In 1965, to get a slightly larger image size and boost sales, Kodak made the perforations smaller, so the picture could be larger, and loaded the film into plastic cartridges for easier handling. Super8 was born.

Film and the 20th Century

Film brought universal ideas to the largest audience in history, and became a common bond. The history of film in the last century is a chronicle of a craft that became the most popular and powerful art form in history, and influenced the globalization of nations, corporations and ideas.

It was a century of nation building--for better or worse. It was a century in which ideas could be presented to ever larger numbers of people in ever shorter spans of time. Never before had so many sat together to watch the same moving images, to share the same common bonds. Universal themes and emotions could be shared across the boundaries of nations, language, and social structure. The record of that evolution is on film.

Over one hundred years ago, the first cinematographers set off to film the world around them. Early locations were the Panama Canal, Egypt, New York, Paris, Berlin, London. One of the first shots of the first cinematographer at work shows a Lumière cameraman cranking away on the Champs Elysée.

Their footage was the beginning of an art form that would introduce universal ideas to the largest audience in history. One of the first film critics said: "Someone went somewhere and saw something and brought it back for us to look at."

The beauty of motion picture camera design is its intrinsic simplicity, which has endured as a worldwide standard for over 100 years. A little pin enters a little hole in a roll of film, pulls it down, and exposes it to light. Perfs and teeth, gears and cranks. Gleaming brass, mahogany and optical elements.

Famous names: Lumière, Eclair, Biograph, Bioscop, Moy, Prestwich, Williamson, Debrie, Urban, Pathé, Ernemann, Cinématographes, Kinarri, Demeny-Gaumont, Arriflex. You can still see these cameras at George Eastman House, American Society of Cinematographers, Museum of the Moving Image, London Science Museum, Barnes Museum of Cinematography in Cornwall, and Deutsches Museum.

One of the first sports films was shot by Billy Bitzer in 1902: footage of NY Athletic Club games. The first commercial was probably one done in 1898, showing a man with a placard advertising Dewars Scotch Whiskey. One of the earliest special effects films was by Méliès, showing a woman swimming in a fish tank (courtesy of double printing.) In 1898, the Edison Company filmed a Native American dance in the American Southwest.

For over a century, motion pictures endured patent wars, rivalries, intrigues, photo-chemical weathering and digital competition. There has been increasing competition to originate on videotape or digital media. But then we are reminded of the persistent vision of the 50 video formats that have come and vanished in just the last two decades. As a film historian pointed out, "the elegance of film is that in 20 or 50 or 100 years, all you will need to recover the recorded imagery is a light and a lens."

Nature is not always renewable, and neither are cultural resources. Both need protection. Audiences, studios, and even governments are finally becoming aware and involved in film preservation. We are learning that the best preservation medium for film seems to be film. Ironically, the matrix holding the image is subject to scratches and tears from the simple act of viewing. That's where digital re-mastering becomes important, along with digital "printing" back to film.

Film can take abundant advantage of new optical, digital and technical innovations such as scanning, digital manipulation, non-linear editing and laser printing. As a universal standard, future-proof and hardware-independent, it can be used anywhere in the world (or universe—as long as there is a light and a lens), on any screen, any television, digital or analog, on tape, disc, computer, CD, DVD, laser, the Internet or formats yet to be devised.

Film endures, entertains, and educates. It is a record of our past, preserved for present and future generations. But, film is only as enduring as its custodians will allow. We laughingly say that the projectionist has final cut, and the colorist is the gaffer. In the wrong hands, film can be as fragile as an endangered rainforest, at the mercy of a splicer's blade or a studio's simple need for more shelf space. Many of Hollywood's great collections were destroyed in the 1950s to make room for parking lots and condos.

The next century approaches with prospects of new and different applications for motion imaging. Just as movies evolved from single-use peep shows to large theatrical presentations, we once again see a return to individual viewing on television, computer, and personal digital devices. Globalization may once again revert to fragmentation, as demonstrated by multiplex theatres, multi-channel television, special interest cable networks, and instant Internet delivery.

The two formats share many ideas. Film cameras are now sprouting on-board video monitors. DV cameras are using optical image stabilization systems dating back to the Dynalens, invented in the 1970s.

DV is now at the point in history where film was in 1923, when Eastman and Pathé devised a cheaper, smaller format to bring an expensive and exclusive professional format to a much wider audience.

How Many DV Camcorders Are out There?

**Professional DV Camcorders Sold Worldwide to Date
for TV news, documentaries, sports, weddings, etc**

Year	DV Camcorders Sold
2000	125,000 to 250,000

**Consumer DV Camcorders Sold in the US alone
for
Amateur, home videos, semi-professional, documentaries,
independent filmmakers:**

Year	DV Camcorders Sold	Sales in US$
1998	177,000	$241 Million
1999	1,077,000	$779 Million
2000	1,857,000	$1.18 Billion

Projected Consumer DV Camcorder Sales

Year	DV Camcorders Projected Sales	Sales in US$
2001	2,778,000	$1.56 Billion
2002	3,858,000	$1.94 Billion
2003	4,749,000	$2.13 Billion

Total DV Camcorders Sold by Beginning 2004

Year	total DV Camcorders: USA	Sales in US$
2004	14,496,000	$7.83 Billion
Year	**total DV Camcorders: worldwide**	
2004	28,000,000	

US sales are estimated 50% to 70% of worldwide market.

*Source: Consumer Electronics Association
eBrain Market Research*

DV Feature Credits

A partial list of feature films originated in DV and distributed theatrically on 35mm release print

Julien Donkey Boy (Dogma 6)

Celebration

Harmony

The Price of Air

Timecode 2000

Famous

On the Ropes

Bus Riders Union

Night Waltz: The Music of Paul Bowles

In Search of Kundun

Signs and Wonders

Bamboozled

The King is Alive

Dancer in the Dark

The Gleaners and I (Agnes Varda)

Five Minute DV Introductory Course

Your daughter's graduation is in five minutes. You just borrowed a DV camcorder from a neighbor.

Or, the CEO has just handed you a mini DV camcorder. He is going to make the speech of a lifetime, and asks if you could please record it. He plans to announce that you are going to be the new president of global DV marketing.

Or, perhaps you are the gaffer on a student DV production. The Director of Photography has just been rushed off to the hospital for massive food poisoning from whatever he ate for lunch. Could it have been the left-over, day-old sushi that you innocently suggested he try? You have been asked to be the new Director of Photography.

Canon Elura 2

You have five minutes to figure out how to use the DV camcorder in your hand.

About 150,000 DVCAM professional camcorders and 3 million consumer mini DV camcorders have been sold worldwide so far. More people are using DV than any previous format. But even more mind-boggling is the thought that of all these users, probably only nine of them have actually read the instruction manual.

Let's face it: if you haven't already lost your manual, you probably lost patience trying to follow intricate flow charts detailing a maze of user settings. Here's some relief: a few quick, concise, hopefully helpful hints on how to shoot DV well, and with style.

First you need a camera

As my mentor Andy Laszlo, ASC used to say, "first you steal a chicken."

First you need a camera. For corporate and documentary work, there's Sony's 3-chip professional model DSR-PD150. It uses three 1/3" CCDs, accepts mini DV and DVCAM tapes, and is lightweight, small and versatile. It is similar to the Sony's consumer division model VX-2000, which only uses mini DV cassettes.

Sony DSR-PD150

Lighter and smaller, but with a picture that's almost as good, is Sony BPC's (Broadcast and Professional Corporation) three 1/4" chip DVCAM/mini DV PD-100a. It's about the size and weight of a plastic quart container of motor oil, turned over on its side.

Sony DSR-PD100a

Sony's consumer division sells a similar three-chip camera, the DCR-TRV900, which uses mini DV cassettes. Sony's single chip DCR-TRV-9, 10 and 11 are similarly styled "handicams."

Canon's XL1 is the largest of this bunch. It is popular with advanced film students and independent feature and docuementary shooters because of its inter-changeable lenses. It uses mini DV cassettes.

Canon XL-1

The smallest DV camcorders are about the size of the "Juicy-Juice" drink containers your kid squirts all over the car while trying to poke the plastic straw into the maddeningly squeazable box.

Most home users, as well as professionals needing to grab shots in precarious places (mountain climbers, snowboarders, skiers), favor the vest-pocket sized mini camcorders like Sony's DCR-PC5, PC100 or PC110.

Rival models include Canon's Elura 2 and the DVM series from JVC, who pioneered these tiny DV camcorders about five years ago.

Sony DCR-PC5

Next, we get to the shoulder-resting professional news, event and wedding photographer size cameras.

The Sony DSR-250 has a traditional news "big gun" camcorder shape, accepts both mini DVCAM cassettes as well as larger 184-minute tapes, and would be a good choice for corporate studio use, interviews, casting, events and weddings.

The DSR-250 is very economical, but remember that it does not have a bayonet mount to accept additional lenses.

Sony DSR-250

For interchangeable lenses, step up to the Sony DSR-300, a DVCAM camcorder with three ½" CCD chips, or the DSR-500WSL, with three 2/3" CCDs.

Panasonic makes similar cameras, and JVC's 3x 1/2" chip GY-DV500 is seen more and more on documentary and news crews.

Sony DSR-300

A Guide for the Perplexed

Most readers will, no doubt, be skilled professionals, but lest I leave anything out, let's assume that you have just returned to civilization, and corporate headquarters, after eight years lost in the remotest part of the Amazon.

You flew into the Patanal eight years ago with a 16mm camera and Nagra. Your job was to have been a simple, one-hour interview with a prominent scientist who had just discovered the cure to all disease. Deep in the rainforest, your dugout capsized. All your equipment was washed away, along with your navigation and communications equipment, and any hope of a speedy return. Even your ARRI 16SR Book, which describes how to fabricate a liferaft from a Thermodyne camera case, was lost.

But now, eight years later, after a long bath, you are back in your office cubicle, which miraculously was not given away during successive waves of ruthless corporate downsizing. The CEO has just replaced your lost equipment with the latest in DVCAM equipment, which you have never seen before. Of course, the camera manuals are nowhere to be found.

Five Minutes and Counting

The easy way to remember how to use a camera is to picture it in your mind. Start at the very front of the lens, and work your way back to the rear. Starting from the front:

1. Sunshade or Mattebox. Use one. It keeps flares off your lens, and has trays to hold filters. Flares are caused when the sun or artificial lights shine onto your lens. For a course on lens flares, rent *Easy Rider*. They're pretty, but you may not want them covering the face of the CEO delivering the annual report. Sunshades usually come with the camera, or you can buy a mattebox as an aftermarket accessory.

2. Filters. Be selective and use them tastefully. A lot of cameramen try to soften the image with diffusion or nets to render a "film look." Instead, the image often looks like it was shot through a shower cap. Tiffen ProMists come in strengths of 1/8 to 3, and can add an elegant, painterly quality—but I would rarely recommend using any grade higher than 1/8 on DV. SoftFX filters soften facial blemishes. There are glass and plastic filters on the market. Use glass. Plastic, even durable lexan, can distort the image at long focal lengths.

3. Focus. Auto Focus is great until the speaker you are interviewing reaches down to find a glass of water. The camera lens starts hunting back and forth, even after the subject is back in frame. Use Manual Focus as often as possible.

4. Zoom. Rule number one: don't zoom unless you really have to. Try to feather the starts and stops of your zoom as gracefully as possible using a delicate touch on the zoom control. Use a remote zoom control when the camera is on a tripod.

5. Exposure. The amount of light entering the lens is controlled by a thin, metal iris that opens and closes. Like auto focus, I prefer to control exposure manually. On most DV camcorders, there is a slide switch called "AUTO LOCK." Sliding it to the middle position will usually allow you to open and close the lens manually. This is particularly important if you are panning from bright to dark areas. The camera will catch up in automatic mode, but there is an obvious delay.

6. Support. Using a fluid head adds elegance to moves and stabilizes telephoto (long lens) shots. Viscous fluid in the head, usually silicone, dampens sudden moves and allows smoother panning and tilting than with a purely mechanical head. O'Connor, Sachtler (DV4 for PD100a and PD150), Manfrotto-Bogen, Gitzo, Miller, Vinten and Cartoni are popular brands. Carbon fiber tripods are about a pound lighter than aluminum, and a two-section tripod will extend from about 16 to 60 inches. SteadyShot image stabilization is great when handheld or bouncing around in helicopters, cars, boats or anything else that moves. I usually leave it on all the time unless the camera is on a tripod, dolly or crane. There are two kinds of image stabilizers: optical and electronic. Sony DV camcorders use motion sensors and compensatory electronic circuits to smooth out bumps and vibration.

7. Remote Control. When using a fluid head, it is essential to have external control of your zooms. Trying to wrap your right hand around the handgrip with a tripod handle poking you in the stomach is both painful and difficult. Tripod handle controls are available from Sony along with aftermarket ones from VariZoom and Libec (PH-9).

8. Sound. The built-in microphones that come with most DV Camcorders are fine for ambient sound. However, these on-board mikes pick up tape transport and zoom motor noise. For serious audio, use an external microphone. Most professional crews have a sound mixer, whose job it is to aim to microphone, set the levels and monitor the audio. The mixer feeds the camcorder with the audio signal, either with a "hard" wire or a radio mike. Because DVCAM tape records on two tracks, you can split the audio—for example, you can put a lavalier output on the right channel, and a shotgun mike for ambience on the left channel. Popular choices of shotgun (directional) mikes include Sennheiser's MKH-416, ME66 and K6 and Audio-Technica's AT815.. Lavalier mikes look like little tie clips, and are plugged directly into the camera or sent by radio-transmitted. Popular lavaliers are Sony's ECM-77B and 44B, and Audio-Technica's AT831B.

9. Lighting. A great fallacy of DV is that you don't need to light. Nothing could be farther from the truth. Like all things photographic, if it doesn't look good by eye, shooting it on DV is not going to rescue your career.

The best way to learn about lighting is to go to the movies and try to figure out how they did the lighting. Study great paintings, and then pretend you have to light the same scene. How would you do it?

Beware the easily portable lighting kits. They can be wonderful tools or terrible traps, ensnaring the unwitting in a downward spiral of poor technique. Because the lights themselves are small, harsh shadows can result if the lights are used un-modified. Remember: the larger the source, the softer and more natural the shadows. So, bouncing the light from these small fixtures into large reflective surfaces will soften the light and its accompanying shadows. Use bed sheets, muslins, foamcore, or even the wall. Large sheets of diffusion material, similar to shower curtain, but fire-resistant, help soften light when bouncing is impractical.

When shooting on location, we usually try to place our lights outside, and aim them through the windows of the room. Using large 12,000 to 18,000 watt HMI lights softened slightly with Lee 216 or Rosco Opal Tough Frost creates a beautiful, single source natural look. A standard location package will usually include a generator and a ten-ton truck to carry all the lights, along with lots of grip equipment to control them, because beautiful lighting is mostly about taking light away, selectively, from certain areas.

Lighting kits large and small are made by Lowel, Ianiro, Mole, LTM, Desisti and ARRI. Remember, the more equipment you have, the larger the vehicle needed to transport it. Keep it simple and small. Kinoflos are cool, soft fluorescents. Your favorite expendable supply store should provide 4' x 8' Foamcore and Beadboard. Chimera Lightbanks, metallic umbrellas, Flexfills and Litepanels are some of the many commercially available products used in the never-ending quest to shape and control light.

10. Cases and Covers. The most important accessory of all—to pack, coddle, ship and protect your investment. Soft-sided shoulder bags, backpacks and wheeled soft-sided cases are best for local work where the equipment is carried by people, cars or vans. My favorite soft-sided bags come from Lowe, PortaBrace, Tenba,Kata, Tamrac and Lightware. For serious expeditions and hostile environments, LowePro makes back packs, along with the Vidcam series of shoulder bags and the Omni /Extreme series of soft bags that fit inside waterproof shells for shipping.

Once you get into air travel and shipping, you need durable, water-resistant ATA style cases from Pelican or Thermodyne. A good source is Nalpak, which also supplies tripod cases and Magliner carts to wheel all the stuff around. To cut out the foam inside these cases, an electric knife left over from your Thanksgiving feast makes an excellent saw and is a lot easier to use than an X-Acto knife. For custom foam jobs, go to A&J in Los Angeles, makers of durable custom cases and wonderful custom foam cut-outs.

DV, DVC, DVCAM, DVCPRO

What Is DV?

DV stands for Digital Video, but Digital Video is not always DV.

Huh?

Digital Video is the broad term describing any video format, including DigiBeta, HD, Digital8, Digital S, DVCPRO, DVCPRO50, DV, DVC, mini DV, DVCAM and Mini DVCAM. The common thread among all these formats is that the video signal is stored in binary code: ones and zeroes. Analog video stores the information as waves that change in frequency and amplitude (think of an oscilloscope or waves in the ocean).

This book is about DV, and its variations: DVCAM and DVCPRO.

DV was introduced in 1995 as a new video format. A consortium of 55 companies worked on the standard. I think the first major consumer product was the tiny paperback book styled JVC Camcorder, which fit into your pocket if you had a large enough one.

DV is also called DVC (Digital Video Cassette), and Panasonic still labels most of its tapes "DVC" on the package.

I think the main ingredient for the success of DV is the digital part of its name, and its seamless import and export to computers. The picture quality is better than Hi8 and just as good, if not better, than BetaSP. Unlike analog formats, the image will not degrade as copies are made. It is much less prone to dropout, which plagued Hi8.

The tape is ¼ inch (6.35 mm) wide, but usually called 6mm. I suppose that is to avoid confusion with ¼ inch audio tape.

DV Cassettes

There are two cassettes sizes in the DV format: mini and standard. The large size records up to 3 hours of video and sound. You can even squeeze 4½ hours of recording time out of a standard cassette at the slow, EP speed (not recommended). The smaller mini-DV cassette will record a maximum of 1 hour of video and audio.

For consumer and general use, the most prevalent is Mini DV. These are the cute, matchbook-size cassettes.

The Mini DV size is the most prevalent for home, corporate and documentary use in small camcorders. It measures 2.6 x 1.9 x 0.5 inches (66 x 48 x 12.2 mm), which is smaller than a business card. You can buy 30 minute and 60 minute mini DV cassettes.

The standard DV cassette shouldn't really be called "standard;" it should be called "Bigger" or "Longer." It is 4.9" x 3" x 0.57" (125 x 78 x 14.8mm). That's a little larger than a 1/8" audio or Video8 cassette. This cassette is reserved for the big gun shoulder-

actual size MiniDV Cassette

resting cameras used by wedding videographers and news crews. The large cameras will accept mini DV cassettes without adapters. Of course, large cassettes cannot be used in small camcorders.

The actual tape width is 6.35 mm (¼ inch) wide, and it moves at 18.81 mm/sec (0.75 inch/sec.) A 60-minute Mini DV cassette uses about 213 feet (65 m) of tape. A standard DV cassette has about 813 feet (250 m) of tape.

Sony cassettes offer the option, for slightly more money, of "Cassette Memory" (CM). This is a small chip in the cassette shell that stores from 4K to 16K (Kilobytes) of information on scene, date, time and so on. It's useful for quickly finding the end of the tape, or indexing scenes. You can tell if you have Cassette Memory by the copper-colored strip at the bottom.

ID Holes

A DV cassette has identification holes on the cassette bottom to indicate tape thickness, cassette grade, and tape grade. The camera or VCR, using this information, will adjust its circuits to obtain the best match between the tape and the recording/playback system.

DV Tape

Many of the early live TV shows are lost forever. Video tape, up to now, has really been ground-up rust (metal oxide particles) glued to a long, thin strip of plastic tape. Just like those photo albums in your closet, the glue dries out when it gets old, and the particles, like the pictures, fall off.

Rust glued onto plastic tape is an over-simplification, of course, but dreaded tape drop-out, in which the picture would become snowy or disappear totally after a number of years, was the result of metal oxide particles flaking off from the tape itself, along with their magnetized analog picture.

DV tape changes all that.

DV tape is stronger than Hi-8, and much more advanced than VHS tapes. It is made from an advanced form of metal evaporated (ME) tape, in which the metal particles are embedded into the tape itself, as opposed to being "glued" on the way tapes were made in the past. The magnetic layer is double coated to give higher output and less noise. A layer of carbon is placed over the magnetic portion of the tape to protect it from wearing out. A back coating reduces friction and jitter, and provides a more even tape speed.

Comparing tape widths:

- Beta, DigiBeta and VHS tape is ½ inch (12.7 mm) wide
- Hi8 and Video8 tape is 8 mm (slightly less than 1/3-inch) wide
- DVCAM, DV and DVCPRO tape is 6.35 mm (¼ inch) wide, although it is usually referred to as 6mm tape.

Comparisons

DV "took off" when news organizations and networks began buying Sony VX1000 cameras.

"Professional" DV was invented, along with another VHS-Beta style format war, when DVCPRO was introduced by Panasonic in 1995, followed by Sony's DVCAM in 1996. The two formats basically use similar video and audio encoding schemes as the consumer DV format, but have different cassette sizes, along with slight differences in speed and track pitch. You can't always play one cassette in the other deck, although some decks do have dual capability.

The recording area on tape of DV is slightly smaller (10 microns) than DVCAM (15 microns) and DVCPRO (18 microns).

DV runs at a slightly slower speed (1/3 slower) than DVCAM, which runs slightly slower than DVCPRO.

DV runs at 18.81 mm per second (¾ inches per second in Standard (SP) mode, and 12.56 mm/s (½ ips) in Long Play (LP) mode.

DVCAM runs at 28 mm/sec, and DVCPRO at 33.82 mm/sec.

A "Standard" DVCAM cassette is the same size as a "Large" DVCPRO cassette. Standard and Large often become confused in catalogs.

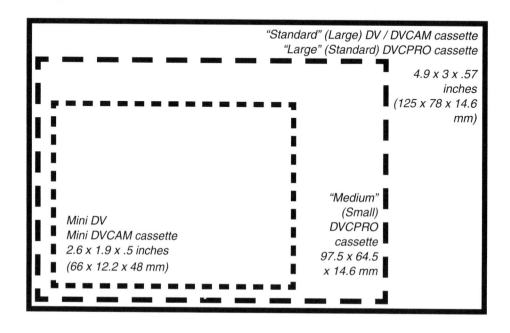

"Standard" (Large) DV / DVCAM cassette
"Large" (Standard) DVCPRO cassette

4.9 x 3 x .57 inches
(125 x 78 x 14.6 mm)

"Medium" (Small) DVCPRO cassette
97.5 x 64.5 x 14.6 mm

Mini DV
Mini DVCAM cassette
2.6 x 1.9 x .5 inches
(66 x 12.2 x 48 mm)

DV Restaurant Guide

Using the Zagat's Restaurant rating system of 1 to 30, where 1 is poisonous and 30 is nirvana, here's where DV stands:

rating	format	introduced	horizontal lines
1	VHS		240
2	Video 8		240
3	8mm film		
4	3/4" Umatic	1972	250
5	NTSC	1948	330-480
6	Hi8		400
7	S-VHS		
8	Super 8mm film		400
13	BetaSP	1982	
15	DV	1995	500
16	DVCPRO 50	2000	
17	Digibeta		
18	HD		1,080
19	16mm		1,750
20	Super16		2,000
25	35mm	1889	4,000
27	75mm		
30	IMAX		

Not bad: DV scores better than BetaSP, which has been used for years in broadcast, documentary and corporate work—and just behind DigiBeta. And with HD (High Definition) DV lurking on the horizon, it can only get better.

Why is NTSC only 330 lines? That's the pitiful amount that reaches your set, after all the blanking, synchronization, captions and timecode take their share from the original 525 lines.

And what about film? These are conversions of pixel information when film is transferred to digital with a film scanner or telecine.

DVCPRO

Panasonic's DVCPRO (sometimes called D-7) uses metal-particle tape instead of metal evaporated tape. The track pitch is increased to 18 microns. Unlike DV, the audio cue track and timecode control track of DVCPRO are recorded on two extra linear tracks set aside in the DV standards specifications.

The tape is transported at 34 mm/sec (DV is 17mm per second, DVCAM is 28 mm/sec.)

Most DVCPRO VTRs, however, can play back DV, DVCAM, and DVCPRO tapes.

Digital8

Digital8 was introduced by Sony in 1999. It has the same specifications as DV, but records onto the familiar Video8 - Hi8 cassette. The picture should look the same. The only drawback is that timecode cannot be sent over the Firewire / 1394 cable. That becomes a serious drawback only if you plan to edit the tapes, and need to return to the original tape for frame-accurate re-editing.

The main reason to buy a Digital8 camera is compatibility with all your old Video8 tapes. Digital8 camcorders will play the older format tapes back. This involves multi-speed design, since Digital8 runs twice as fast as Hi8. Digital8 cameras are cheaper, but they're also bigger and bulkier. Unless your Hi8 camera is broken and you don't have a Hi8 deck, buy a DV camcorder instead.

Digital S

Digital-S (called D-9) is JVC's format that delivers 50 Mbps of video data compressed at 3.3:1, with 4:2:2 sampling. This is similar to DigiBeta, and some decks can play back your old S-VHS tapes. Remember, S-VHS and Beta are both ½" formats

DVCPRO50

DVCPRO50 from Panasonic uses regular DVCPRO tape, but moves it faster to achieve a Mbps data rate. Compression is 3.3:1.

What is DVCAM?

DVCAM Format

DVCAM is Sony's name for its professional version of DV. The main differences between DVCAM and DV are track pitch and tape speed.

Track pitch is the width of the recorded area on the tape. DVCAM is 15 microns. DV is 10 microns. DVCAM runs about 1/3 faster than DV.

The DVCAM cassette itself is supposed to be a little more durable, and a little more reliable for professional editing. However, I've dissected both cassettes, and can't see any real difference. They both seem extremely durable. Both formats use the same metal evaporated tape.

A DVCAM camera or deck can play back a tape recorded on DV.

DVCAM Tape

The maximum recording time of a Standard DVCAM cassette tape (PDV Series) is 184 minutes (PDV-184ME), and the DVCAM Mini cassette tape (PDVM Series) is 40 minutes. Each cassette contains a 16K integrated circuit which stores data about scenes and contents to help in editing and identification.

Consumer DV cassettes with 4K of IC memory, or without, can be used in DVCAM camcorders.

The Mini DVCAM cassette measures 2.6 x 1.9 x 0.5 inches (66 x 48 x 12.2 mm).

In comparison, a Video 8 cassette is 3.7 x 2.5 x 0.6 inches (95 x 62.5 x 15 mm). A VHS cassette is 7.4 x 4.1 x .98 inches (188 x 104 x 25 mm). The mini-DV cassette takes up less than half the overall space (43.4%) of an 8 mm cassette.

The tape inside a VHS cassette is ½ inch (12.7 mm) wide, Hi8 and Video8 tape is 8 mm (or slightly less than 1/3-inch) wide, and DVCAM/Mini DV tape is 6.35 mm (¼ inch) wide. The DVCAM/Mini DV cassette uses a reel lock system to prevent tape sagging or unspooling.

Cassette Labeling

DVCAM cassettes are identified by the DVCAM logo in the upper right. The lower left has a number, referring to minutes of recording time. ME stands for Metal Evaporated—the kind of tape used. A 32 minute mini DVCAM cassette will read: "32 AdvancedME" on the tape cassette and "PDVM-32ME" on the cassette jacket.

Mini DV cassettes have the Mini DV logo in the upper right. The number in the lower left identifies minutes of recording time. So, a 30 minute mini DV cassette will read: "DVM30." A two hour standard cassette will read: "DV 120." This labeling is the same whether the tape is for NTSC or PAL recording.

Labeling Your Cassettes

After you finish shooting a cassette, slide the Safety Lock slider to the "SAVE" position. That prevents accidental re-recording over your once-in-a-liftetime shots.

To identify the tape, you'll have to do some origami tricks. Since the DV cassettes are so small, the adhesive labels on which you'll write scene information, date and contents are about the size of your thumbnail.

Suggestion to manufacturers: use a matte-finish white plastic on the cassettes so we can write on them directly. Save paper. Don't bother with the adhesive labels. They are a nuisance.

Write-Protect = Playback Only

Like other video formats and floppy
disks, standard and mini-DV cassettes
have write-protect tabs. These sliding
"windows" are similar to those found in
the Hi-8 and Video8 formats—unlike the
break-off tabs of the VHS cassette, the
red button of Umatic, or the up-down tab
of Beta. A DV cassette shows an open
hole to prevent recording, while a closed
hole allows recording. This is similar to a
3½" computer floppy disk and a VHS
cassette (open hole protects data, closed
hole permits recording). The opposite
scheme applies to Video/Hi-8 (where an
open hole allows recording).

IC Memory

You can get cassettes with and without a
memory chip. Cassettes containing the
chip can be readily identified by their
gold band just below the **REC-SAVE** tab.
The memory chip adds about a dollar to
the cost of each cassette, but provides the
following benefits:

> Date, title of tape, table of contents
> Search tape by date of recording, searching tape by title or scene
> Labeling a cassette, titles

Emergency: Middle of a Shoot, Can't Find More DVCAM Tapes

DVCAM cameras and decks can accept widely available home-use Mini DV
cassette tapes as well. Mini DV cassettes labeled for 60 minutes of DV recording
can record up to 40 minutes of professional DVCAM in a DVCAM machine. The
tape's the same. The cassette is not as rugged, and it may be lacking the 16K
memory chip, but it will still work.

Don't...Because

The cautions for handling digital video tape are pretty much the same as for any video or audio tape:

1. Do not touch the tape itself. Oil from fingers can damage tape.

2. Do not expose the tape to strong magnetic fields. That means, don't put the tape on top of a TV, monitor or speaker (they all emit magnetic fields), keep it away from magnetized screwdrivers, and of course, away from bulk tape erasers unless you really want to delete all contents.

3. Try not to leave tapes in your car, especially in the sun.

4. Do not use the tape if it has gotten wet or has had anything spilled on it

5. If the cassette is cold, let it warm up for at least 2 hours before using. Coming from cold outdoors to warm indoors, put the tape in a Zip-Lok plastic bag, and seal it tight. Any condensation formed in the warming process will cling to the outside of the bag, not the tape.

6. When using tapes in hot, humid or dusty locations, store them in plastic bags, out of the sun.

7. Do not leave the cassette in the DV recorder for longer than necessary.

8. Keep the cassette in its case. That will help protect it from dust and dirt.

9. Tapes that are moist with humidity will shut down all cameras immediately.

A Short Catalog of DV Tape

The following tables are included to show the varieties of tape stock available.

Prices are approximate street prices, based on quanitites of 10, and are included only to show differences.

Note: the speeds of DV vary depending on recording mode—in SP, an 80 minute cassette will run for 80 minutes; in LP, it will run for 120 minutes, and in DV, it will run for about 50 minutes.

Sony DVCAM (6mm) Tape

ID	minutes	Mini or Standard Size	$ Street Price
SONY DVCAM with 16K Memory CHIP			
PDVM-12ME DVCAM	12	Mini w/16K Chip	14.50
PDVM-22ME DVCAM	22	Mini w/16K Chip	15.95
PDVM-32ME DVCAM	32	Mini w/16K Chip	16.70
PDVM-40ME DVCAM	40	Mini w/16K Chip	19.00
PDV-34ME DVCAM	34	Standard w/16K Chip	24.65
PDV-64ME DVCAM	64	Standard w/16K Chip	27.90
PDV-94ME DVCAM	94	Standard w/16K Chip	34.20
PDV-124ME DVCAM	124	Standard w/16K Chip	38.80
PDV-184ME DVCAM	184	Standard w/16K Chip	46.20
SONY DVCAM MASTER (W/16K CHIP)			
PDVM-32MEM DVCAM	32	Mini w/16K Chip	20.30
PDVM-40MEM DVCAM	40	Mini w/16K Chip	23.00
PDVM-64MEM DVCAM64	64	Standard w/16K Chip	33.80
PDVM-124MEM DVCAM124	124	Standard w/16K Chip	47.00
PDVM-184MEM DVCAM184	184	Standard w/16K Chip	56.00
SONY DVCAM (CHIPLESS)			
PDVM-32N DVCAM	32	Mini (No Chip)	11.75
PDVM-40N DVCAM	40	Mini (No Chip)	14.00
PDV-34N DVCAM	34	Standard (No Chip)	19.95
PDV-64N DVCAM	64	Standard (No Chip)	22.70
PDV-94N DVCAM	94	Standard (No Chip)	29.00
PDV-124N DVCAM	124	Standard (No Chip)	33.45
PDV-184N DVCAM	184	Standard (No Chip)	40.75

Mini DV (6mm) Cassettes

SONY			
ID	*length*	*type / chip*	*street price*
DVM-30PR Mini DV	30	Premium Chipless	6.00
DVM-60PR Mini DV	60	Premium Chipless	6.75
DVM-30EX Mini DV	30	Excellence Chipless	8.50
DVM-60EX Mini DV	60	Excellence Chipless	9.50
DVM-30EXM Mini DV	30	Excellence w/4K Chip	12.50
DVM-60EXM Mini DV	60	Excellence w/4K Chip	15.20
MAXELL			
DVM-30SE Mini DV	30	Chipless	8.20
DVM-60SE Mini DV	60	Chipless	6.50
FUJI			
DVM-60AME Mini DV	60	Chipless	6.50
PANASONIC			
AY-DVM60 Mini DV	60	Chipless	6.50
AY-DVM80 Mini DV	80	Chipless	10.50

Standard (Large) DV (6mm) Cassettes

SONY			
DVM-120MEM DV	120	Excellence w/4K Chip STANDARD SIZE	22.50
DVM-180MEM DV	180	Excellence w/4K Chip Standard Size	26.75
PANASONIC			
AY-DVM120 DV	120	STANDARD SIZE	22.00

DVCPRO (6mm) Cassettes

FUJI				
DP121-12M	DVCPRO	12	Mini	7.15
DP121-24M	DVCPRO	24	Mini	8.70
DP121-33M	DVCPRO	33	Mini	11.25
DP121-46M	DVCPRO	46	Mini	12.80
DP121-66M	DVCPRO	66	Mini	19.45
DP121-34L	DVCPRO	34	Standard	14.35
DP121-66L	DVCPRO	66	Standard	20.45
DP121-94L	DVCPRO	94	Standard	30.70
DP121-126L	DVCPRO	126	Standard	39.95
MAXELL				
DVP-12M	DVCPRO	12	Mini	6.90
DVP-24M	DVCPRO	24	Mini	8.40
DVP-33M	DVCPRO	33	Mini	10.85
DVP-66M	DVCPRO	66	Mini	18.75
DVP-34L	DVCPRO	34	Standard	14.00
DVP-66L	DVCPRO	66	Standard	19.75
DVP-94L	DVCPRO	94	Standard	29.60
DVP-126L	DVCPRO	126	Standard	38.50
PANASONIC				
AJ-P12M	DVCPRO	12	Mini	7.60
AJ-P24M	DVCPRO	24	Mini	9.30
AJ-P33M	DVCPRO	33	Mini	11.85
AJ-P46M	DVCPRO	46	Mini	13.75
AJ-P66M	DVCPRO	66	Mini	18.70
AJ-P34L	DVCPRO	34	Standard	15.30
AJ-P66L	DVCPRO	66	Standard	19.80
AJ-P94L	DVCPRO	94	Standard	26.40
AJ-P126L	DVCPRO	126	Standard	38.50

DV Theory

Video 101

Television is not a recent invention. The picture we watch today was conceived in the 1940s.

Movies, television, and even computer displays rely on a phenomenon called "persistence of vision," described by Peter Mark Roget in 1824. When you watch a movie, you are seeing 48 separate pictures flash on the screen every second. The film was shot at 24 frames per second, and it is projected at the same frame rate. But a "butterfly" shutter between the lens and the light breaks up each frame into two flashes of light, giving us 48 images per second. Each frame is displayed two times before being "pulled down" while the shutter closes off the light.

Because each frame appears on screen so quickly, your brain is "fooled" into thinking it's a single image instead of a series of individual ones. So, the pictures blend seemlessly, as a single scene showing movement. The early movies were called "flickers," and you really did see the image flickering. There were two reasons. Early films were usually projected at 16 frames per second. And early light sources were carbon arcs that sometimes sputtered and fizzled.

You can demonstrate persistence of vision at night with a flashlight. Shine the beam onto your ceiling. Move the beam slowly around the room. It looks like a point of light. Now wave it quickly back and forth. It will look like a line. It's still made up of the same point of light, but your eye is fooled into thinking it's a line.

Television is displayed at the rate of 30 complete pictures per second in North America and Japan (NTSC), and 25 pictures per second in Europe and almost everywhere else (PAL). In both film and video, each individual picture is called a frame. Video is further broken down into "fields," with 2 fields per frame. This is called interlaced scanning.

The picture you see on a regular television is actually created by electron beams scanning a phosphorescent coating on the back of the screen. It's very much like your waving flashlight. Three electron beams (Red, Green, Blue) scan from the top left corner (as you face the screen), continuing in left-to-right down to the bottom.

The electron beams vary in intensity to control the brightness of the scene. The three electron guns are aimed in slightly different paths, one for each primary color. When the electrons hit the phosphor pixels, they glow varying shades of Red, Green and Blue. When all the pixels glow in the same area, the picture is white, because it is an additive color system.

When television standards were adopted, committees met and argued over which was the better system. Politics and business mingled with self-interest and nationalism. The consumer benefited the least, because we now have three totally different, incompatible systems worldwide. Sounds a bit like the HD and Wireless Telecom standards of today.

North America, Japan, Philippines, and some other countries, use NTSC (National Television Standards Committee—more often laughingly called "Never The Same Color"). It consists of 525 scan lines and 30 frames per second (60 fields). England, Germany and most of Europe and Asia use PAL (Phase Alternating Line), with 625 scan lines and 25 frames per second (50 fields). France and parts of Russia use SECAM (Sequentiel Couleur a Memorie).

In NTSC, of the 525 scan lines, only 480 lines are actual picture information, and by the time it gets to your set via cable or transmission, it can be down as low as 330 lines. In PAL's 625 scan lines, only 576 lines are picture information. The other lines are used for internal timing.

The NTSC system is also called 525/60, PAL and SECAM are called 625/50. The first number is the number of scan lines, the second number is the number of fields per second. So, NTSC 525/60 means 525 scan lines at 60 fields per second, which is 30 frames per second. PAL / SECAM 625/50 means 625 lines, 50 fields per second, 25 frames per second. The 60 fields of NTSC and the 50 fields of PAL happen to correspond to the line frequency of the power in the respective countries.

Next, we get to the story of interlace. Early television flickered, just like early movies, because the phosphors in the picture tubes would lose their glow before the electron beam had finished its horizontal scanning at 30 times a second. Persistently visual viewers could see it flicker, so the answer was to record half the image every 1/60th of a second.

The NTSC and PAL committees fixed this by dividing each frame into two parts, called fields. It is somewhat like the projector shutter dividing each film frame into two flashes. There is a difference. The committees numbered each horizontal scan line, starting at the top (1 to 480 for NTSC and 1 to 576 for PAL). The first field of each frame consists of the odd-numbered scan lines. The second field is made up of the even-numbered scan lines.

Our persistence of vision thinks the interlaced lines are one frame, and they go by so fast, we can't see the flicker. This is called interlaced scanning. To convert fields to frames, divide by two.

When you hear the term progressive scanning, it means each frame is a complete scan of the entire screen. Computer monitors and High Definition Television use progressive scanning.

How DV Camcorders Work

Through a Lens Darkly

In a film camera, light passes through a lens and activates tiny particles of silver on the motion picture film. A mirror shutter blocks the light 24 times a second while the film is advanced by a pull-down mechanism to the next frame. While the film advances, the mirror bounces the light into your viewfinder, so you can see the image. The film stops again, the next frame is exposed, and so on. The film has to stop during exposure; otherwise, the picture would be blurred.

In a DV camcorder, light passes through the lens and activates tiny silicon particles on a computer chip, called a CCD for Charged Coupled Device. This image sensor converts the light into an analog electrical signal that is sent to associated circuits, where it is converted to digital and compressed to make it smaller and more manageable.

Three Chip Cameras (3 CCDs)

Most of the smaller and cheaper cameras use one CCD (charge coupled device) to gather picture information.

Higher-end cameras use 3. Each CCD handles one of the three primary colors: Red, Green and Blue. The light passing through the lens is separated into red, green and blue by a beam-splitting prism, and then each color is sent to its own CCD. This process provides better picture detail, more accurate color reproduction, a wider dynamic range and virtually no color noise.

This will change in time. The beam-splitter introduces optical problems and lens-design compromises. Professional video lenses take the beam-splitter into consideration in adjusting the back-focus of each of the three colors. Motion picture and still lenses go to great lengths to assure accurate focus of all colors in the same place on the film plane. As chips get better, achieving higher resolution and fidelity of color, there will no longer be a need to divide the work up among three separate chips. Shorter flange to chip distances can be used, and the millions of excellent still and motion picture lenses can be used.

Luminance and Chrominance

Black and white would consist of one channel: luminance, which means brightness. Absence of luminance (brightness), is black. Maximum brightness would be white. All the steps in between are the shades of gray. Chrominance is color.

Components

DV is usually color. And it's component.

Component video breaks the video signal down into 3 separate "tracks," or "channels" of information. To save space on the video tape, the engineers took a shortcut. A video signal really should have at least five tracks: red, blue, green, brightness and contrast. But, by combining some of the information, they eliminated two of the five "tracks." The result is the somewhat baffling Y, R-Y, B-Y scheme. It's arcane, but it somehow works.

The three "tracks" of video information are:

1. Y (luminance, or brightness)

2. R-Y (Red color, or chrominance, minus the luminance signal)

3. B-Y (Blue color, or chrominance, minus the luminance signal).

What happened to green, you may ask? To find out, try this experiment. Play a component video tape back onto a component monitor. A BetaSP video tape recorder attached with three BNC cables to a PVM monitor will demonstrate this admirably. First, attach only the Y cable. The picture is black and white. Next, attach only the R-Y cable only. The picture looks greenish-reddish. Finally, attach only the B-Y. The picture is greenish-blue. This shows that the Red and Blue channels also carry some green color information.

The Y signal is the largest of the three "tracks." In addition to brightness, it carries information about contrast, resolution and sharpness.

Composite Video

By the way, composite video is what you're probably watching on your TV set at home, along with VHS, Video8, Hi8, 3/4" Umatic and 1". The signal is analog. All the picture information of color, brightness and contrast is lumped together, composited, on one "track" on the video tape.

DV Components and Conversion

So the signal is divided into three components: Y, Y-R and Y-B.

The next thing that happens inside your DV camcorder is the analog to digital conversion, which is a three-part process consisting of sampling, quantization and digitizing.

Sampling

"Sampling" means how many times a second the signal is divided into millions of sections. The black & white component is sampled 13.5 million times a second (13.5 MHz). That means it is divided into 13.5 million sections. "Sampling" is a measurement of the speed at which the three components are checked for information. It's measured in Megahertz, and the bigger the number, the faster the information is gathered. This measurement of speed is similar to the way your 100MHz computer pokes along much more slowly than your brand new 966 MHz Pentium or 733 MHz G4.

The big difference is that, in video, all the information has to come out 30 times a second, or 25 in PAL. So, if there's a bottleneck in the sampling, you don't get a picture. Your TV can't wait, fingers drumming, while the information is slowly being processed.

The Y component (luminance) of the DV signal is "sampled" at 13.5 MHz, which means that the black and white (along with brightness and resolution) video signal is checked 13.5 million times a second. Each of the two color components (R-Y, B-Y) is sampled 3.375 million times a second (3.375 Mhz).

When you see the number 4:1:1, it is referring to the ratio of the luminance to the chrominance sampling (13.5 divided by 3.375 is 4).

Why so fast? Since there's more information in the Y component (luminance) than the other two—not only black and white but also shades of gray, level of picture detail, brightness and contrast—it has to be checked more often. Remember, all the information has to be read and translated into a digital stream.

4:2:2, 4:1:1, 4:2:0

D-1 and Digital Betacam (DigiBeta) encode the video signal at a ratio of 4:2:2. DV encodes the signal at a ratio of 4:1:1 (4:2:0 in PAL).

These numbers are the ratios of the way the video signal is broken down into the 3 separate "tracks" of information.

When we say DigiBeta is 4:2:2, and DV is 4:1:1, we are comparing the different ratios of brightness to color information. The numbers don't actually refer to any real, absolute values. They are ratios. The numbers 4:1:1 could just as well be 8:2:2 or 16:4:4 or 1:¼:¼.

In 4:2:2, the first number, "4", refers to the 13.5 MHz luminance (brightness and green) sampling rate in the video signal. D-1, DigiBeta, BetaSX, Digital-S, DV, DVCam and DVCPro all sample at 13.5 MHz.

The second and third numbers in "4:2:2" or "4:1:1" are the ratios of the other two "tracks" of color information compared with the luminance "track."

So, 4:2:2 (D-1, DigiBeta, BetaSX, Digital-S, and DVCPRO50) means that the two "tracks" of color information are sampled at half the rate of the luminance, which would be 6.75 MHz.

4:1:1 (NTSC DV, DVCAM, DVCPRO) means that the color information is sampled at ¼ the rate of the luminance signal, or 3.375 MHz.

What this really means is that DigiBeta and the 4:2:2 formats let us have 360 colors per horizontal scan line of video. DV and the 4:1:1 formats let us have 180 colors per scan line. What, only 180 colors? But my computer displays millions of them.

Lest we become seriously panicked by this paucity of colors, remember that BetaSP, that venerable standard of the last twenty years, only has a color sampling rate of 1.5MHz. Although it's not digital, and the comparison is not totally accurate, BetaSP would translate to a ratio of 4:½:½.

No one ever said NTSC and PAL were great display formats. Each scan line is made up of 720 pixels (dots of color) going across the screen. And, as we've pointed out, although NTSC is supposed to scan 525 of these horizontal lines up and down, by the time it gets onto your TV set, it's far fewer. Figure on 480 pixels (dots of color) going up and down. That is certainly worse than your computer monitor.

Quantizing

Sampling tells us how often the three channels are being checked, but we also need to know about their quanitities. Quantizing is the process of deciding how many colors and how much brightness we're going to see. You can adjust your computer to display 256 colors, thousands of colors, or millions of colors. Try it. Setting 256 colors will let the computer run faster. Millions of colors slows things down. The same holds true of our video signal. If we quantize too many colors, things will bog down, and our picture will be a blob.

The Y component is quantized as 256 shades of gray, ranging from pure white to deep black. The other two components, R-Y and B-Y, are quantized as 256 colors each. This is also called 8 bit depth. But, as we just read earlier in the discussion of 4:1:1, we're really only getting 180 colors, not 256.

Digitizing

Next, all this information has to be converted to binary file format, since DV is, after all, digital.

Every pixel will be represented by binary numbers, defining placement, color, brightness, and picture detail.

Compression

The technology that really makes digital video possible is the process of compression, in which the actual file size of each frame is made smaller by using mathematical formulas to describe areas of similar color or brightness. Let's say our picture has a big blue sky in it. Rather than define each pixel with the same numbers, compression schemes tell the file to repeat the same shade of blue, for example, for the next 20 horizontal pixels.

DV images are compressed at a rate of 5:1. Here we go again with more ratios. DV information travels back and forth from the camera to your computer or monitor at a constant digital "stream" of 35 Mbps (millions of bits per second), which is the same as 3.5 MB/ sec (Megabytes or Millions of bytes per second).

Think of your modem. A standard modem has a "bandwidth" of 56Kbps, which lets information travel along at 56,000 bits per second, and a paltry 5,600 bytes per second (divide by 10). By comparison, the hard drive in your computer probably has a transfer rate of 5 Megabytes per second.

So, the signal is compressed to 1/5 of its original data size. Without compression, the camcorder and computer would have to stream data five times larger, at rates of 350 Mbps or 35 Megabytes per second. That's too fast even for most hard drives, whose average transfer rates are 8 Megabytes per second. Not to mention the size of video cassette we'd have to use.

Unlike JPEG, MPEG and other video compression schemes (called codecs) used on computers, the compression here is done by the hardware, so it's fast and consistent, not variable. NTSC DV only has color in every other pixel. PAL DV has color in every other line. That's how "they" save so much space.

By the way, JVC's Digital-S (D-9) and Panasonic's DVCPRO50 is compressed 3.3:1, with a data rate of 50 Mbps (5 MB/sec). Sony's DigiBeta is compressed 2:1.

Heads and Tape

DV Tape is 1/4" wide, and a mini DV cassette is less than ¼ the size of a VHS cassette. Yet it has to store much more information. Like most video systems, DV tape is pulled along a rotating drum to which are attached two tiny electro-magnetic "heads" for recording and playing back video and audio. The heads are made of small coils of wire that magnetize the DV tape when an electrical pulse is applied. Since it's digital, the pulse is either on or off. A zero is represented by absence of magnetizing. A one is represented by a magnetized portion of tape.

The drum, which is about an inch in diameter, rotates 150 times per second, 9,000 rpm. The drum is angled so that the heads travel in a diagonal direction along the width of the tape, laying down information in bands—called tracks—from top to bottom. This is called helical scanning.

Each time the head comes in contact with the tape, it records a "track." There are 10 tracks per frame of NTSC DV (12 tracks in PAL). Each track contains picture information for approximately 48 video scan lines. Extra tracks are used for timecode and audio.

This is true micro-miniaturization. Each track on DV tape is 10 microns wide (10 millionths of a meter). A human hair is 60 microns thick.

Audio

The DV format uses digital audio. Almost all DV camcorders automatically record sound onto the tape, whether you need it or not. You can also add better microphones. Whatever, the audio is recorded onto the DV tape as a digital signal, similar to a CD or DAT.

Sampling

As with the video signal, audio is sampled and quanitized. The camcorder ususally offers you a menu of sampling rates, typically 48 KHz, 44.1 KHz or 32 KHz.

Sound is sampled at a much slower rate than video because there isn't as much information to gather. A 48KHz sampling rate means the sound is checked 48,000 times a second. By the way, DAT (Digital Audio Tape) uses 48 KHz sampling and CDs use 44.1 KHZ sampling. The audio in the DV format is not compressed.

Quantization

When setting up audio on your camcorder, you are sometimes offered the choice of 16 bit or 12 bit audio. This is the quantization, or quantity of choices being made while sampling.

Higher sampling and quantization rates will yield better sound. 48KHz with 16 bit sound is the best. However, remember that 16 bit audio gives you two tracks of sound, while 12 bit audio lets you record 4 tracks. This should rarely be a problem until you start recording your son's string quartet, and want to isolate each instrument with a separate microphone.

16 bit

16 bit is 2 to the 16th power, which means there are 65,536 choices of tonal variation.

12 bit

12 bit is 2 to the 12th, which is 4,096. 12 bit audio is usually sampled at 32 KHz.

Comparing DV with DigiBeta

DV camcorders work pretty much the same way as high-end digital camcorders like DigiBeta. Both are component formats, which means the picture information is recorded onto tape as three separate "tracks." The three tracks separate out the three primary colors, along with brightness and contrast. The components are: brightness (luminance, Y), Red-Y (chrominance, R-Y) and Blue-Y (chrominance, B-Y).

By the way, S-Video is also a component format, but with only two "tracks" or channels of picture information. And composite video lumps everything together.

DV has a sample rate of 13.5 MHz, which is the same as DigiBeta.

However, DigiBeta uses 4:2:2 encoding compared with DV's 4:1:1 encoding.

DigiBeta, therefore, will have truer color (chrominance), and a better signal-to-noise ratio (less grain or noise) because of its 10-bit encoding (1,024 colors) versus DV's 8-bit (256 colors).

DigiBeta compresses the signal 2:1, while DV compresses it 5:1.

Comparing DV with BetaSP

Now, let's compare DV with BetaSP, which has been a broadcast, industrial and documentary standard for twenty years. I think DV is as good as, if not better than, analog Betacam SP.

DV has a video signal-to-noise ratio of 54 dB. BetaSP is 51 dB.

DV has a luminance bandwidth of 5.75 MHz. Betacam SP has a lower 4.1 MHz.

Recently, the good lenses of BetaSP and DigiBeta camcorders have become available on higher-end professional DV cameras. And better glass is being used on the consumer models.

Progressive Scan CCDs

Some cameras use a Progressive Scan CCD image sensor. Every pixel on the CCD is used to produce a full frame video image. In contrast, the conventional interlace-type CCD produces only half a full frame, known as a field, in the same amount of time. Progressive Scan Mode produces sharper stills. HOWEVER, it does not gives us better video—no matter what you may have heard. If you shoot video in Progressive Mode, the CCD cannot keep up, and it simply repeats the same frame. This can cause jittery images. We'll see Progressive Scan for full motion video very soon.

Cameras

There are basically 3 styles of cameras, which for lack of any better nomenclature we'll call "Juicy-Juice Box," "Oil Can" and "Big Gun." More shapes will evolve as components become smaller. "Lipstick" cameras will proliferate. Lenses will be separated from recorders. The rapidly decreasing time from idea inception to product release should propel more inspired ergonomic designs.

"Juicy-Juice Box" describes the shape of the tiny, upright cameras made popular for home video. They almost fit in the palm of your hand, almost fit in your pocket, and are getting smaller with every new model introduction. The first ones came from JVC, quickly followed by Sony and Canon.

"Oil Can" is the next size larger—about the size and weight of a quart of motor oil in a "handy" plastic container.

"Handycam" is Sony's trademark for this style of camera body—basically a handgrip you hold in your palm with a lens sticking out the front. I think Panasonic has a trademark on the term "palmcorder," which is a better name.

The one thing not so handy is the ergonomics. After a couple of hours of handholding, your hand and wrist will most likely become very sore.

However, this is the most versatile of DV cameras, with features and 3-chip circuits that approach the level of professional camcorders twice the size, weight and price.

"Big Gun" or "Shoulder-Resting" camcorders have the traditional shape we're all familiar with from 16mm handheld cameras and video ENG (news) cameras.

Most of the "professional" video cameras used by news crews and wedding videographers are this size. The image quality can be slightly better than the two smaller siblings, because of better lenses, larger chips, and special electronic options.

These "big guns, " with a few exceptions, accept the larger of the two DV size tapes, making it possible to record up to 3 hours on one tape.

Image Stabilization

When you have a tiny camera, of no apparent weight, appended to your hand with a thin leather strap, every move you make and every breath you take will show up on screen in headache-inducing magnification.

The remedy for home-video induced nausea is image stabilization. There are two kinds: optical and digital. The idea is to shift the image in the opposite direction of the camera's movement. Suppose you're shooting a Western. The bad guy is galloping in front of you on his horse. You're shooting from a camera car. The car hits a bump. Your arm bounces up. The bad guy is no longer in frame. The only thing in frame are a couple of buzzards circling overhead, waiting for the imminent demise of your career. Had you turned on your image stabilizer, you would have been saved. When your arm bounced up, actuators would have told the lens elements to aim down, keeping the cowboy centered in frame.

Optical Stabilization

Optical stabilization dates back to the 1970s when two optical-mechanical devices were invented: the Dynalens and the ARRI Image Stabilizer. Both attached to the front of existing lenses; they were large and heavy. Built-in gyroscopes adjusted the optical path to compensate for camera movement and shake. The Dynalens was a sandwich of two optical elements with silicon fluid inside. Whenever the camera shook, the elements compensated in the opposite direction. The silicon helped dampen the vibration, but it also degraded the image by diffusing it a little. ARRI's Stabilizer came out a few years later, adapted from British Aerospace technology used in binoculars. It was lighter and didn't soften the image; but wouldn't work on wide-angle lenses. It consisted of mirror pairs that shifted to keep the picture smooth.

DV camcorders use two similar methods of optical stabilization, but improve the original concept enormously through miniaturization and electronics. Heavy gyros have been replaced by motion sensors and microprocessors.

Sony's system improves on the ARRI system by actually moving an element inside the zoom lens up-down, left-right in reaction to all your best efforts to make your audience dizzy.

Canon applies the Dynalens idea with glass elements and a thin layer of silicon, controlled by microprocessors and motion sensors, which essentially creates a variable angle prism. The two optical flats, supported by bellows, shift in reaction to movement to keep the target centered.

Electronic Stabilization

The digital answer to wobbly-vision, developed about 1996, is to use a smaller area on the CCD as the actual picture-taking area. When the camera moves, electronic circuits find a fixed point, like a nose or an eye, and keep it in the same relative position on tape. Electronic stabilization can add noise to the picture, and can also be fooled when you pan or tilt quickly.

Electronic stabilization can also be done in post-production. Be sure to frame a bit wider than the final composition, allowing it to be repositioned frame by frame.

This had to be done on the title sequence of the movie *Bonfire of the Vanities*. It was shot on film, but the idea applies to DV as well. Our camera was placed on scaffolding on top of the Chrysler Building in New York, on some particularly windy days in hurricane season. The camera was a highly sophisticated, computer-controlled motion-control rig. Yet watching our tests in dailies, we noticed all of New York swaying back and forth in the background. The next day, someone heard the elevator operator casually mentioning that the entire building sways something like seven feet back and forth. So, to stabilize the shot, the optical wizards at R/Greenberg Associates had to reposition each frame of film, frame by frame. Like digital stabilization, they had to pick a fixed point that would serve as a reference point, and around which everything else would be moved equally.

Autofocus

Otto Focus is the little camera assistant living inside your camcorder, who keeps everything in focus. When he sleeps, a special circuit takes over that analyzes the contrast of the scene. A picture that is in focus has more contrast than when it is out of focus. Check it out with a reflex still camera. Look at a black area next to a white area. As you turn the focus barrel to put the image out of focus, the black area starts looking gray. Anyway, the camcorder checks the scene many times a second, and sends its commands to a miniature servo motor in the lens assembly.

FireWire IEEE1394

More than 50 broadcast and consumer video equipment manufacturers have adopted IEEE 1394, also known as FireWire and i.Link, as the standard digital audio/video interface for all DV equipment. If you're planning to buy a DV camcorder and it doesn't have Firewire, forget about it.

FireWire is the Apple trademark, i.Link is the Sony term, and IEEE 1394 is the generic industry name for a standard that was agreed upon by a consortium of engineers, making the specs much more complicated than the actual product—which is really just a wire with plugs on each end, and a bunch of technical specs on how the signal should travel down those wires.

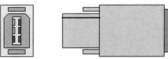

FireWire makes DV possible, bcause it lets you plug a DV camcorder into your computer to transfer all the video as digital data for editing or emailing. And when you're finished editing, FireWire lets you plug the camera back into the computer to make a tape from your digitally edited show. However, FireWire is not just DV—there are FireWire hard drives, scanners, CD burners, and all kinds of peripherals.

FireWire was invented by Apple Computer in 1986 as a high speed serial bus intended to replace its ADB connectors for keyboards, printers, scanners and other peripherals.

But FireWire didn't catch on until 1995, when it appeared under a different, licensed name—i.Link—on the first DV camcorders from Sony. Apple retained the FireWire trademark.

DV really was the spark that got FireWire going, because it needed faster transfer rates than USB, and SCSI was slower still. In December 1995, FireWire was adopted by the IEEE (Institute of Electrical and Electronics Engineers), and officially called IEEE 1394. FireWire works with both Macs and PCs.

FireWire cables have either 6 or 4 conductors.

The standard FireWire cable has six conductors. Data travels over two individually shielded twisted pairs. Two additional wires carry power (8 to 40 v, 1.5 amp maximum), although they are rarely used. Most camcorders don't even bother with the power wires.

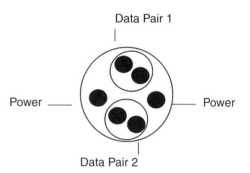

Data Pair 1

Power — Power

Data Pair 2

The wires end in either 6-conductor gameboy-style plugs, or smaller 4-conductor ones.

Sony usually uses a 4-conductor cable and 4-pin receptacles on its DV camcorders, DVCRs and i.Link-equipped computers. They are like the 6-pin connectors, but without the power wires. To connect a Sony DV camcorder to a standard IEE1394 FireWire device or interface card, you can buy cables with 4 pins on one end and 6 pins on the other.

Data Rates

IEEE 1394 FireWire has a data rate of 100 to 400 Megabits per second, which translates to 40 Megabytes per second, over a 4.5 meter (14') cable.

By comparison, an RS-232 serial port handles 20 kilobits per second, a USB port will move about 12Mbits per second (1.2 Megabytes), and SCSI devices have a data throughput of 5 to 320 Megabytes per second (50 to 3200 Mbits per second).

Cable

The data cable is 28 gauge, and the power pair in the standard cable is 22 gauge. Longer cable runs are possible with thicker cable or by lowering the bit rate. Sony DV camcorders have put out data through FireWire/i.Link cables at about 100 Megabits per second. So it should be possible to have cables 60 to 90 feet long (20 to 30 meters).

FireWire is not DV. First you buy a DV camcorder. Then you either buy a FireWire/i.Link/IEEE 1394 equipped computer (Mac or Sony), or buy an add-in IEEE 1394 PCI board or PCMCIA card.

Companies that make 1394 cards include Adaptec, Texas Instruments, Radius, Promax, Canopus, Orange Micro, and others.

Mulitple Devices

You can, although I've never tried it, connect up to 63 FireWire devices together at one time, provided the cables aren't too long. The 400 Mbps data rate permits simultaneous full-motion, full-frame, 30-frame-per-second video and CD-quality stereo audio. FireWire is Plug and Play, meaning you can plug it in without shutting down the computer.

Up to 63 devices can be connected simply by connecting them with FireWire cables. ID numbers do not have to be set. Even though they are "daisy-chained," turning off a device does not prevent the next peripheral in line from being used. Devices can be plugged and unplugged at will, and they will be automatically recognized. This is called "hot-pluggable."

Data Throughput Speed Chart

Device	Mbps Megabits per second	MB per second MegaBytes per second
FireWire	100-400	10-40
USB	12	1.2
RS-232	.2	.02

SCSI

And then there's SCSI: SCSI, SCSI-2, SCSI-3, Fast SCSI, Fast/Wide SCSI, Ultra SCSI, Wide Ultra SCSI, Ultra2 SCSI, Wide Ultra2 SCSI, and SCSI-3, not to mention Ultra160 and Ultra320.

SCSI Names	8-bit - Narrow	16-bit - Wide
	speeds measured in MegaBytes per second	
SCSI (aka SCSI-1)	5 MB/ps	n/a
Fast, SCSI-2	10 MB/ps	20 MB/ps
Fast-20, SCSI-3, Ultra	20 MB/ps	40 MB/ps
Fast-40, SCSI-4, Ultra2	40 MB/ps	80 MB/ps
Fast-80, Ultra3, Ultra160	80 MB/ps	160 MB/ps
Fast-160, Ultra320	160 MB/ps	320 MB/ps

Five Minute Videomaker's Guide

How to Use a
DV Camcorder

How to Use a DV Camcorder

Sony DSR-PD100A

Despite the number of DV camcorders available, the way most of them work is fairly similar. There are some subtle differences. But thankfully, learning to shoot with a DV Camcorder is something like learning to drive a car. Once you learn how to use one model, most others will be familiar. But, like learning to drive with a stick shift, DV has its own manual controls that can help promote your work to a higher level of performance and quality.

In the next chapters, we'll learn how to shoot with a DV Camcorder. The camera we'll use is a Sony DCR-PD100A.

It is a DVCAM camcorder that uses mini DVCAM or mini DV cassettes.

This camera, in my opinion, represents most of the features used on most DV cameras. If you learn the PD100A, you'll be comfortable with most other DV camcorders.

We are not endorsing this camera. Having said that, the PD100A is the camera I recommend very often, because of its high quality, good picture, ease of use, and number of features.

After examining the PD100A, we'll look at some other popular cameras.

Sony DSR-PD100A

Sony's DSR-PD100A camcorder is the quintessential "Handycam." For that reason, we'll use it to describe the basic operation of most DV camcorders, and examine it in greater detail than other models. As they say in the car commercials, your mileage may vary, but these instructions should still get you there.

The PD100A has the familiar shape of the majority of consumer camcorders, along with an adjustable strap that presses your hand firmly against the body of the camera. Perhaps it is this cradling of the hand that gives it the odd name of "handycam."

The PD100A is one of the smallest professional video cameras that doesn't really look "professional." It looks like millions of other consumer miniDV cameras, and bridges the gap between consumer and larger professional models.

It accepts both DVCAM and mini DV tape. The "A" means it is the NTSC model; the PAL model is called DSR-PD100AP. DSR-PD100 is an older model.

Three ¼" CCDs convert light into digits, capable of rendering an NTSC image of 500 TV lines horizontal resolution. Each CCD records 380,000 pixels interlaced (for video), or 480,000 progressive.

Minimum illumination is 4 lux. Most functions and camera status are displayed in the viewfinder. 480p (progressive as opposed to interlaced) is available for both video or still images.

The camera has a built-in PCMCIA slot for Type II PC flash memory cards, and comes with a PCMCIA-to-Memory Stick adapter for still image storage. Up to 150 640x480 JPEG pictures can be stored on one chewing-gum sized Memory Stick. About 340 stills can be recorded on a 40 minute tape for 7 seconds each, which I find is an easier way to go than the proprietary Sony Memory Stick.

Aspect ratios are switchable from 4:3 to 16:9 .

The viewfinder is color, and there is a swing-out 3.5" LCD display panel on the camera right side. Purists may prefer the black and white viewfinder of the next "higher" model, Sony's PD150. A black and white finder is sharper, which is helpful for critical determination of focus. A color finder has the advantage of being, well, color, and truer to what is actually being recorded.

The 12x zoom lens has Sony optics, auto and manual focus, and electronic image stabilization. The lens is not removable, but various wide-angle and tele lens adapters are available.

An XLR adaptor mounts on top to connect either electret or dynamic microphones.

The PD100A is handled by Sony's Broadcast and Professional Group.

List price is $2,825. Street price may be less.

Sony's Consumer Division sells the similar DCR-TRV900 for about $500 less than the PD100A.

The TRV900 has three chips, like the PD100A.

The main difference is that the TRV900 records only on mini-DV tape (not on DVCAM), lacks timecode and XLR audio input.

TRV900

TRV900

Sony's consumer line includes similar camcorders with a single chip CCDs.

These consumer mini-DV camcorders are Sony's DCR-TRV8, TRV10, TRV11, and TRV20.

Almost anything in the Sony line named TRV will be a Handycam, but that could include 8, Hi8 or Digital 8.

TRV20

TRV20

PD100A Camera Views

FRONT

filter ring

lens

stereo microphone

handgrip strap

IR remote control sensor

REAR

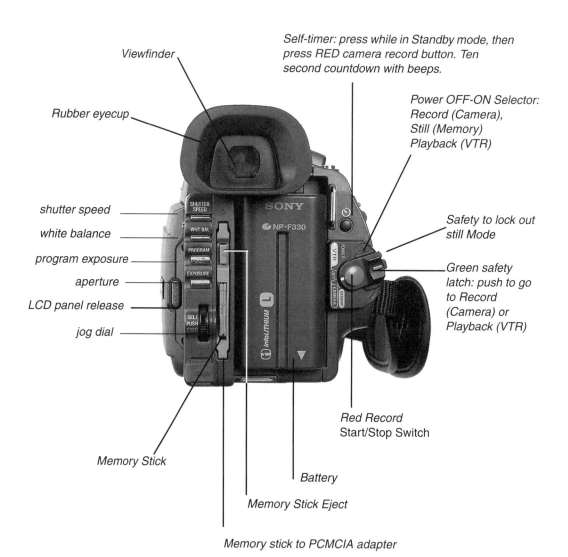

Viewfinder

Rubber eyecup

Self-timer: press while in Standby mode, then press RED camera record button. Ten second countdown with beeps.

Power OFF-ON Selector: Record (Camera), Still (Memory) Playback (VTR)

shutter speed

white balance

program exposure

aperture

LCD panel release

jog dial

Safety to lock out still Mode

Green safety latch: push to go to Record (Camera) or Playback (VTR)

Red Record Start/Stop Switch

Memory Stick

Battery

Memory Stick Eject

Memory stick to PCMCIA adapter

TOP

focus ring

hot shoe

edit search

timecode reset

zoom control

still photo button

fader

backlight

ND filter

VTR controls

BOTTOM

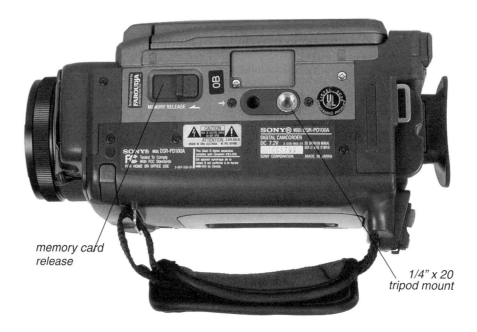

memory card
release

1/4" x 20
tripod mount

CAMERA LEFT

ND filter

focus

LCD display: timecode, battery status

Auto/
Manual
control

momentary
auto focus

CAMERA RIGHT

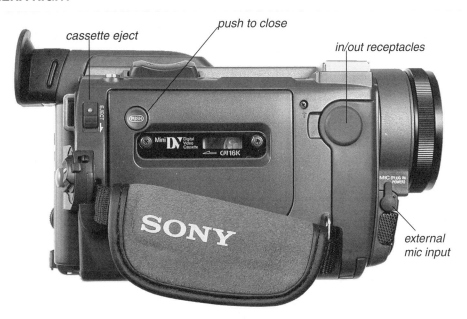

cassette eject

push to close

in/out receptacles

external
mic input

Quick Start: Shooting with the PD100A

Removing and Attaching Battery

Most DV camcorders use Lithium-Ion or Nickel Metal Hydride Batteries that slide or snap onto the back. The battery is held in place by a push-button latch.

Rechargable batteries do NOT last forever. Depending on brand and how they were used, you can expect to buy new batteries after about 200 charge-discharge cycles.

Sony now uses Lithium Ion batteries. They do not have the dreaded "memory effect" of Ni-Cads, which required careful attention to discharging to prolong longevity.

Removing Battery

1. Lift up on the eyepiece to get it out of the way.

2. Push the Batt Release (Battery Release) button in— in the direction of its arrow.

3. It's easiest to use one hand: push the Batt Release button with your index finger, and lift up on the battery with your thumb.

4. Pull the battery away from the camera body.

Attaching Battery

To install a new battery, do the opposite.

1, Line up the top of the battery just below the **Batt Release** button.

2. Slide the battery toward the camera. (You'll see the **Batt Release** button being pushed in).

3 Push down until it locks in place with a click.

Recharging Battery

Plug the battery charger cable into the receptacle marked **DC IN** at the back of the camera.

Plug the power cord of the charger into a wall outlet. The charger is auto-sensing for 100 to 240 V AC.

Charging time for the NP-F330 battery that comes with the camera is about 2.5 hours.

When charging is complete, the battery/timecode display window will read *FULL*. The time shown is estimated battery life for recording in minutes. NP-F330 battery will last about 40 minutes.

The largest battery, NP-F950, takes about 6.5 hours to charge, and will last for about 4 hours of recording time.

Loading Tape

To load the camera with tape, a battery (or power supply) must be connected.

However, you do NOT have to turn the camera on.

1. To open the tape cover, press the little blue button and, at the same time, push the **EJECT** button in the direction of its arrow.

2. The spring-loaded door is released by a servo, and pops open. Note: If the handgrip strap is too tight, it may prevent the tape door from fully opening.

3. Load a mini DVCAM or miniDV cassette into the tray.

4. The clear window on the cassette, which shows tape remaining, faces out.

Be sure the REC - SAVE slider on the bottom of the cassette is set to the Record position. If it is in the SAVE position, you will see a flashing tape icon with a slash through it, telling you the camera cannot record on the tape.

5. Slide the cassette all the way down into the chamber. Close the tape cover by pushing on the button labelled "**PUSH**." If you don't push on **PUSH**, the cover probably will not latch closed.

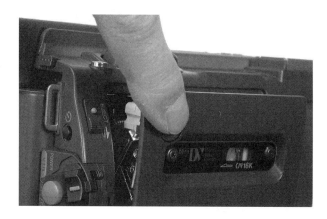

Shooting: Quick Start

This is the emergency chapter. You just pulled the camera out of its case, and you have to shoot in a hurry. Here's a quick checklist on default settings and auto-everything.

1. I'm embarrassed to say it, but remove the lens cap.

2. The camera's Main Power Switch has 4 positions: **CAMERA** (to record), **MEMORY** (still pictures), **OFF**, and **VTR** (playback).

    The green button in the center of the Main Power Switch is a safety latch to help prevent accidental changes.

3. But first, there's another safety slider that can actually make things a lot easier. The little, un-labelled slide switch lurking at 2 o'clock—above and to the right of the Main Switch—can help prevent accidentally going into Still Photo Mode when you really want to be shooting Video. Slide the switch toward the rear of the camera to LOCK OUT Still Photo Mode.

4. Push the little green bar in with your thumb, and move the 4-position lever to the **CAMERA** position. You are ready to shoot. The camera is in the sublime state of readiness called "Standby," indicated by the abbreviation **STBY** in the viewfinder.

    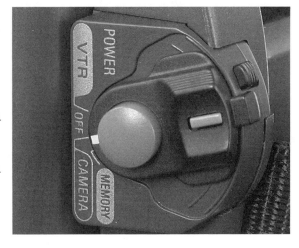

5. Press the red button once to begin recording. You'll see **REC** for "Record" in the viewfinder. Press again to stop tape. Press again to resume shooting. And so on.

Turn the Main Power Switch **OFF** when you want to conserve power. If the camera stays in standby more than five minutes, it turns off by itself.

Auto Everything

The most beautiful stampede of zebras the world has ever seen is taking place right in front of you. No time to read the rest of this manual, nor to fumble with the other kind of manual—the manual settings you painstakingly entered last night for that low-light animals-in-the-watering-hole sequence illuminated by vehicle headlamps. If you use the same exposure settings now, you'll be about 20 stops over-exposed.

Auto Lock and Auto Focus

On the camera left side, set the **AUTO LOCK—HOLD** switch to the top (**AUTO LOCK)** position.

This setting basically "locks" out manual settings, and lets the camera automatically set exposure, shutter speed, and white balance.

Set the **FOCUS** switch to **AUTO**.

Viewfinder Warnings

Check the viewfinder, and if you see the following warnings, push the appropriate switch until the warning disappears:

ND ON — press the **ND FILTER** switch to activate the ND filter (cut down light).
ND OFF — press the **ND FILTER** switch to allow more light through the lens.

Square with quarter sun icon — press the **BACK LIGHT** switch
FADER, **MONOTONE**, **OVERLAP**— press the **FADER** switch

Eyepiece

The viewfinder contains optics that magnify the
image displayed on a small internal color LCD
screen. You should set the correct diopter for your
eyesight by moving the adjustment lever until the
letters displayed in the viewfinder are sharpest.
(This is easier and more accurate than focusing
the diopter on a distant object).

When the rubber eyecup becomes encrusted with
donut goo, buy a box of Isopropyl Alcohol Swabs
from your local drugstore. The swabs come in handy foil packets.

Cleaning the eyepiece lens with the same Isopropyl Swab will smear the element.
Use lens cleaner and lens tissue instead.

Handgrip

Do not carry the camera by its eyepiece or the
microphone. Use the handgrip.

When handholding, the strap should be snug
against the back of your hand. Lift up the velcro
cover with the SONY logo, and tighten the strap.

Lens and Sunshade

Clean the lens with lens cleaner and tissue or a good photographic microfibre cloth.

The included sunshade screws onto the lens. Line up the locating pin at 3 o'clock on the lens with its matching indentation on the sunshade.

locating pin

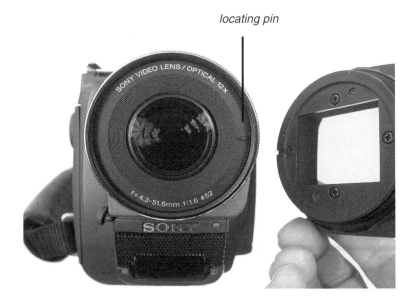

LCD Screen

It's usually easier to shoot while looking at the flip-out LCD monitor than into the viewfinder, except in very bright sunlight. Framing with the LCD screen allows much smoother hand-held shots, because you are not transmitting any body movement to the camera, and your arms are working almost like a Steadicam.

To open the LCD monitor, press the silver OPEN button, and swing the monitor panel out.

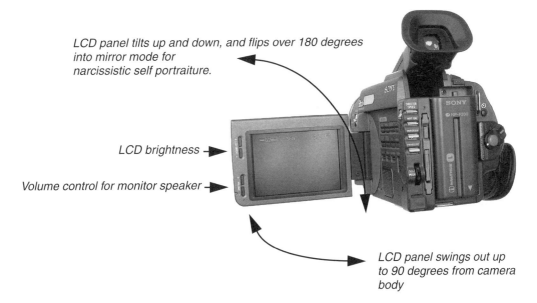

LCD panel tilts up and down, and flips over 180 degrees into mirror mode for narcissistic self portraiture.

LCD brightness →

Volume control for monitor speaker →

LCD panel swings out up to 90 degrees from camera body

The viewfinder shuts off when the LCD screen is out, except in mirror mode.

The LCD screen must be in its original vertical position to close.

Try not to touch the plastic LCD screen. It inevitably becomes smudged, and you can clean it off with a dry microfiber optical cloth. Do not use alcohol, solvents or lens fluid.

Stiffened nylon and velcro monitor hoods are very useful for keeping glare off the screen in bright sunlight. The original ones were made by Hoodman, but a number of companies make them.

Focus

With the lens zoomed in "tight" (T), the closest you can focus is about 30 inches from the front of the lens, which will cover an area (called field of view) that is about 1 3/4" high x 2 1/2" wide.

With the lens zoomed out (W), you can focus to about 1/2 inch from the front element, with a field of view about 1" high x 1 1/2" wide.

So, to get a gorgeous macro shot of that tarantula sitting on your pillow, you'll have to go in close and wide.

Auto Focus

Auto Focus is great until the speaker you are interviewing bends down to retrieve the notes that just fell onto the ground. The camera lens jumps to the next distant object, and then may hunt back and forth for the speaker, even after he or she is back in frame.

Auto Focus should be avoided particularly when shooting scenes with little contrast (sky, walls, ocean, snow), scenes with very low light levels, and still lifes.

Use manual focus as often as possible. Slide the focus selector to **MANUAL** position. An icon of a hand with the letter "F" appears in the viewfinder or on the LCD screen to indicate you are in manual focus mode.

The best way to assure correct focus is to zoom in all the way (T), turn the lens focus barrel until the image appears sharp, and then zoom out to whatever focal length you like. The image will stay sharp throughout the zoom range.

Sliding the focus selector momentarily down to **INFINITY** can be helpful to reset focus when shooting landscapes. An icon of mountains appears in the finder.

focus barrel

Press the **PUSH AUTO** button momentarily to get a quick automatic focus lock on a subject.

Slide the selector back to **AUTO** to get out of manual focus mode.

Zoom

Rule number 1: Don't

Rule number 2: Most people zoom too often.

Try to feather the starts and stops of your zoom as gracefully as possible by using a delicate touch on the zoom rocker control.

No, the PD100A does not have manual zoom capability.

The PD-150 does.

When the camera is on a tripod, use a remote zoom control. It plugs into the LANC receptacle under the rubber cover on the forward camera right side.

Varizoom and Coolzoom are two excellent remote zoom controls.

Speaking of tripods—the 1/4"x20 threaded tripod receptacle at the bottom of the camera is rather shallow. Do not force the tripod mounting bolt too deep. If the bolt is too long, it could crack the housing and damage electronic parts inside.

Manual Control

When the action is slower and less controlling of your destiny than, for example, racing with the bulls of Pamplona, controlling manual exposure will yield better pictures.

AUTO LOCK Switch

Turn off the camera's autopilot by sliding the **AUTO LOCK** switch to its middle position.

The center position is Manual Control, should be labeled as such, and probably would have been if there were room to say Manual Control of Exposure, Shutter, White Balance and other things.

The bottom position is **HOLD**, where you can lock in your manual settings.

This switch is useful to compare automatic and manual exposure settings.

You can switch out of Auto, set a manual exposure, as described next, and then flip back and forth with this switch between the two modes.

EXPOSURE (Aperture)

1. Press the **EXPOSURE** button on the back of the camera to turn manual exposure on.

A linear scale appears in the upper left corner of the eyepiece or LCD screen. The minus sign means darker (closing down the iris), the plus sign means brighter (opening the iris).

The actual F stop is displayed in the finder in 1/2 stop increments at the lower left of the display.

2. Turn the control dial up or down to adjust the F stop. Pushing in on the control dial will have no effect. To lock it in, slide the **AUTO LOCK** switch to **HOLD**.

The aperture is adjustable from F2 to F11. Closing down further than F11 shuts out all light, as indicated by CLOSE in the finder. Opening wider than F2 kicks in electronic gain, indicated in 3 dB increments up to +18 dB. Electronic gain introduces grain, or "noise," to the picture.

There are no click stops for the aperture settings, nor are there end stops for the dial.

Backlight

There is a **BACKLIGHT** button on top of the camera. It only works in **AUTO LOCK** mode. It's a quick way to open the aperture about a stop when a backlit subject looks too dark against a bright background. For example, when you're shooting a close-up of your daughter on the ski slope, the ambient brightness of the snow fools the camera into thinking the whole scene is the brightness of snow. So your little darling's face will be too dark. Press the **BACKLIGHT** button to brighten her up. Better yet, use manual exposure control.

Shutter

With the **AUTO LOCK** switch in its center, manual position, you can adjust the shutter speed of the camera from 1/4 to 1/10,000 second (1/3 to 1/10,000 on PAL model).

1. Press the **SHUTTER SPEED** button on the back of the camera.

2. Turn the control dial.

3. The shutter speed will be displayed at the lower left of the viewfinder or LCD screen.

High shutter speeds are useful for freezing quickly moving action either as still frames or in post production. Remember, you're still shooting at 30 images per second (25 in PAL), so it's not slow motion; you are simply capturing each one of those images in a much shorter span of time.

There can be a few disadvantages to fast shutter speeds—similar to the ones encountered when using a motion picture camera. Vertical objects may strobe when panning, and car wheels sometimes look like they are turning the wrong way.

Slow shutter speeds

Slow shutter speeds of 1/4 and 1/8 second provide a smeared, semi-slow motion look similar to filming at 6 frames per second and transferring that footage to video at 6 frames per second. In essence, the camera is recording the same image for a duration of 1/4 second, smearing it electronically with motion blur, and then recording the next image for 1/4 second. So, in one second, you get about 6 discreet images.

White Balance

The human eye is very tricky. It can be tricked into thinking that a series of flashing images are really continuous. That is why televisions, computer monitors or films projected in movie theatres appear not to flicker after a while. It's called persistence of vision. The longer you look at something, the more your eye and brain adapt.

Try adjusting your computer monitor to different refresh rates. You'll notice flicker, even at 60 Hz. But soon you adapt, and the flicker seems to disappear.

Try another experiment with your eye's "white balance." Turn on a lamp with a standard tungsten filament bulb. Now, look at the sky outside for a couple of minutes. Then, look at the lamp or the wall behind it. It will appear orange-yellow. After a couple of minutes, however, the lamp will appear normal and neutral in color.

The color of light is measured in degrees Kelvin. Daylight averages around 5600 degrees. Household light bulbs are around 3000 degrees. Quartz and tungsten bulbs for film and video lights are 3200°. And HMI lights are daylight balanced 5600°. It's a good idea to buy a color temperature meter when you get into lighting, to keep the different units consistent. Bulbs have a habit of shifting color temperature as they get old. HMIs in particular can look green or magenta, and can be corrected with gels.

To check color temperature, I like to use the Minolta Color Meter IIIF.

When you buy still film, you have a choice of tungsten or daylight-balanced film. Film is not as clever in adapting as your eye. Neither are video cameras. You have to tell them something about the lighting conditions.

The camera has four white balance settings: manual, indoor, outdoor and auto.

The camera defaults to automatic white balance when the **AUTO LOCK** switch is in the **AUTO** position.

Setting White Balance

1. To set white balance yourself, slide the **AUTO LOCK** switch to the middle position.

2. Press the **WHT BAL** button at the back of the camera.

3. Rotate the jog dial to choose one of three white balance modes: manual, daylight or tungsten. You will see an icon depicting the mode on the middle left of the viewfinder or LCD screen.

Manual White Balance 🎥

This is the setting to use for consistent color in studio lighting, as well as correcting fluorescents or sodium vapor lamps that tend to look green. Manual mode also helps compensate for off-color HMI lights. To set Manual White Balance, hold a white showcard, foamcore, or piece of white paper in front of the camera. Zoom in to fill the frame with white. Or aim at a white wall.

Press the control dial momentarily. You do not have to keep pressing on it. The 🎥 manual icon will flash quickly. When it stops flashing, manual white balance has been set, and will remain stored in the camera's memory for as long as you have power, and for an additional hour after the battery is dead or removed.

It's a good idea to use the same white card for the duration of the shoot. If you use different cards with different values of white, the scenes will not match. White balancing this way makes all the whites look white, of course. This could become boring after a while.

What if you want your video to have a warm, amber look? You can shift the color balance of your scenes away from normal by using a white balance reference light, sometimes called a slate light. Keep an inkie or small 3200° unit available to illuminate the white card. Have both accessible for the duration of the shoot. Set your white balance for the card and its reference light. Then gel your lights according to the color shift desired: CTO for a warmer look, CTB for cooler, CTS for an amber-straw tone, chocolate for a sepia tint. Rosco and Lee are two major manufacturers of gels, which are actually made of acetate and other temperature resistant plastics. The word gel comes from the early days of photography, when color control really was done with gelatine.

If you're frugal or pressed for time, you can let the laws of complementary colors work for you. Again, let's say you want a warm, orange look—but you are on such a low budget, you can only afford a couple of tiny gels for the inkie. Experiment with CTB (blue) gels. Try shooting your white card and setting white balance with 1/2 CTB on the inkie. You will be fooling the camera into thinking this extra blue light is actually white. So when the camera "sees" normal tungsten lights, they will appear extra orange, without your having to gel each one.

Remember, the slate light should be the complementary color of what you want things to look like.

What if we want our video to have a cool, blue look? Add CTO (orange) gel to the slate light, and set your white balance for that. The camera is now fooled into shifting everything towards a bluer tone.

Daylight (Outdoor, 5600°K) White Balance

Even though it is called "daylight," the color temperature outside varies throughout the day. At sunrise and sunset it can be as orange as a tungsten light (3200°). A foggy, early morning can be so cool your color temperature meter reads above 12,000°. Be careful to check your image when using this setting.

Tungsten (Indoor, 3200°K) White Balance

Indoor mode is useful when shooting in studios or controlled lighting situations. You can avoid manual white balancing this way. You can also gel your lights, as we described in the manual mode, to shift the color away from normal.

ND Filter

When you see the words "ND ON" flashing in the viewfinder or on the LCD screen, the scene is very bright, and the camera suggests you activate the internal Neutral Density filter. It's like sunglasses for the video pickup chips. The ND filter is actually a piece of optical glass tinted gray.

When the words "ND OFF" flash in the viewfinder, the camera is telling you it needs more light. Press the **ND FILTER** switch on top of the camera near the lens.

Zebra Stripes and Exposure

Unfortunately, video cameras do not have built-in lightmeters like still cameras and some movie cameras. It would be nice if they did. A simple, center-weighted match-needle or spot-meter electronic display would help maintain consistent exposure.

The problem with relying on our eyepiece to judge scene brightness and contrast is that old problem of how easy it is to fool the human eye. As with white balance, the longer we look at something, the more normal it appears. Also, the eyepiece is pretty small, and not as accurate as a good studio monitor. So we can shoot ten different scenes thinking we are keeping them very consistent. Much to our horror, when we see the ten scenes displayed as thumbnails side by side in our editing room, we notice how easily our eye was fooled.

It's not always practical to lug a studio monitor around in the field. Fortunately, there are two things that can help us maintain consistent exposure.

Zebra stripes quickly show where a scene is over-exposed (too much light).

The three-position **ZEBRA** switch is either **OFF**, **70**% IRE or **100**% IRE.

The zebra stripes appear as white diagonal zebra lines in the viewfinder or LCD. Obviously, they are not recorded on tape.

At 100%, you'll see stripes over areas of the picture where reflected brightness is greater than Video 100%, and the 70% setting will display stripes on portions of the scene greater than 70%.

What this means is that a picture is assigned brightness values of 0 to 100. "How can anything be brighter than white?" you ask. Hold a piece of white foamcore up to a backlit window. Both appear white. But the window is much brighter.

How can something be darker than black? Again, look at the difference between a black showcard and a piece of black felt or velour.

The great debate between film and video always ends up in a discussion of contrast. Film has much greater "latitude," meaning the ability to record a far wider range of contrast. Video has a narrower latitude, and one of two things happen when you exceed the limits. Areas that are over-exposed on video will be totally "blown out," meaning that the image looks white with jagged, weird edges. Or the camera's electronic circuitry compresses the over-exposed areas, and renders them 100% white.

The same will happen in the blacks. In video, under-exposed areas will look muddy, murky and grainy. If the camera has the circuitry, the blacks will be "crushed," and under-exposed areas will be recorded as 0 black.

For comparison, if video has a scale of 0 to 100, film would have an equivalent scale of 0 to 1000.

Anyway, back to our zebra stripes.

They can be helpful in maintaining consistent whites. Don't try to close down your aperture totally to eliminate the white zebra stripes. A little over-exposure looks good.

Try to remember how much area was covered by stripes in your previous scene. Let's say you were doing a political spot. Your politico is standing against a white wall in Scene 1, a wide shot. In Scene 2, you go in for a close-up or him making a speech. The same wall is in the background. The white level should be the same, with the same amount of zebra stripes.

Having said all this, I prefer a lightmeter. More on lightmeters later.

Menu and Navigation

Nokia gets my award for best digital menus. Nokia cell phones have the most logical layout and the best menu structure, which make navigation a breeze. They use "soft keys," which are simply buttons whose identification labels show up on the LCD screen. To save space, reduce clutter and use fewer buttons, the function that each button performs can change from time to time. However, it is still consistent and logical, and always clearly labeled.

The worst digital menus are the ones on your VCR or fax machine. A six-year-old, and most adults, can figure out Nokia's text-driven soft keys and up-down buttons. I urge all engineers to seriously look at a Nokia cell phone before designing their menus.

The menu, mode and dial system on Sony's PD100A isn't bad, but you won't praise its virtues, either, when you have to quickly change settings during that spectacular takeoff of five thousand flamingoes against the blood-orange setting sun.

To use the menu, press **MENU**

Turn the jog wheel to navigate.

Press in on the jog wheel to accept a choice.

The jog dial on this camcorder makes navigation much easier than on most other cameras, but I still live in the hopes of a return to the simpler analog dials and switches for dedicated functions that we are mercifully returning to still cameras like the Nikon F4 and F5.

CAMERA Menu

When the Main Power Switch is set to **CAMERA**,

you have the following choices when you push the
MENU button:

(note—default values are shown first)

(my recommendations starred)

MANUAL SET -	AUTO SHUTTER - ON */ OFF
	PROGRESSIVE SCAN - OFF */ ON
CAMERA SET -	DIGITAL ZOOM - OFF */ ON
	16:9 - OFF */ ON
	STEADYSHOT - ON */OFF
	AE SHIFT - *- set with jog dial*
	GAIN SHIFT - 0DB */ -3 DB
	FRAME REC - OFF / ON
	INTERVAL RECORD - OFF / ON
	RETURN
LCD / VIEWFINDER SET -	LCD BACKLIGHT - BRIGHT / NORMAL *(only with battery)*
	LCD COLOR *- set with jog dial*
	VIEWFINDER BRIGHTNESS - *set with jog dial, LCD closed*
	RETURN
CASSETTE MEMORY SET -	TITLE ERASE
	TAPE TITLE - SET WITH JOG DIAL
	ERASE ALL - RETURN / OK
	RETURN
TAPE SET -	AUDIO MODE - 32K / 48K *
	MIC LEVEL - AUTO */ MANUAL *- set with jog dial*
	TAPE REMAINING - AUTO */ ALWAYS ON
	TIME CODE - DROP FRAME / NON DROP FRAME *
SETUP MENU -	CLOCK SET - SET WITH JOG DIAL
	LETTER SIZE - NORMAL / 2X
OTHERS -	WORLD TIME (TIME ZONE ADJUSTMENT)
	BEEP - MELODY / NORMAL / OFF
	COMMANDER (REMOTE) - ON / OFF
	DISPLAY - LCD / V-OUT /LCD
	REC LAMP - ON / OFF
	COLOR BAR - OFF / ON
	RETURN

MEMORY Menu

When the Main Power Switch is set to **MEMORY** for shooting stills, you have the following choices when you push the **MENU** button:

```
MANUAL SET
CAMERA SET
LCD / VF SET
MEMORY SET -    CONTINUOUS - OFF / ON / MULTI SCREEN
                QUALITY -   STANDARD / FINE / SUPER FINE
                PROTECT -   OFF / ON
                SLIDE SHOW -
                DELETE ALL - RETURN / OK
                FORMAT      RETURN / OK
                RETURN
SETUP MENU
ETC
```

VTR Menu

When the Main Power Switch is set to **VTR**,
you have the following choices when you push the
MENU button:

VTR SET -   HI FI SOUND - STEREO / 1 (LEFT TRACK) 2 (RIGHT TRACK)
                   AUDIO MIX (BALANCE)-

LCD / VF SET
MEMORY SET
CASSETTE MEMORY SET   CM SEARCH - ON / OFF
                         TITLE ERASE
                         TITLE DISPLAY - ON / OFF
                         TAPE TITLE
                         ERASE ALL
                         RETURN

TAPE SET
SETUP MENU
OTHERS   BEEP
                         COMMANDER
                         DISPLAY
                         DV EDITING
                         RETURN

Program AE

Programmed Auto Exposure is a carry-over from the world of still photography. You probably will not use it very often, but sometimes it can be very useful.

1. With the **AUTO LOCK** in the middle position, push the **PROGRAM AE** switch at the rear of the camera.

2. Spin the jog control dial to one of five exposure settings. You will see an icon at the lower left of the viewfinder or LCD display: Aperture Priority, Shutter Priority, Sports Lesson, Sunset and Moon, and Low Lux.

3. **A** and **S** indicate Aperture Priority and Shutter Priority. To select either one, push in on the control dial, and then rotate the control dial to select either your aperture or shutter speed. Push the control dial again to lock in the setting.

Aperture Priority

In Aperture Priority, you pick an aperture from F1.6 to F11. The camera automatically selects the correct shutter speed, and will boost gain if there still is not enough light. Aperture Priority is useful when you want to shoot with minimim depth of field—meaning that almost everything except your subject will be out of focus. The wider open the lens (F1.6), the less depth of field. Shallow depth of field overcomes video's drawback of having too much in focus, which makes things look "flat." Note that the lens is not as fast in telephoto as it is in wide angle. The widest you'll be able to open at 51.6mm is F2.8, while at 4.3mm, you can open all the way to F1.6. This is inherent to the design of the lens. Having a uniform aperture throughout the zoom range would make the lens much bigger and heavier.

Shutter Priority

In Shutter Priority, you select a shutter speed from 1/60 to 1/10,000 of a second (1/50 to 1/10,000 in PAL), and the camera sets the aperture (and ND filtration).

Sports Lesson Mode

The fast shutter speeds used in sports lesson mode help to sharpen motion blur, and are useful only for reviewing the tape frame by frame later on.

Sunset and Moon

This should actually be called Magic Hour Mode, or Dusk Exposure. Magic Hour is the time between the dark and the daylight, when the night is beginning to lower—and the light is great for shooting cars, landscapes, and architecture against glowing skies. Clients, producers and agency folks would much prefer to forego the overtime usually incurred by their crews chasing around after sunset instead of safely ensconced at the bar enjoying Happy Hour instead of Magic Hour.

In Magic Hour Mode, the camera compensates for dark backgrounds behind point sources of light. It's good for neon signs, fireworks, sunsets, buildings lit at night—all those situations where there are points of light that would otherwise be washed out if the camera based its exposure on the overall dark scene.

Low Lux

Low lux lets even more light into the camera than Magic Hour Mode. The shutter speed becomes slow, and you get an interesting, slightly blurred and jittery look if you're panning. This is not quite night vision—but you can shoot in some pretty dark places without too much grain or noise from gain boosts.

Timelapse

Timelapse is the effect you see in almost every airline and technology company commercial—clouds zipping by at high speed, arrays of satellite dishes re-aiming simulaneously, car headlights blurred into a ribbon of light.

Timelapse is basically an animation technique for live action. By shooting single frames with extra time between them, we are, in essence, compressing a long period of time into a much shorter time. Let's say it takes one hour for a beautiful sunset to occur. It begins with the sun a few degrees above the horizon, and ends as the sky has gradually changed from a multitude of red and pink hues with wispy clouds into a rich purple-blue with just the hint of a glow where earth meets sky.

Now, what if we want to do a title sequence, and show all this in 2 minutes? We need to do a little math. 60 minutes is 3600 seconds. Let's take one shot (one frame) every second. We'll have 3600 exposures. How much real-time is that? Well, our results, even though they were shot at a rate of 1 frame per second, will be played back at 30 frames per second—or 25 frames if we're using PAL. So, we divide 3600 exposures (frames) by 30 frames, and the result is 120 seconds, or two minutes.

Timelapse is a combination of: burst—how many frames are exposed at any given time, interval—how long we wait between bursts, and exposure—combination of aperture and shutter for each frame exposed.

Interval Recording

Few camcorders, the PD100A included, can do true frame by frame timelapse because it is difficult for them to record just one frame. You can approximate the effect using the Interval Recording mode. Think of it more as a surveillance type of mode, like they have in banks. It records a burst as short as 1/2 a second, with intervals as short as 30 seconds, going up to 10 minutes.

To get to Interval Recording mode, press the **MENU** button while the Main Power Switch is turned to **CAMERA.** Turn the jog wheel to the *CAMERA SET* menu, and press to accept the following sequence: *INT. REC* - *SET* - *INTERVAL* (choice of *30 SEC, 1, 5, 10 MIN*) - *REC TIME* (choice of *.5, 1, 1.5, 2 SEC*) and then press **MENU** to accept your choices.

Cut Recording

Cut Recording is the closest most camcorders can come to true Stop Motion. The difference between this mode and Interval Recording is that you control the time between exposures. Each time you push the Record Button, six frames of video are recorded. To get there, in **CAMERA** mode, push **MENU**, and turn the jog wheel to *FRAME REC-ON*, and push the **MENU** button to accept your choice.

Playback

The moment has come to review your masterpiece.

Turn the Main Power Switch to VTR, which stands for Video Tape Recorder.

Remember: your camcorder is actually a camera attached to a video tape recorder.

The VTR panel on top of the camera lights up. Microswitches beneath the rubbery-plastic membrane control the movement of the DV tape within.

Press **REW** to rewind.

Press **PLAY** first, and then **REW** to rewind and see the picture at the same time.

Press **PLAY** first, and then **FF** to fast forward while watching the picture.

It's easiest to watch on the swing-out LCD screen.

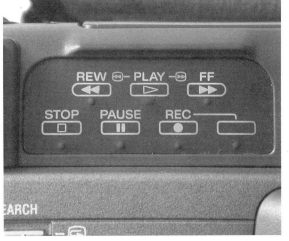

Whatever you do, DO NOT press **REC** and the blank button to its right. That will erase and record over your tape.

End Search

The **END SEARCH** button provides a quick way to find the last recorded portion of a tape.

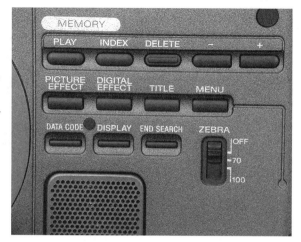

It works with the Main Power Switch set to either **CAMERA** or **VTR**.

It is especially helpful when using DV or DVCam tapes with cassette memory (you can tell because there's a copper-colored metal strip just below the **SAVE-REC** slider).

Without cassette memory, **END SEARCH** will not work after the tape is ejected from the camera.

HOWEVER: I do not recommend relying totally on **END SEARCH**. It will not behave correctly if there is a blank portion between scenes (you popped the tape in and out a couple of times, or reviewed footage in between recording).

Therefore, always double check your footage with the **PLAY** button.

Edit Search

Edit Search is a bit tricky—not intuitive, and an easy way to erase footage.

It is used to review tape while the Main Power Switch is in **CAMERA** mode.

Let's say you're shooting, and want to make sure the last take looks good.

Without having to open the LCD screen, you can momentarily push the button of the **EDITSEARCH** control at the top front of the camera.

The tape rewinds two seconds, and then plays back the last two seconds on the LCD viewing screen or in the Viewfinder.

But, what if you keep pressing the - button? You see the recorded image while the tape plays back in reverse as long as you hold the button. When you release it, the picture goes "live." If you momentarily push the - button down again, just two seconds will play back. After two seconds, the tape stops, and the picture goes "live" again.

To review in the forward direction, press the + button of **EDITSEARCH.** You will see recorded tape as long as the button is pushed down.

The danger with all this is that you're in the middle of the tape, with the Main Power Switch precariously parked on **CAMERA** and ready to record. Use this function with caution.

So, if you use **EDITSEARCH,** be sure to use the **END SEARCH** control to make sure you're at the end of the tape, or use the **PLAY** button.

In/Out and Dubbing

Audio and Video Input and Output connectors lurk beneath the rubber cover on camera right.

Analog video and audio comes out of the yellow mini-plug receptacle. Plug in the special 4-conductor A/V cable that comes with the camera.

At the other end of the cable, Composite video comes out of the yellow RCA plug. The red RCA jack is Audio-Right, and the white one is Audio-Left.

Plug these connectors into your TV, monitor or VTR.

S-Video, which separates the video signal into luminance and chrominance for higher quality, is accessed from the S-VIDEO receptacle on the camera. You still need to use the special A/V cable for sound, but you can disconnect the yellow composite video RCA connector.

These same connectors can be used to dub video onto the DV tape. Set the Main Power Switch to VTR, and use the top **REC** controls.

The **DV IN/OUT** receptacle provides both input and output of the digital video and audio signal. Dubbing from another DV camcorder or deck is done with one FireWire/i.Link cable for both digital video and audio.

The **LANC** receptable is for edit control. It also provides access to camera functions for external controls like zoom control and camera start/stop.

Still Photos

There are two ways to use your DV Camcorder as a still camera: grabbing 7 seconds of the frozen image on tape, or capturing the same image on a chewing-gum shaped Memory Stick.

The advantage of shooting stills on tape is that you can capture up to 340 images on one 40-minute DVCAM cassette, using a very cheap form of storage, compared to the relatively expensive Memory Stick. The same tape can be used for both stills and full-motion video, alternately taking stills and shooting video.

The disadvantage of using tape is that you have to wait 7 seconds for each one to be stored. It would be nice if there were a fast mode, perhaps called New York Stills, which only records for one second.

The second way to shoot stills on the PD-100, and many other cameras, is the Memory Stick. The image is the same size and resolution, but is recorded much faster to a flash memory chip.

As of this writing, neither form of still photo capture will make you want to give away your megapixel digital still camera. The photos are 640x480, producing a 4" wide x 3" high, 160 dpi, 900K BMP bitmap file or 65K JPG file.

Progressive Scan

Many camcorders provide progressive scan mode for shooting stills. The advantage is that every scan line is employed. If you shoot a still in interlace mode, you only wind up with half the scan lines. In that case, many cameras cheat, by line doubling the field.

Recording Stills

On Tape

It's easy to quickly go between full motion video and stills on tape.

Keep the main power switch in the **CAMERA** position.

1. Now you can either push the red button to start recording video, or...

2. Gently, push down on the **PHOTO** button on top of the camera until the image freezes and you see an icon of a still camera and the word "*CAPTURE*" in the upper right of the finder.

3. If you like what you see, push down harder on the **PHOTO** button to begin saving the image to tape. The word "*CAPTURE*" is replaced by seven red dots, that count down to 1. When it's over, the camera beeps twice, and goes back into Standby, ready for another still photo or video recording.

4. If you don't like what you see when lightly pressing on the **PHOTO** button, release it, re-compose, and press down lightly again.

5. You can also shoot a still while recording video. While the tape is rolling, simply press down all the way on the **PHOTO** button. The image is frozen for 7 seconds, and then the camera goes into standby.

Remember—the camera records sound during the interminable 7 seconds of grabbing the still, so any nasty things you have to say will be recorded.

Progressive or Interlace Scan

The PD-100A can record with either progressive scan or interlace scan. Interlace is the normal way we have been accustomed to watching video: half the horizontal lines are displayed in one 1/60th of a second, and then the rest of the scan lines are displayed in the next 1/60th second (1/50th second in PAL).

In progressive scanning, all the horizontal lines are recorded every 1/30th of a second (1/25th second in PAL), which means that every 1/60th field is "printed twice," or duplicated.

The camera's default setting is Interlace scan.

Shooting video under fluorescents, HMIs and even some light bulbs may cause flicker when using Progressive Scan.

StillPhotos recorded on tape will have more picture information if recorded in Progressive Mode.

1. To change the scan mode, push the **MENU** switch while in Standby.

2. You will be in the *MANUAL SET* Menu. Press in on the control dial.

3. Turn the control dial to *PROG SCAN*. Press in on the control dial.

4. Turn the control dial to select ON. Press in on the dial.

5. Press the **MENU** switch.

The words "*PROG. SCAN*" appear in the left center of the finder.

To return to interlace scanning, repeat the steps above, but select "*OFF*" in step 4.

Recording Stills on Memory Stick

Recording to the Memory Stick is very similar to recording to tape.

Set the Main Power Switch to the **MEMORY** position.

If it will not move past the **CAMERA** position, the safety lock-out is engaged.

To record still photos onto the Memory Stick, slide the little safety tab forward (towards the front of the camera).

Pressing the red record button will no longer work.

To take a still photo, gently push the **PHOTO** button on top of the camera.

You will hear the simulated sound of a still camera shutter. This is misleading—do not assume the image has been recorded yet. The word *"CAPTURE"* appears in the upper right of the finder.

To record the image to the Memory Stick, push the PHOTO button down all the way. A red bar graph display appears in the upper right. It takes one or two seconds to record to the Memory Stick.

There are three levels of image resolution, displayed in the finder at top center: standard (*STD*), fine (*FINE*) and super fine (*SFN*). As far as I can tell, the file size and dpi is the same in all three resolutions. The difference is in anti-aliasing and some other subtle differences.

Changing Image Quality

1. To change image quality, swing the LCD screen out.

2. Turn the Main Power Switch to **MEMORY**.

3. Push the **MENU** switch.

4. Turn the control dial to the 4th icon from the top: Memory Stick settings.

5. Push in on the control dial to get to the next level in the menu tree.

6. Turn the control dial until "*QUALITY*" is highlighted.

7. Press the control dial.

8. Choose Standard, Fine, or Super Fine.

9. Press the **MENU** switch to accept your choice.

Memory Stick Picture Quality Menu

MANUAL SET		
CAMERA SET		
LCD/VF SET		
MEMORY SET---------	CONTINUOUS	
	QUALITY----------------	STANDARD
	PROTECT	FINE
	SLIDE SHOW	SUPER FINE
	DELETE ALL	
	FORMAT	

Playing Back Stills

Stills on Tape

The easiest way to see your stills is to simply play the tape. Since the pictures were recorded for 7 seconds each, it's like a slide show.

The memory chip in the cassette automatically indexes stills by date and time. The Remote Commander (Remote Control) can find these pictures. Be sure "*COMMANDER*" and "*CM SEARCH*" are both *ON* in the menu. Then, press SEARCH MODE on the Remote Commander, and press the forward or back arrows.

Viewing Stills on Memory Stick

To review the pictures on the Memory Stick:

1. The Main Power Switch can be in either the **VTR** or **MEMORY** position.

2. Open the LCD display panel.

3. Directly below the word "**MEMORY,**" prominently displayed in a white bubble, are 5 switches that work on the Memory Stick.

4. Push **PLAY**. The still photo most recently shot is displayed on screen.

5. Push "**+**" or "**-**" to cycle through the stills stored on the Memory Stick.

6. All kinds of information is displayed at the top of the LCD screen, beginning at the upper left:

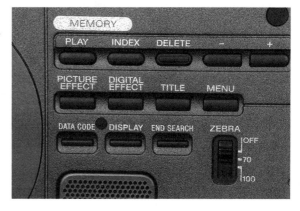

filename, image resolution, image number out of total image shot, and *"MEMORY PLAY,"* in case you've forgotten what you're looking at.

7. Push **INDEX** to see 6 images at a time. Press **+** or **-** to cycle through the index. Press **PLAY** to see a specific photo full-screen.

8. Press **DELETE** to get rid of photos. The camera asks for your blessing. Press **DELETE** again. If the images won't go away, eject the Memory Stick, and chances are that the write-protect tab is in the **LOCK** position.

9. Press **PLAY** again to get out of Memory playback and back to live.

Transferring Stills to Computer

Now the fun begins. There are numerous permutations of places your stills can go: Memory Stick to tape, tape to Memory, and so on. But the most useful function of all is getting a still onto your computer, where it will be ready for email to defenceless relatives and friends, gracing the company's new website, or on the cover of this month's real estate brochure.

Plug Camera into Computer

Open the rubber cover at the forward end of the camera right side.

Plug 4-pin FireWire/IEEE 1394/ i.LINK cable into the **DV IN/OUT** receptacle. Remember, there are two kinds of connectors: the small, 4-pin Sony style, and the larger, 6-pin variety.

Plug the other end of the cable into your IEEE 1394 equipped computer. You can purchase 4-pin to 6-pin cables and adapters at most computer stores, including CompUSA. PCConnection can mail you one overnight.

Almost all Sony computers made after January 2000 have a small i.LINK port, connected to the motherboard. Most Macs made within the last couple of years have a larger, 6-pin FireWire connector. Dell, Gateway, Compaq and HP towers introduced after January 2001 have 6-pin IEEE 1394 connectors. Many aftermarket PCI boards and PCMCIA cards are available for Windows machines—although 300 MHz is probably the slowest chip speed that works reasonably well.

Not surprisingly, Sony computers work almost flawlessly with Sony DV cameras. So do Macs.

Once you turn the camera on, the hot-pluggable IEEE 1394 connection is automatically detected. When all else fails, reboot the computer with the camera's main power switch set to **VTR**.

Using Sony DVgate Still

Most Sony laptops and towers come with DVGate Still, a good Windows program for grabbing stills from the DV Camcorder and saving them on the computer.

1. Launch the program (Start-Programs-VAIO-DVgate-DVgate Still).

2. Open all three windows: Control Panel, Monitor and Still.
    (Click on the Window Menu of the DVgate Still Control Box,
    and check Monitor and Still)

3. If the camera is off, the Control Panel says "OFFLINE." You must turn on the camcorder. Turn the power switch to "VTR;" the Panel now displays "ONLINE."

4. Click on SETUP of the Monitor Window. Go down to SETTINGS. Select High, Medium or Low Resolution. Suggestion: use High Resolution. You can always compress file size later.

5. Control the camcorder with the control panel. Click on the PLAY arrow to begin. Hovering the mouse over the different controls shows a description of the particular buttons.

6. The tape plays back everything you've recorded: stills and full motion video.

7. Click on "CAPTURE" whenever you want to grab a frame. The frame will be displayed in the STILL window.

8. The reason for the 7-second still duration becomes evident when you quickly scan through the tape.

9. To grab a single frame of moving images, click the STEP button, and FREEZE when you get the shot you like.

10. To grab a full second of video—30 frames—click in the Control Panel Window on Settings - Capture - Capture Frames Continuously.

11. But wait. The stills are grabbed, but not saved.

12. To copy a still to the clipboard, find the shot you like in the STILL window by clicking on one of the arrows. Click COPY to save a bitmap image to the clipboard, which then must be pasted into another application.

13. To save images to disk, click on SAVE in the STILL window.

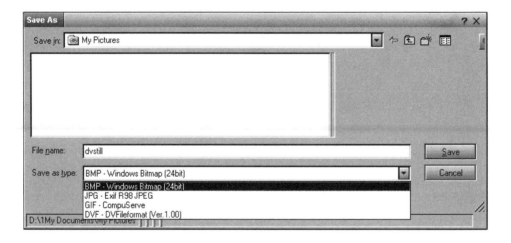

14. Select your destination. Suggestion: keep all your DV stills in a directory called DV Stills. Select the file type.
    A Windows Bitmap will be about 900K
    JPEG files are about 65K
    DVF (Digital Video Format) files are about 90K

I usually save files as bitmaps, and then convert them to TIF files in Photoshop.

If the files are just going on the Internet, I'll save as a smaller JPG file. I avoid GIF files because of limited color depth, and DVF because they don't import easily into other applications.

Downloading Memory Stick Photos

When transferring images recorded on Memory Stick using DVgate Still, the control panel camera controls will not work.

View the pictures as described earlier, using **MEMORY PLAY**, **+** and **-**.

The pictures will appear on the Monitor window, and can be grabbed in the STILL window with the CAPTURE button.

As the following two pictures show, there is no discernable difference between pictures recorded on DV tape or on Memory Stick.

Still image recorded onto tape and saved as a 640x480 2.5 inch wide grayscale 260 dpi TIF file.

Similar shot, recorded onto Memory Stick, and saved as a 640x480 2.5 inch wide grayscale 2.5 w b&w 260 dpi TIF file.

Sony Smart Capture

Sony Smart Capture is another software application that can be used to get still and moving images onto your computer. Although you cannot control the camcorder from the computer, it offers a quick alternative.

Be sure to set the image size under "OPTIONS:" 640x480, 320x240, 160x120, or 80x60.

Click CAPTURE in the Smart Capture window, and SAVE in the Still Viewer.

The EFFECTS button provides all kinds of gratuitous image adjustments, including sepia, outline, emboss and negative.

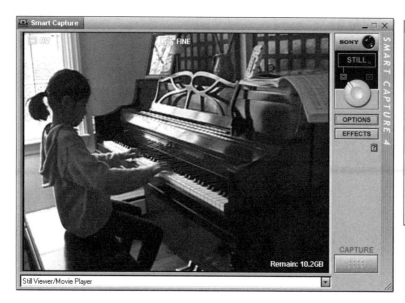

Touching up Your Pictures

Pixels, Dots and DPI

Picture files on your computer are made up of lots of little dots, called pixels. Hold an 8x magnifying glass up to your computer screen. You'll see them. Color pictures are made of red, green and blue pixels, arranged side by side. Black and white photos on a color monitor are still displayed with the same color pixels, but they are blended to look like shades of gray.

When you have an image that measures 640x480, it means the picture has 640 dots going left to right, and 480 dots going from top to bottom. So, a 640x480 pictures consists of 307,200 pixels. Actually, multiply that number by 3 and you get 921,600—since each pixel really has 3 dots: red, green and blue.

When you buy a computer monitor, its display properties are given in pixel count. Monitors from the late 1980s couldn't display anything larger than 640x480 edge to edge. Most monitors now routinely display 1024x768 pixels, and go up to 1600x1200.

But that's just part of the story. The size of each dot also determines resolution and sharpness. Most monitors have a default screen resolution of 72 dots per inch. That means there are 72 pixels arranged side by side for each inch. This is fine for most NTSC video at 640 x 480.

Let's say our monitor is set at 640 x 480. A 640 x 480 72 dpi video image would take up the entire sceen. Let's change the monitor's resolution to 1280x1024. A 640x480 picture with a resolution of 72 dpi (dots per inch) would most likely take up just half of the screen's real estate. But what if we change the resolution to 36 dpi? We'll still have 640 dots going left to right, but they will be spread out farther apart. The picture will now take up the whole screen, but it won't look as sharp because of the space between each pixel.

Now, what if we increase resolution to 144 dpi? The pixels are displayed closer together, making the image look sharper. And, those 640 pixels will take up just 1/4 of the screen. There is a direct correlation between number of pixels, dpi, picture resolution and picture size.

Look at a newspaper photo and a picture from an inkjet printer with a magnifying glass. They're made of similar red, blue and green dots, along with black for extra contrast.

However, dpi on the computer screen does not translate directly into dots on the page. Dots on the page are better measured in LPI, for Lines Per Inch, which are really lines or rows of pixels going across the page.

Printer DPI to LPI

To see how DPI on screen relates to LPI on the page, divide the printer's advertised dots per inch resolution by 16.

DPI / 16 = LPI

So, a 1200 dpi laser printer will yield the following:

1200 / 16 = 75 lines per inch. Aha! That's why photos from your laser print don't look so great.

The pictures in this book are printed at 2400 DPI, so we get 150 lines per inch.

Current inkjet printers are capable of up to 2880 dots per inch, which is 180 lines.

Screen DPI to Printer DPI

The opposite also holds true. Multiply the DPI (pixels per inch) of your photo by 12 to see what the corresponding printer resolution will be. If you have a 96 pixel/inch (96 dpi) image file:

96 Pixels/Inch x 12 = 1152 printer DPI.

So, the picture is not going to look great.

What does this all mean?

When you transfer a still image from the camcorder to your computer, it is usually a BMP bitmap image of 640x480 pixels, 96 pixels/inch (DPI), measuring 6.66 inches wide x 5 inches high, that takes up 900Kb of disk space. If you're lucky enough to have a camcorder that can save stills as JPEG files, they'll take up only 70Kb for the same size image because they compress the file.

Now, we know that a 96 pixel/inch photo isn't going to look very good when printed out. What should we do?

We'll open the picture in an image editing program, and by making it smaller, we'll increase the resolution. Remember, we still have all those pixels to work with. We just need to bunch them closer together.

The smaller you make a picture, the sharper it will look when printed out. By setting a new size of 300 dpi in the lower box will give you good results. Anything larger than 4" x 6" will become grainy. If you just want to send the picture by email, 72 dpi is fine.

Adobe PhotoDeluxe

Not everyone wants to shell out $600 for Photoshop. Adobe PhotoDeluxe is much cheaper, and often comes free with many digital still cameras and Sony Vaio computers.

Open PhotoDeluxe.

Click on the Advanced Menus button, which lets you see more menus on top instead of having to use the tedious step-by-step wizards.

Open your picture file (File-Open)

Click on Size-Photo Size to see the screen shown at right.

At the top of the box, you will see the original resolution of your photo in pixels/inch and size.

The bottom of the box is where you work to change size and resolution. Make sure the CONSTRAIN: Proportions and File Size Boxes are checked. This changes image size as you change resolution.

In our example above, we changed the Width to the size of paper on which we wanted to print: a 4"x6" photo paper. This increased our resolution to 300 pixels/inch.

To send pictures by email, 72 pixels/inch is an unofficial Internet standard. However, if we leave the Constrain boxes checked, we'll be making the picture much larger by going to a lower resolution because we'll still have the same number of pixels, but they'll be spread apart more. We don't need all those pixels. To "throw" some of them away, un-check the Constrain: File Size box to avoid sending your uncle Basil a 24 inch wide picture.

Further adjustments can be made to color, brightness/contrast, and so on from the QUALITY Menu. Don't forget to save your work. Use the EXPORT command from the FILE menu to save as a JPG file for the web or a TIF file for print.

Adobe Photoshop

Adobe Photoshop is the industrial strength, industry standard image editor. Not only can you use it to edit images from your camcorder, but you can also export titles, logos and graphics to your nonlinear editing programs.

It can be overwhelming at first if you try to learn all its features at once. There are scores of books on Photoshop. One of the best is Adobe's "Photoshop Classroom in a Book."

For our one-page Photoshop Lesson, we'll learn how to adjust image size, just as we did with PhotoDeluxe.

Open your image from the menu with FILE-OPEN.

Click on IMAGE-IMAGE SIZE.

To make your pictures higher in resolution (sharper), but smaller in size, uncheck the RESAMPLE IMAGE box. (Yes, the Constrain commands of PhotoDeluxe are more intuitive). Be sure "Constrain Proportions" is checked—if it's grayed out, but checked, that's fine.

To make pictures smaller and lower resolution for the web, be sure RESAMPLE IMAGE is checked.

Photoshop does its work in layers. To save to a TIF or JPG file, you may have to combine all the layers. Click on LAYER-FLATTEN IMAGE. Then, click on FILE-SAVE AS, and select your file format.

By the way, the picture above measures 1024 x 1535 pixels. This is what is known as a "megapixel" image, and where we're headed in digital photography: more and more pixels.

Audio

Most camcorders come with built-in microphones. The picture on the right shows the PD100a, with its two stereo microphones hidden behind a black screen just below the SONY logo.

Sony PD100A

This kind of mike is fine for ambient sound, and has received the seal of approval from millions of home movie makers the world over.

Problem is, it picks up motor noise from the camcorder's tape transport, and isn't very selective about cancelling out wind or background noise. If you're far away from your subject, you'll probably hear yourself more clearly than anything else.

Sony VX-2000

So, sticking a microphone on the front of your camera is probably the worst way to record sound.

Sure, most camcorders come with stereo mikes pointing towards the front. They are convenient, and record on command. But you can do better.

Canon GL-1

However professional it makes you feel to attach an expensive mike on top of your camera, and despite the fact that every news camera in the world has one, the secret to good sound recording is having another microphone as close to your subject as possible.

Watch carefully next time you see a reporter doing a stand-up. You'll notice two things. First, you'll see why it's called a "stand-up." Have you ever seen a reporter sitting down while on camera? They must teach this in reporter school. Second, the reporter is holding the mike. The station logo is inevitably as big as the mike. But, the mike is not in the shot lest the viewer forget the name of the station. It is there because as it is positioned closer to the person speaking, it records clearer sound and cancels out distracting ambient background noise.

To keep the mike out of the shot, professional sound engineers will fasten it to the end of a lightweight pole, called a boom.

If the shot is wide or the subject moving around, a small lavalier microphone will be hidden under the talent's clothing. The lavalier is connected to a radio transmitter, also hidden. A radio receiver tuned to the same frequency receives the sound, and passes it by cable into the camcorder. The arrangement is called a radio mike (also spelled "mic").

Audio Input

There are two ways to get audio recorded onto tape: using the internal microphone, or plugging an external one into the MIC input.

And, there are two types of microphone receptacles.

The one pictured here is a mini plug. It is the same size as the one you use to plug headphones into a Walkman.

The Audio/Video receptacle is a line input connection.

48K Audio

Be sure to set the Audio Mode to FS48K in the menu settings. This will provide two 48K (16-bit) audio tracks, as opposed to FS32K, which records four tracks at 32K (12-bit).

Professional microphones use 3 pin XLR connectors. The cables are shielded in such a way as to cancel out hum and noise. This is called balanced audio.

The PD100a has an accessory box that attaches to the "hot shoe" on top of the camera. A microphone plugged into the XLR connector sends its audio signal through the contacts in the hot shoe to the camera and tape.

To attach the accessory box, slide it from front to back, and tighten the knurled ring.

The microphone holder attaches above the box.

Plug the microphone into the XLR receptacle.

To remove it, first push on the shiny tab marked **"PUSH."**

The **+48V** switch provides 48 volts at low amperage to power many professional microphones. This is called phantom powering. Turn it **ON** if your mike requires it.

The 3-position **LEVEL** switch on the left should usually be set to the middle **STD** position. If sounds are too loud, slide it to **ATT** (attenuate). If the audio is really faint, slide it to **GAIN**.

It's a good idea to watch the level indicator in the eyepiece. Activate it from the menu.

Headphones

It's a good idea to connect a headset to the headphone terminal to monitor your audio selections before and during recording.

Audio Accessories

There are a number of audio accessories that can seriously improve the sound you record.

You can add professional XLR input and mechanical dials for level control on most DV camcorders. This is a vast improvement over the menu-driven level control settings on most cameras. Two companies that make these after-market adapters are BeachTek in Canada and Studio 1 Productions in Florida.

Beachtek Audio Baseplate

Split Tracks

Take advantage of both audio tracks. If you're using a single microphone, get an audio splitter and feed the output into both tracks. Set the right manual level control for normal peaking. Set the left manual level control 15dB lower, so loud sounds will not totally over-modulate. That way, you are protected from severe audio distortion without having to rely on automatic level control.

Recording Audio Separately

The sure way to infallible audio is simultaneous recording on a separate DAT machine, with a simultaneous feed directly into the camcorder.

No matter how ambidextrous the camera operator, it is, nevertheless, counter-productive for one person to be expected to execute graceful pans and tilts, with elegant zooms and follow-focus, while carefully keeping the frame perfectly composed, consistent in continuity, properly lit, appropriately white-balanced—all the while monitoring audio and adjusting levels to avoid over modulation or excessive ambience.

There is no doubt that the one-man-band camera operator is the key to network news and ENG field production. Economically, it swept aside the three-man network film crews. The cameraman manned a heavy Auricon or Frezzi. The mixer handled the sound. And the third member of the crew was irreverently called "Statue of Liberty," because it was his job to hold high the torch light of a single sun-gun, powered by the heavy battery belt slung around his usually ample waist.

But, when quality is at stake, there is no question that having a separate sound system provides not only an extra set of ears, and hands, but it also serves as a backup system that protects the original tape. This can be especially helpful when the final project is going to be mixed in a studio. Handing over the DAT is much simpler, and safer, than giving up the cassette holding all the original pictures.

Many documentary and news crews employ an audio person to handle the microphone and mix the audio. The sound is fed into a mixer, whose knobs control audio input levels. The signal is then passed along to a wireless transmitter, which sends it to the camcorder, where it is picked up by a wireless receiver attached to the back. The audio is then fed to the XLR audio inputs, and recorded on tape.

In either situation, the audio can be split onto separate tracks. You can put a lavalier output on the right channel, and a shotgun mike for ambience on the left channel. Popular mikes are Sennheiser's ME66 and ME67 shotgun modules for the K6 battery/phantom power unit, and Sony's ECM-77B and 44B lavalier.

For dramatic productions, using an electronic slate jam-synced to the timecoded DAT will save lots of agony in the editing room, even if it takes a few seconds more on set. You can identify scene and take number, but more importantly, have a "head sticks" synchronization point to enable laying in audio over the reference track of the camcorder.

Editing
and
Post

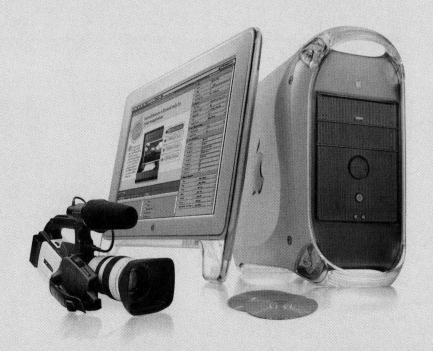

photo courtesy of Apple

Editing
and
Post

Simple Editing

It has been said that the worst editor is the cinematographer who shot the footage. The reasoning is that the shooter is too in love with the footage to cut it out, or figures that cutting a scene that was incredibly difficult to capture would lessen the experience.

It is always good to have a fresh set of eyes and metaphorical scissors to excise gratuitous material.

It is also good for the shooter to know how to edit, because knowing about transitions, divisions, scenes and continuity can only help improve ones skills. Although a wag once said "anything cuts" (it might have been Orson Welles himself), certain shots definitely cut better than others.

Software

In the beginning (1983), there were many word processing software programs. Remember Leading Edge, Wordperfect, Ami Pro? Works?

We appear to be at that early pre-Microsoft stage of competition in DV nonlinear editing software. It comes in all sizes, flavors and prices. Many can be downloaded from the web for free demos. Some programs are software only—MGI's Video-Wave and Ulead's VideoStudio; some come with an IEEE 1394 card, such as Pinnacle System's StudioDV or Digital Origin's IntroDV; and some come bundled with the computer you buy, like Apple iMacs and Sony Vaios.

There are basically three flavors of interface—the way the software looks.

Storyboard editing starts with a row of empty boxes. You drag each scene into a different box. You see the first frame of each take. It sort of looks like an arrangement of 3" x 5" still photos arranged in a row. You can change the order of events by swapping and sliding pictures around. Windows Movie Maker and Apple iMovie are storyboard based.

Timeline editing shows the various video and audio tracks as a graphic representation. Dragging each shot onto the timeline shows where it appears relative to other shots. Higher end programs switch quickly from timeline to storyboard views, and often combine a hybrid of both. Avid, Final Cut Pro, Media 100 and Cinestream are examples of this.

Text view shows statistics and descriptions of shots.

Let's start with the simplest way to chop up your footage, and work our way up. We'll begin with the free programs that come with Macs and Sony VAIOs.

Windows Movie Maker

Not to be outdone, Microsoft hurriedly bundled Windows Movie Maker with Windows ME.

It is easy to load DV footage, but useful only for the most rudimentary tasks like sending email movies.

Footage is saved in the Windows Media Video Format, which is a little baffling.

Apple iMovie

Apple iMovie comes free with most Macs, iMacs, iBooks and Powerbooks. It and the advertising campaign that heralded its appearance were the "killer aps" that made DV what it is today.

It's simple, and it works.

I wouldn't cut a feature with iMovie—but it's good for assembling your sample reel, cutting a short subject or learning editing fundamentals.

Suggestion: save your project, and then export it to: Quicktime file.

Working with Quicktime

Once you have exported your iMovie to Quicktime, you can change the file size if it's larger than you'd like. Although there are special programs like Media Cleaner 5, the Quicktime on your Mac or PC will do an adequate job of making files smaller. But first you need Quicktime Pro. It's a simple online upgrade if you have the free version of Quicktime. Go to *Edit, Preferences, Registration*, and click *Register Online*. The nice thing about Quicktime is that it works on PC or Mac.

Open the Quicktime file (*file, open*). It will have a .moov or .mov extension.

Next, choose *file, export*. Click in the box next to *Export*:
Select *Movie to Quicktime Movie*.

Click *options* (on the right side). Click *settings* under video. Choose *Sorenson Video* (because it's the best.) Pick *Medium Quality, 30 Frames per Second, Key Frame every 60 frames*. Use 320 x 240 for size. No filters.

Check your sound settings: *Qdesign Music 2, 44.100 kHz, Mono, 16 bit*.

Check *Prepare for Internet Streaming* and *Fast Start*. Then click *OK*. Give the file a name, and click *Save*. A 30 second piece of video, with audio, at 320 x 240, should compress to about 4 Megabytes—a decent size to send by email or post on the web.

Sony DVGate Motion Capture

If you have a Sony VAIO computer, laptop or tower, it comes with DVGate Motion Capture, which is similar to its still capture cousin. (Don't bother with DVGate Assemble or Movie Shaker.)

DVgate Motion offers you two options for capturing video:

Manual Video Capture

This is another name for Log and Batch Digitize. You watch the video on your computer monitor and manually mark multiple start and stop points throughout your recording.

Just follow these simple steps:

1. Connect DV camcorder to Sony VAIO computer using i.LINK cable.

2. Set camcorder to "VTR" mode.

3. Launch DVgate Motion software.

4. Set the mode to "IMPORT - Auto" in the control panel.

5. Click the "Play" button on the DVgate Motion control panel.

6. As video plays, click the "Mark" button to select a beginning (in) point for capture.

Click "Mark" again to select an end point (out). Multiple sections can be marked, with each section appearing in the In/Out List window.

7. Once you're finished marking sections, click "Capture All" to save each scene. Clicking "Capture" will only capture the highlighted clip in the In/Out List.

8. Indicate a file name for your captures, along with a destination folder, and click "OK".

9. Your camcorder will rewind and begin the capture process.

DVGate Motion Automatic Video Capture

This method automatically marks all of the recording start and stop points in your video for fast and easy editing. Just follow these simple steps:

1. Connect the DV camcorder to your Sony VAIO computer using an i.LINK cable.

2. Set your camcorder to "VTR" mode.

3. Launch the DVgate Motion software.

4. Click the "Scan" button on the DVgate Motion control panel.

5. The camcorder will rewind and then start playing. It will automatically mark ins and outs for each scene by detecting cuts or abrupt changes in picture. Sometimes it can be fooled, but not often. Each scene will be logged in the In/Out List window.

6. Click "Capture All" to save all of your marked video segments. Clicking "Capture" will capture just the highlighted clip in the In/Out List.

Files are saved in AVI (.avi) format, which can be imported into Premiere or Windows Movie Maker.

Boards and Software only

What if your PC doesn't have an IEEE 1394 port? Well, you could buy a new Mac or Sony VAIO, since both come with FireWire on the mother board. Here are some cheaper alternatives and home remedies. a rundown on some of the DV editing packages available that might help a shooter become better.

Try to get software with batch capture and logging—a process in which you mark the beginning and end of each shot you want downloaded into your computer and type a brief description of the shot. After you have finished logging, the computer automatically goes back and captures your selected takes.

Digital Origin IntroDV 2.0

Digital Origin IntroDV is an inexpensive, PC-only introduction to DV. You can download it for a 30 day free trial period from www.digitalorigin.com; $79 buys the DV editing software package and $149 gets you the software and FireWire card.

It's aimed at first-time owners of DV camcorders. Software includes PhotoDV, for capturing still images from your DV camcorder. Camera control from the keyboard. Built-in color preview window. Media Cleaner EZ for Windows Media, a special version of Media Cleaner by Terran Interactive, which you can use to make ultra-compressed web movies for viewing with Microsoft's Windows Media Player.

Digital Origin CineStream (previously EditDV)

Media 100 has purchased Digital Origin, and EditDV is now called CineStream. the next frontier in streaming media production. It handles Windows Media, Real MPEG-1, or QuickTime. This software-based nonlinear editor integrates Media 100's streaming media output. Handles editing, compositing, animation and special effects functions into a single editing environment available for the desktop. Includes MotoDV capture/playback software.

Available for Mac or Windows, as software only for $499; or $599 with FireWire card and cable.

Pinnacle Studio DV

One of the cheapest ways to go is Pinnacle Studio DV.

Pinnacle Studio DV is a PCI card that adds 3 IEEE 1394/FireWire ports to your PC (2 external, 1 internal).

For around $99, you get FireWire/ IEEE 1394 on your PC, which not only enables you to capture and edit DV, but also lets you add FireWire hard drives and other peripherals.

Be aware, however, that you cannot simultaneously access video stored on FireWire hard drives and output the video to your camera or DV deck. So, if you don't have enough drive space in your computer, you should either add additional internal ATA drives, or external ones via a SCSI card.

With Studio DV, you can transfer digital video directly from your camcorder to your PC hard drive. Studio DV then lets you to edit and create digital videos on your PC.

Studio DV addresses a fundamental problem: transferring a single 1 hour digital camcorder tape to a PC requires 13GB of free disk space.

With Pinnacle Systems' SmartCapture technology, you initially transfer a reduced resolution "preview" version of the video to your hard drive. One hour of preview-quality video requires only 150MB of disk space. Once you've selected your favorite scenes, added any additional elements desired such as voice-over narration, titles, background music and special effects, SmartCapture automatically transfers the full resolution data only for the scenes needed to complete the movie at full DV quality.

Standard features of the Studio software include: Instant Previews, which lets you instantly view your edited scenes and special effects to see how the final product will look; TitleDeko, enabling the creation of professional, Hollywood-style titles; Voiceovers, which lets you record your own narration while viewing the video; Timeline, for adjusting the duration of scenes frame-by frame; Storyboard, for quickly and easily arranging the order of scenes in a movie; and Sonic Desktop SmartSound, which generates a custom music soundtrack that exactly matches the duration of a movie.

Pinnacle Studio DV Interface

The package includes Studio DV software, a rudimentary editing program that lets you transfer digital video from your DV camcorder to your PC, and then begin editing.

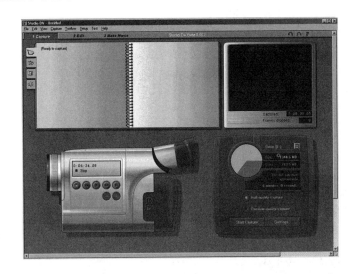

Preview compression allows an entire 60 minute tape to be captured in as little as 150MB.

Simple interface controls for camera, destination, drive space and clips.
Drag clips from the album to the timeline.

There are 100 scene transitions, and over 300 styles of cheap video effects for titles, including neon, metallic, drop shadows and more.

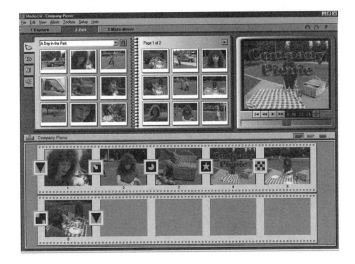

Recommended:
- Win 98 (Second Edition)
- 64MB recommended
- 30MB hard disk space for software (and 50MB for every 20 minutes of video captured at preview quality and 4GB for every 20 minutes of finished movie)
- Hard disk drive must be capable of sustained throughput of at least 4MB/sec. (All SCSI and most UDMA drives will work.)
- 233MHz or faster Pentium or equivalent
- 1 Free PCI slot
- Minimum 256-color DirectX 6.0 (or higher) compatible graphics board
- DirectX 6.0 (or higher) compatible sound board
- DV camcorder or VCR with DV (FireWire/iLink/IEEE 1394) port required
- CD-ROM drive

Pinnacle DV200

I just saw Pinnacle Systems' DV200 listed on their website for $329—which is cheaper than buying the Adobe Premiere 6 software that comes with it. DV200 (previously called miroVIDEO) consists of a PCI card and software. It is one of the cheapest IEEE-1394 editing packages with lots of advanced features. Includes Pinnacle Systems' DVTools for tape scanning with automatic scene detection, visual database logging, drag-and-drop batch capturing, and frame accurate DV device control. Also includes Adobe Premiere 6 for editing.

DV200 has two external and one internal IEEE-1394 connectors. The card features DV CODEC technology from Sony that enables the device to produce near real-time playback in quarter-size. The device captures at a maximum rate of 30fps and features a maximum resolution of 720 x 480. Runs on Windows 95, 98, Me, and NT 4.0.

ADS PYRO

This has to be the cheapest way to add 3 IEEE1394 ports to the PCI slot of your PC. ADS Technologies PYRO BasicDV costs around $70, and includes Video Studio 4.01 and Photo Explorer for Windows. This is the card recommended by AVID for XpressDV. (www.adstech.com)

ADS has a $130 PCMCIA card for laptops, providing two FireWire ports.

Canopus EZDV

Canopus makes a number of boards and editing packages for simple home and professional use. The simplest is EZDV, a $229 NTSC PCI board and software combination with a single IEEE 1394 connector. Includes EZDV Editing for Windows 98/2000/NT4.0. Includes EZDV Applications (EZ Edit, EZ Video, EZ Audio, EZ Navi), SoftXplode, SmartSound CD and cable. (SoftXplode does not run under Win NT)

Serious Editing

Serious editing usually means buying an entire system from one place: computer, boards, software and tech support. As Zorba the Greek said in the movie, "wife, house, children—the full catastrophe."

If you shoot or edit for a living, time wasted installing incompatible cards and resolving hardware conflicts is more expensive than the extra cost of buying an all-in-one editing system. Anyone who has ever tried upgrading from Windows 95 to 98, or 98 to Windows ME, knows the agony of hours spent on hold trying to reach intelligent signs of life at the other end of the phone.

When you buy a Mac, you usually can be comfortable in the knowledge that everything works when you plug it in. I use both Mac and Windows, and cannot in good conscience say that a Dell, Gateway or Sony will perform flawlessly and without tweaking when first switched on. It's not the hardware—it's the lurking conflicts of multiple software programs all vying for the attention of a giant operating system that may or may not have shared every kernel of all its code.

Mac-based editing was probably easier and less headache than PC/Windows systems until Avid's Xpress DV 2.0 was introduced. For serious DV editing, it is now a close race between AVID on the PC platform, and Apple Final Cut Pro on the Mac. What would I buy? Probably both!

Titanium PowerBook from Apple

Apple Final Cut Pro

Apple Final Cut Pro runs on G4 Mac computers and Powerbook laptops. You can use SCSI or IDE hard drives, but not FireWire drives.

Features in Final Cut Pro include match frame editing, sequence trimming and batch recapture, scriptable effects, JKL navigation controls (K=stop, L=play forward, J=play backward), support for the 16:9 picture aspect ratio, and other nonlinear editing tools. These are the most widely used and required functions for video editing; previously they were found only in systems priced significantly higher than Final Cut Pro editing systems.

With Final Cut Pro, you can work with opacity control, motion blur, and After Effects compatible plug-ins. Photoshop files can also be imported—maintaining their layers.

Final Cut Pro uses DV-based video as well as 2:1 compressed M-JPEG, along with uncompressed standard-definition (SD) and high-definition (HD) systems through after-market boards.

Avid XPress DV

I have been using an Avid Media Composer for about five years. Learning the basics took two days at an intensive class given by Future Media in New York. Becoming familiar with the ins and outs, advanced features and keyboard shortcuts happened more gradually.

I first saw Avid Xpress DV 2.0 at NAB 2001. Apple's new Final Cut Pro 2.0 was being demonstrated a few paces away. Since both programs compete both in cost and features, there will be much debate on which one to buy. Some excellent comparisons of the two are available at www.2-pop.com (named for the audio "pop" used by editors to sync picture with sound on film count-down leader.)

Avid XPress DV 2.0

I think it mostly comes down to the system with which you're most familiar, and whether you want to use a Mac or Windows 2000 computer. With a background in Media Composer, I was able to figure out Avid Xpress DV right away. Commands and shortcuts were similar. Avid XPress DV is based on the Media Composer interface.

Avid Xpress DV 2.0 brings Avid editing to laptops equipped with Windows 2000. The only additional piece of hardware required is an inexpensive ($80) DV In/Out PCMCIA card. Avid has prepared a list of "qualified" notebooks and desktops that have been tested.

Avid Xpress DV 2.0 can be purchased as stand-alone software for Windows 2000 computers for around $1,699. Bundled with an IBM Intellistation or Dell tower, it can cost as little as $4,500, with hardware, drives and an IEEE 1394 DV card. Xpress DV was originally targeted at corporate, educational and government users. It is already in place in many schools and universities. It shares the familiar AVID features seen on Media Composers and Avid Xpress that cost up to twenty times as much. Projects can be imported and exported from one machine to another. The compelling advantage of Xpress DV is that 95% of professional editing is done on Avids, and a low-cost compatible system can be very useful.

Based on Avid's 11th-generation editing technology, Avid Xpress DV 2.0 includes editing, effects, audio, titling, compositing, graphics, and several choices of output. Projects are compatible with Avid Media Composer, Symphony and Avid Xpress systems. Entire projects can be imported and exported to other Avid systems, including titles, layers, dynamic audio levels and mix, keyframes, customized effects, color correction, and batch import information.

There are a number of helful new features in version 2.0 of Avid Xpress DV, including new dual monitor support (workstations only), separate audio and video marks, smart trim, trim a rendered clip, copy source locators, and find bin command.

There are lots of effects, one-step export to Media Cleaner and 16:9 widescreen support. It's a DV-only package that includes boards, software and hardware—combining professional video editing with the ability to output your video to the Web, CDs, DVDs, DV tape, analog tapes, and more.

Export to Web video is done with integrated Media Cleaner EZ program as MPEG-1, MPEG-2, RealMedia, Windows Media/ASF, and QuickTime. Import/export of OMF (Open Media Files) ensures compatibility with other Media Composers.

Xpress DV has 4 video tracks (nestable for unlimited tracks), EDL support, Batch digitizing, IEEE 1394 and RS-422 deck control, and DV camera compatibility with Sony, Panasonic, Canon and others. Audio editing handles 8 tracks with real-time mixing and real-time equalizing options.

The compelling argument is that 95% of all commercials and features are cut on Avid's big brother Media Composer and Film Composer, which have a similar look and feel.

Avid Xpress DV Interface

The user interface is more customizable, with a mappable keyboard and command palette, resizable source monitor, and configurable timeline toolbar. There are more than 80 built-in digital video effects.

For output, there is a "Create DVD" command and Sonic AuthorScript for direct MPEG 1 & 2 output. You can output to DVD, RealMedia, QuickTime, Windows Media, MPEG 1 and 2, as well as DV formats. Enhanced DV Camera, Deck and Card Support includes a wider selection of optional DV In/Out cards, single-wire connection, and improved machine control.

Software that comes with Xpress DV includes: Boris FX LTD (2D/3D effects), Boris Graffiti LTD (2D/3D titling), Sonic Solutions DVDIt! LE ("burning" your project to DVD), and Media Cleaner EZ (compression of project for output to CD or the web). It also comes with an interactive tour and tutorial.

Avid XpressDV Powerpack

For another $1,300, you can add "PowerPack," which adds about $4,200 in additional software, including:

- Avid ePublisher Companion Edition, for web pages synchronized to video
- Pinnacle Commotion DV 3.1 for compositing, rotoscoping, and paint
- Knoll LightFactory AVX plug-in, for lighting and lens flare effects
- Sonic DVDit! SE for enhanced DVD creation tools
- Stabilize Effect AVX plug-in for correcting shaky camera work
- Avid FilmScribe with Matchback, based on Film Composer technology, for editing 24FPS film-originated projects and creating frame-accurate cut lists
- Script-Based Editing for "syncing" shots to a script
- Dupe Detection to indicate duplicate shots
- AutoSync feature for synchronizing separate audio and video

Qualified Systems

Avid Xpress DV version 2.0 is qualified for use, so far, on Dell Latitude C600 laptop, IBM ThinkPad A21P with DV In/Out card ADS PYRO 1394DV for Notebooks, SIIG NN-PCM012 or NN-PCM212, or IBM 9K5679. Workstations include IBM IntelliStation ePro, Dell Precision 330 or 220, or Compaq DeskPro EN with DV In/Out card ADS PYRO 1394DV or SIIG NN-400012, NN-440012 or LP-N21011. Configurations are also available from Ocean Systems and ProMax. More details and updates can be found at www.avid.com/products/avidxpressdv/.

Media Composer

There are currently four Media Composer models. Version 10.5 adds DV support to:
- Offline XL
- Film Composer XL: for feature film editing
- Media Composer 1000 XL: for online editing, with uncompressed resolutions
- Media Composer 9000 XL — The all-in-one Media Composer system designed for offline, film and online editing. Includes all Media Composer features and options as standard features.

Adobe Premiere 6

Adobe Premiere 6.0 is a nonlinear editing program for Windows and Mac.

In its earlier iterations, it was mostly used by web and CD authors, and was developed by some of the people who went on to work for Apple Final Cut Pro. The latest release, 6.0, addresses a criticism shared by many professional editors—that it had a corporate audio-visual "feel," as opposed to a filmmaker's tool.

Having said that, AVID on Windows requires Windows 2000. So there are very few choices of a Final Cut Pro rival on Windows 98 or Windows ME. The list price is $549. It is often bundled with some of the high-end DV and video capture cards like Pinnacle's Targa 3000 or DC2000.

Premiere took off with version 5.1, and version 6.0 adds improved audio tools and more DV device drivers. It works pretty seamlessly with other Adobe programs like After Effects and Photoshop. You probably wouldn't want to cut a feature on it, but it will be fine for short subjects, commercials, music videos and web films. Premiere supports both IEEE 1394 and analog video. Its device drivers let you pick from a list of cameras and decks.

There are a few things you cannot do. You can't work on more than one sequence per project. For example, let's say you have 10 versions of a commercial. You might want to use the beginning of version 4, the middle of version 6, and the end of version 9. This should be addressed in future updates. And you can't import an EDL (Edit Decision List). And the control buttons are very small.

Most editing functions can be done directly in the timeline. Premiere 6.0 has a history palette like Photoshop's. Premiere 6.0 comes with Terran's Cleaner 5 EZ, which is very useful for compressing your project to Quicktime or Windows AVI Media File.

Batch-capture operates similarly to Avid and Final Cut Pro. You mark in and out points on the DV tape. Then, a button in the Batch Capture window plays the tape back and imports the selected shots.

Premiere 6 saves window positions and sizes, like Photoshop and Illustrator. The history palette graphically displays recent actions so you can easily undo and redo them. Unlike Photoshop, however, Premiere 6 does not automate tasks.

A command palette assigns keyboard shortcuts and lets you create toolbar buttons.

Premiere 6 can be purchased alone, bundled with DV Cards, or bundled by companies as "turnkey" systems.

System Suggestions:

Large hard disk (capable of 5MBps for DV)

Windows

300MHz Pentium; Windows 2000, 98SE, or ME; 128MB RAM; 85MB hard disk space for install (40MB for application); IEEE 1394 interface and video display adapter.

Mac

300MHz PowerPC; OS 9.0.4; 128MB RAM; 50MB hard disk space for install; QuickTime 4.1.2.; Apple FireWire 2.4 software install; QuickTime-compatible FireWire (IEEE 1394) interface.

Adobe Premiere 6 Interface

Media 100

Media 100 i

There are currently four different Media 100 i models of this Quicktime-based, Mac-platform non-linear editing system, with various data rates from 200 Kb per frame to 300Kb (360 PAL). What distinguishes Media 100 is the variety of formats it can handle

Video Signal (I/O)	Audio Signal (I/O)	EDL
Component Analog+	AES/EBU+	Avid
Composite Analog	Balanced Analog (XLR)+	CMX 3400
DV (IEEE-1394)+	Unbalanced Analog (RCA)	CMX 3600
SDI, S-Video Analog		Grass Valley, Sony

Video File (input)	Video File (output)	Image File (output)
Animation	Animation, Cinepak, Component	Bitmap (.bmp)
Cinepak	Video, DV-NTSC, DV-PAL	GIF (.gif)
Component Video	H.261, H.263, Hinted Movie	Photo-JPEG (.jpg)
DV-NTSC	Intel Indeo Video R3.2	PICT (.pict)
DV-PAL	Intel RawMotion JPEG A	PNG (.png)
Graphics	MPEG-1, 2, 4; Motion JPEG A, B	QTIF
Hinted Movie	QuickTime .mov	Targa (.tga)
Image Sequence	RealNetworks .rm	TIFF (.tif)
Motion JPEG A, B	Real 4, Real 5, Real G2, 8	
QuickTime (.mov)	Sorenson Video,	
Sorenson Video	Windows Media .asf	

Audio File (input)	Image File (Input)	Audio File (output)
AIFF (.aif, .aiff)	Bitmap (.bmp)	AIFF (.aif, .aiff)
CD-Audio	Photo-JPEG (.jpg)	ALaw 2:1
QuickTime (.mov)	PICT (.pict)	CD-Audio
Sound Designer II	QTIF	IMA 4:1, MACE 3:1, 6:1
	TIFF (.tif)	MP-3
		QDesign Music 1, 2
		Qualcomm PureVoice
		Sound Designer II
		Wave (.wav)

iFinish 4

iFinish 4 is a Windows 2000 system similar to the mac-based Media 100. There are four models, ranging from $5,995 to $18,995—handling component, composite, DV, SDI and S-video formats.

Serious Boards and Software

Pinnacle DV500 PLUS

$899 buys you a single PCI Card with IEEE 1394 and analog connectors for DV Editing With Real-time Effects, Titles and Filters. Real-time editing with connectors for both analog and digital (IEEE1394) inputs and outputs. Input analog or digital video sources. Windows 2000/NT/Me/98SE/98.

Includes Adobe Premiere 6.0 for editing, Minerva Impression for CD-R & DVD authoring, Pinnacle Systems' FreeFX and Hollywood FX Copper for 3D transitions and TitleDeko for titling. DV500 PLUS is a real-time editing package that takes full advantage of all Adobe Premiere 6.0 capabilities with professional quality features such as real-time multi-track audio mixer for volume adjustments, 16:9 widescreen effects, transitions and titles, TitleDeko RT with video output for title creation previews, image correction for color and brightness controls.

Matrox RTMac

Matrox has recently introduced its RT Mac card to speed up realtime editing and effects in Final Cut Pro on the Power Mac G4. A Matrox RTMac in your Apple G4 lets you work with three layers of video and graphics in real time and create effects instantly—without rendering delays. Rendering is the time spent while the computer processes complex video and audio effects, such as titles, dissolves, fades, and so on.

Matrox RTMac adds analog video capture and output to Apple's pre-existing FireWire support built into Power Mac G4 computers. Using its breakout box, Composite and S-Video source material can be digitized from analog decks, such as BetaSP, Umatic or VHS, without having to go through an analog to digital FireWire converter. Once digitized, the material can be used with DV projects. Full resolution viewing on NTSC or PAL video monitors is made possible, where previously you had to hook it up through an analog to FireWire digital converter, deck or camcorder. Dual-screen editing is an added benefit of Matrox RTMac, allowing a second computer monitor to be hooked up for increased viewing real estate. Street price is around $999.

Matrox RT2000 MEGA Pack

This is an IEEE 1394 card and software package that competes with Pinnacle's DV500 on Windows 98 computers (Pentium 3 recommended). The package includes a DV capture card, a G400 graphics accelerator card, Adobe Premiere, Sonic DVDit! LE DVD authoring and more. A breakout box provides DV, composite and S-Video input and output.

It includes MPEG-2 output for DVD, Video CD, and web video streaming applications. , with 1394 and analog video output. Street price is around $999.

Canopus DVRexRT Professional

DVRexRT Professional competes with Pinnacle's Targa 3000 for PC as a DV and uncompressed analog video board with external break-out box. It is compatible with Adobe Premiere 6.0. It features component video I/O, balanced audio I/O, RS-422 analog deck control, a rack-mountable 19" breakout box, balanced XLR audio connectors, and many real-time features. DVRex RT Professional incorporates Sony's DVBK-1 hardware DV CODEC on-board for digitizing analog video into the standard DV format and outputs to DV in real-time. MPEG-1 and MPEG-2 encoding is done by the Panasonic hardware MPEG CODEC. You can transfer DV footage via the IEEE 1394 (i.LINK) interface. Composite, component and S-Video are connected to the breakout box.

- Dual PCI bus board design
- Component video input/output
- Real-time DV and analog input/output
- Real-time capture through DV IEEE1394 interface
- Real-time capture through analog (Y/C, composite, and component) input
- Frame accurate DV & RS-422 analog deck control for capture and output
- Real-time video tracks, Real-time moving titles
- Real-time transitions and filters
- Color correction, Picture-in-picture, Luma-key, Chroma-key
- Output to DV AVI, MPEG1, MPEG2 and streaming video (WMV) files
- Hardware MPEG encoder
- 19" Professional breakout box
- Analog level meters and input gain control
- Software bundle includes Canopus RexEdit 2.91, Adobe Premiere, Canopus SoftXplode, Boris Graffiti Ltd., Sonic Foundry ACID Style, SpruceUp (full version), SoftMPG Encoder, Canopus Web Video Wizard
- List price approx $4599

Uncompressed Video

DV compression is 5:1. Compression is done by the hardware. It looks for adjacent pixels with the same colors that take up a lot of space, and assigns them mathematical values. Unlike software compression (Quicktime) and variable rate hardware compression (Avid AVR75—which was around 3:1), the rate of DV compression is fixed.

With variable compression, complex scenes sometimes had more grain or jagged "artifacts" than simple scenes. A complex scene would be one with a lot of detail, like trees against a blue sky. A simple scene would be a close-up of a face.

For DV format (FireWire/IEEE1394), you need 240 megabytes of hard drive space per second of video.

Pinnacle 3000 / Cinéwave

As we climb up the food chain of compression and pass BetaSP and reach the lofty heights of D1, Digibeta, DVCPro HD and HD, you won't want to use FireWire to get the signal into your computer. Instead, you'll reach into your wallet for a few more thousand dollars and purchase a Pinnacle Cinéwave card for your Mac or Targa 3000 for your PC (pretty much the same PCI board with different names and software configurations).

The board connects to a breakout box with audio XLR along with component and composite video BNC connectors.

How Many Hard Drives Do I Need?

DV Firwire/IEEE1394 requires 240 Megabytes of hard drive space per minute. Here's a brief chart to help calculate your storage requirements:

Running Time	Drive Space Needed
1 second	4 Mb
1 minute	240 Mb
10 minutes	2Gb
20 minutes	4 Gb
30 minutes	6 Gb
60 minutes	12 Gb
90 minutes (feature—final cut)	18 Gb
120 minutes (2 hours)	24 Gb
20 hours (feature—dailies)	240 Gb

Remember, you can't use FireWire drives. They should ideally be SCSI, though IDE will also work.

Some programs, such as Pinnacle Studio DV and others, allow capturing at lower resolution to reduce storage requirements. Studio DV has an option that records DV with additional compression (preview quality) at 2.5 Mb per minute, 416Kb per second, 150 Mb per hour. When you complete your edit, you recapture only the footage you need at normal resolution.

Uncompressed Video

Uncompressed video is not DV. However, since AVID, Final Cut Pro with Cinewave and other vendors are offering uncompressed video options, it's worth mentioning. If you have shot your material on HD, DigiBeta, BetaSP or film transferred to tape, you might not want the 5:1 compression of DV.

Uncompressed Quicktime requires about 1.3 Gigs per minute and a throughput rate of 22-30 megs per second.

Uncompressed AVID is about the same: 45 seconds per 1 Gig of drive space.

For uncompressed video, you are usually steered toward AVID, Medea or JEMS SCSI drives.

Running Time	Drive Space Needed
138 min	180 Gb
230 min	300 Gb
345 min	450 Gb

Buying or Renting Extra Drives

Sooner or later in your DV career, you'll run out of hard drive space. There are dazzling choices of storage devices with SCSI specifications that will surely make you doze.

Do not use FireWire drives. Even though the data rate is very high, it gets bogged down with the multiple demands of simultaneously handling the DV signal from the camera or to a monitor. Use SCSI or IDE drives.

Compatibility is a complicated matter, and it is best to seek professional advice from a dealer, rental agent or manufacturer.

Where Does It All Go?

Your opus is complete. Where can it go?

> DV Tape
> Analog Tape
> Web
> Quicktime
> Windows Media
> Real Player
> CD
> DVD
> Film
> Festivals
> Theatrical Release

The fastest way to release your DV is to eject it from the camera and hand it over to cop who is towering above you and inquiring why you are working without a permit on private property in full view of the No Trespassing signs.

The next higher level of DV distribution is copying it to another tape. Using a direct FireWire connection from one camcorder or deck to another, your tape can be "cloned" onto another tape. Analog audio and video outputs or S-Video connections let you copy your DV to non-digital tapes, such as VHS, 3/4", BetaSP and so on.

Farther up the evolutionary chain, nonlinear DV editing on computer opens up vast possibilities and many choices of formats, compressions and destinations. The final project can be output as DV, analog video, Quicktime, Windows Media, streaming media, or still frames to be uploaded to the web, broadcast on television, mastered and released on VHS, sent as an email attachment, or written to CD or DVD.

Apple's iDVD lets you "burn" your completed video to a standard DVD, which can be viewed by anyone with a standard DVD-equipped TV or computer.

In the old days, up to the year 2000, it could take as long as 25 hours to record one hour of video to DVD. Apple's SuperDrive reduces that time to two hours.

The iDVD software facilitates importing iMovie or any QuickTime file and making menus. Don't you hate those DVD menus? Why can't the disk just play when you put it in the machine, like a laserdisc or CD?

DV to Film

Even though DV distribution promises a surfeit of formats in numerous venues, the holy grail, the Everest, the promised land of DV distribution is film.

And there's the paradox. The medium that vies with film for attention and economy still aspires to ultimate release on film.

ARRI Laser

The reasons, like almost everything else economic, are fear and greed. Greed, because most movie theatres and film festivals around the world use 35mm film projectors that have been paid for long ago. Fear, because if they invest in a new digital computerized projection system today, they are assured of its imminent obsolescence within eighteen months, replaced by something twice as good at half the price, as predicted by Moore's law.

Nevertheless, manufacturers are hard at work raising resolution and lowering prices on digital projection systems. But until a $100,000 digital projector becomes cheaper than the $3000 per print cost of a 90 minute feature on an already amortized projector in Kazakhstan, you're probably going to have to "blow up" your DV epic to 35mm film. Most theatres still project 35mm film. You don't shell out $10 for a ticket, along with concommitant popcorn and junk food, to watch DV in a theatre on a projection TV.

The machine looking like a freezer on wheels, pictured above, is one of the devices that makes possible decent conversion of DV to film.

It works essentially like the laser printer attached to your computer. The DV data is "printed" frame by frame onto 35mm motion picture film, which becomes the new master.

It is safe to say that most of the material shot on DV will be viewed once, never be seen again, and soon relegated to the same dusty drawer reserved for previous generations of home movie and video ephemera. There are the inevitable spools of 8mm film, and the projector whose burned-out bulbs aren't even available on eBay, and, of course, lots of Betamax tapes, because you were an early adopter of every superior technology, which did not guarantee its longevity or acceptance by everyone else.

Auteur Theory

I think anyone who ever picked up a movie or video camera has dreamed of becoming an auteur, darling of the film festivals, pursued by rival studios, loved by critics, adored by all.

Up to now, there have been a few surmountable impediments to such dreams, the most notable of which have been cost and crew.

Making movies is not cheap. Nor is it easy. Francois Truffaut once said that making a movie is like riding a stagecoach in the Wild West. You begin your journey with high expectations. Halfway through the journey, you just wish you had arrived at the destination. It's a complex process requiring a team of highly skilled people working together for long periods of time under difficult conditions. Truffaut also said, "if prisoners were forced to do what film crews willingly do, they'd rebel."

Enter the DV

DV is small, lightweight, fast and cheap. Almost anyone can use it—I regret to say, even without reading this book. The results may not look good, but there will most likely be an image. You will not wake up at three in the morning, in a cold sweat, wondering if you remembered to close the eyepiece during the remote-controlled stunt shot, or whether the entire scene has been irreparably fogged, because there are another six hours to go until dailies will be viewed at the lab. With DV, what you see is what you get.

The other DV aphorism is "you can pay now or you can pay later." Meaning, you can spend big bucks now and shoot your independent feature on 35mm, or you can spare every expense now, and shoot it on DV. You, or the major studio that has just purchased worldwide distribution rights, can pay later to blow the DV material up to 35mm.

And that is why there is so much excitement about this format. Most first film efforts are like first novels. They are put in square cans so they don't roll off the shelf where they remain in unappreciated obscurity.

ARRI Laser film gate

But there is always the exception, and that is what we all dream of.

Low Budgets

How much does it cost to make a 90 minute, low budget feature? That's sort of like asking "how much does it cost to build a house?" For the purposes of comparison, let's say there are no above-the-line costs; director, producer, actors are all doing it as a labor of love. All production services have been donated, along with grip, electric and sound equipment. We'll only budget for actual shooting costs, and pretend it's a four-week shoot. A lot of numbers are rounded out and approximated for easy math. We're assuming a 10:1 shooting ratio, that you're buying real filmstock instead of recans, and you're making a workprint to view dailies (more expensive but highly recommended because it's the only way to see if that critical shot really was in focus).

Shoot on DV

4 weeks	DV camera rental	1000 - 1600 / week	$ 4,000 (you could almost buy the camera for this price)
15 hours (900 mins)	DV tape	$ 35 / hour (about .60 / min)	$ 525
			total $ 4,525

Shoot on 35mm Film

4 weeks	35mm camera rental	4,000 / week	$ 16,000 (another $ 60,000 might buy you an old ARRI 35BL3 system
15 hours (900 mins)	35mm film, processing, workprint	$100 / minute (90 x 1000' rolls)	$ 90,000
			total $ 106,000

Shoot on 16mm Film

4 weeks	16 mm camera rental	3,000 / week	$ 12,000 (another $ 8,000 might buy you an old ARRI 16SR system
15 hours (900 mins)	16mm film, processing, workprint	$35 / minute (90 x 400' rolls)	$ 31,500
			total $ 43,500

Peddling the Project

So far, shooting on DV has saved you $101,475 compared to 35mm, and $38,975 compared to 16mm.

Next, you need to find a distributor—a search conducted by word of mouth and by sending video dubs of the project to various companies. You enter some of the festivals that accept video. But, you soon discover how difficult it is to find a buyer of your video. You decide to plunge forward, spend the big bucks, and enter some of the major festivals. For that, you now begin the process of DV to 35mm Film. Here are some ballpark figures—they are constantly changing, and often negotiable.

DV to 35mm Film Costs

Method	Cost	Total for 90 minutes
Laser Film Printer	$550-750 / minute (3000-4000 / minute on spots and shorts)	$ 50,000
Electron Beam Recorder	$ 395 - 900 / minute	$ 36,000
Swiss Effects		$ 33,000
Kinescope	$ 230 / minute	$ 20,700

DV to 16mm Film

Method	Cost	Total for 90 minutes
Kinescope	$ 75 / min	$ 6,750

Since we're trying to spare every expense, as my producer friend Mel London used to say, transferring from DV to 16mm using a Kinescope is the cheapest. For around $75 per minute, you get a color negative and timed composite release print along with sound.

16mm to 35 Blowup

9,000 feet (90 minutes)	$ 5 / foot	$ 45,000 - 50,000

If you subsequently find that a festival will only accept 35mm prints, you're back in major spending mode. Blowups from 16mm to 35mm average around $5 per foot, based on the final 35mm footage (90 minutes at 90 feet/minute=8100 feet). That will total around $50,000 for a 90 minute show, once you add extra cost of leader and a few other things, including interpositive, interneg, and composite check print with sound.

DV to Film Transfers

Laser Film Recorder (Printer)

The big names in laser "printing" systems are ARRI, Eastman Kodak (Cineon Lightning), Digital Cinema Systems (Lux) and Pthalo Systems (Verité). These are commonly used in big budget, effects-heavy major motion pictures. The original 35mm negative is often scanned into a "sister" companion laser scanner at high resolution. The digital image is then manipulated, composited, matted or keyed, and the final product goes back to film via the laser film printer, at a rate of about three to six seconds per frame. Light from the laser exposes a fine-grain internegative (5244) film, whose ASA is around 1. The native rate is 4K resolution, with a 2K option. The laser does not use lenses, and works somewhat like your home computer laser printer.

ARRI Laser

CRT Film Printer

Slower and sometimes cheaper than laser printers, Cathode Ray Tube (CRT) devices use a film camera to shoot three consecutive exposures on each frame (through red, green and blue filters) of a high resolution monochromatic monitor. They are made by Management Graphics (Solitaire) and Celco. It takes about five to forty seconds per frame at 2 or 4K resolution.

Swiss Effects

Swiss Effects is a company in Zurich that has devised a proprietary CRT technology. It is curently the "hot" place to convert features shot on video into film. Its appeal is a combination of speed and personal attention. Standard definition DV is "up-rezzed" (increased resolution) to 2K on the fly, and recorded at rates of 5 seconds per frame. Native 2K images, either from HD or 35mm film, is recorded at .7 to 2 seconds per frame. They can use different camera negative films, such as 5245, instead of traditional print and intermediate stocks. Each frame is exposed three times, but at a much faster rate than other CRTs. So, while other machines are still chugging along at three to six seconds per frame and the deadline is looming for your film festival premiere, Swiss Effects is akin to FedEx—absolutely, positively getting it there on time.

Electron Beam Recorder

Electron Beam Recorders (EBRs) use a method similar to the way electron beams scan the phosphors on the back of a TV screen. EBRs use electron beams to expose black and white film. Three passes are made: red, green and blue, something like the old Technicolor 3 strip process. The three strips are printed in three passes back to color film through color filters. Most EBRs are 16mm, except Sony's, and require a blowup to 35mm. Most agree that this technology will be obsolete soon.

Kinescope

Kinescopes are as old as live television, when there were video cameras, but video tape had not yet been invented. Many of the early shows were recorded directly onto film with a kinescope, which was basically a black and white NTSC video monitor photographed by a motion picture camera. Ironically, most of these kinescoped shows have survived better than the early videotapes, which suffered from demagnetization or dropouts.

I suppose if you were really desperate and broke, you could improvise your own kinescope by having your cousin the film student borrow a camera and shoot your own screen. It would look horrendous, but it would certainly be cheap.

2K - 4K Resolution

When you discuss laser film printers and scanners, talk inevitably revolves around 2K or 4K scans. They refer to digital resolution of 2000 or 4000 pixels per horizontal line, and the difference is a matter of time and money. It costs more to work at 4K because it takes the machine longer to do the work.

The image in video is made up of pixels; film consists of light-sensitive, microscopic (.003 to .0003mm) grains of silver halide crystals, arranged in layers that take on colors when processed.

The more pixels there are, the greater the detail. That's why a Megapixel digital still camera looks better than one shooting at 640 x 480.

The finer the grain of motion picture film, the sharper and more detailed it looks. That's why Kodak EXR-50D 5245, a 50 ASA film stock, looks sharper and richer than Kodak Vision 800T 5289, an 800 ASA stock.

A frame of NTSC video consists of approximately 307,200 pixels, and a PAL frame has about 368,640 pixels.

The image on a frame of film is made by lots of little grains, not pixels. But, if we were to make a mathematical or analytical conversion, each frame of film would be 5000 x 3760 (18,800,000) pixels.

If we scanned a frame of film at 5000 x 3846 resolution, we would need 58Megabytes of storage space for that one frame (5,000 x 3,846 x 3 colors). That's 1.4 Gigabytes per second, which, at the moment is not easily manageable. So the image is scanned and printed at lower resolutions, usually 2K.

There has been much debate about the maximum resolution that can be seen by the human eye. Inevitably, the figure 2500 pixels is tossed about. Problem is, it depends where you're sitting in the movie theatre. The industry standard is to watch from a distance that is 1 1/2 screen widths away from the screen. (If the screen is 60 feet wide, you sit 90 feet away.) Not fair! How far away were you during the time warp sequence in "2001: A Space Odyssey?" I'll bet you were in the front row, like me.

Keeping DV to Film in Mind

What does all this mean?

It means plan ahead. If you are going to shoot an independent low-budget feature on DV, prepare for all contingencies in advance.

1. Shoot tests.

2. Do a test of the DV-to-film system you'll be using.

3. Get prices in advance.

4. Know the aspect ratio of your release print (1.33:1, 1.66:1, 1.78:1, 1.85:1) and frame accordingly while shooting. You can cut a piece of gray neutral density gel to serve as a frame line in your viewfinder.

5. On Sony cameras, shoot in 16:9. On Canon cameras, use 4:3. Even better quality will be realized if you shoot with an anamorphic adapter.

6. Do not use the digital zoom.

7. Do not use electronic image stabilizers. Optical stabilizing is OK, and highly recommended.

8. Beware of strobing. If you pan too quickly in film, objects can look jittery. A rule of thumb, often broken, is to pan no faster than the time it takes for an object at one side of the frame to get to the other side. Whip pans are fine. They're supposed to be blurred.

9. Turn manual shutter off.

10. Use a separate tape recorder for audio, preferably DAT, as audio backup. Get as good a feed as possible to the DV camera. It will be a lot easier for the editor to use audio from the DV tape. The DAT will be available for looping and special audio work. Use clapsticks at the beginning of each take, if possible. The editor will sing your praises daily.

11. The envelope please.

Film Look

The question of "film look" pops up constantly on Internet discussion forums, including the one I moderate at www.cinematographer.com.

A number of companies offer "film look" effects and electronic plug-ins to try to make video look more like film. I don't think so.

The fact that film runs at 24 frames per second is not what gives it a film look. Run the same film at 30 fps, and it still looks like film.

The next argument is that the film look is created by the inherent grain pattern. Again, not a good reason. Look at an IMAX film. You can't see the grain in the 70mm print.

So what is film look? It's exposure and latitude. Film has a much wider dynamic range, meaning it will properly record an image that has an exposure range of 11 to 13 stops. You can see details in the dark shadows. You can see details in the highlights. Imagine you're filming a dark room with a window, and trees outside. Film would allow you to see the cat on the rug, and the bird in the tree outside the sunlit window. In video and DV, we're lucky if we have an exposure range of 7 stops.

Incidentally, my favorite suggestion on how to achieve the film look on video is to put a Tiffen 1/8, and sometimes 1/4, Black or White Promist filter on the lens. It will create a slightly romantic look, with a nice glow to highlights and softening of harsh shadows.

Relative Format Sizes

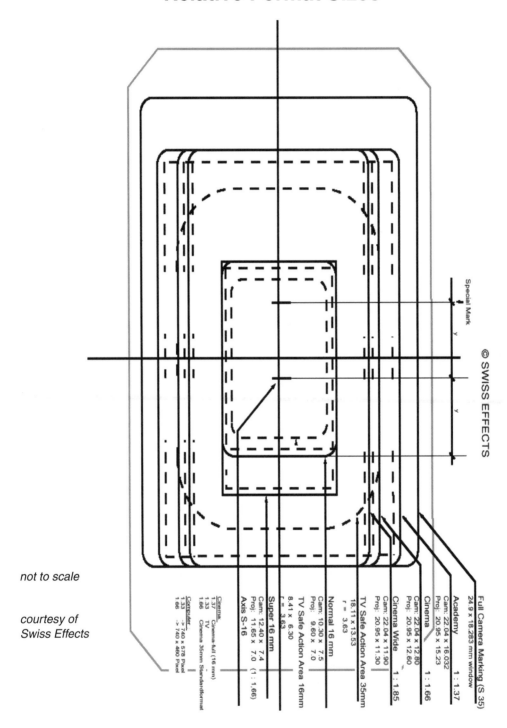

Special Mark

© SWISS EFFECTS

not to scale

*courtesy of
Swiss Effects*

Full Camera Marking (S 35)
24.9 × 18.283 mm window

Academy   1 : 1.37
Cam: 22.04 × 16.032
Proj: 20.95 × 15.23

Cinema   1 : 1.66
Cam: 22.04 × 12.80
Proj: 20.95 × 12.60

Cinema Wide   1 : 1.85
Cam: 22.04 × 11.90
Proj: 20.95 × 11.30

TV Safe Action Area 35mm
18.11 × 13.53
r = 3.63

Normal 16 mm
Cam: 10.30 × 7.5
Proj: 9.60 × 7.0

TV Safe Action Area 16mm
8.41 × 6.30
r = 3.63

Super 16 mm
Cam: 12.40 × 7.4
Proj: 11.65 × 7.0 (1 : 1.66)

Axis S-16

Cinema
1.37   Cinema-full (16 mm)
1.33   TV
1.66   Cinema 35mm Standardformat

Computer:
1.33   → 740 × 578 Pixel
1.66   → 740 × 460 Pixel

Accessories and Techniques

Accessories and Techniques

Lenses

Comparison of CCD Size and Film Apertures

The chart at right is a lifesize drawing showing the relative sizes of different CCDs and how they compare with the image area on 16mm and 35mm film.

CCDs are measured diagonally. So a 1/2" chip is measured along opposite corners. The aspect ratio is 4:1, which is the same as a 1.33:1 film gate.

Notice how 16mm and the 1/2" CCD are the same.

The amazing thing is how small a 1/4" CCD really is.

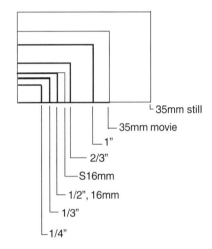

- 35mm still
- 35mm movie
- 1"
- 2/3"
- S16mm
- 1/2", 16mm
- 1/3"
- 1/4"

In case you're wondering, 16mm and 35mm are measurements of the width of the film, including sprocket area.

Here, on the right, is a sample of 16mm film, which is indeed 16mm wide. The picture area in this case is composed in the Super16mm format, which is 1.66:1 (not quite the 16:9 of the video world, which can also be expressed as 1.77:1.)

You can't take an off-the-shelf film lens and attach it to a DV camcorder. The back-focus is different. Back-focus is the distance required from the lens mount to the chip, and in a film camera, from the lens mount to the film itself. Three-chip cameras add their own limitations because of the beam splitters. Therefore, manufacturers have specific lines of DV lenses. Some of these are modified film lenses, re-housed.

DV Lens Specs and 35mm Still Equivalents

When you see specifications for DV lenses, you'll see something like this:

4.2-42mm f1.8-2.8

This is a 10x (10 times) zoom. If you divide the telephoto end (42mm) by the wide end (4.2mm), you get 10.

The letter "f" is the maximum f-stop of the lens (wide open).

In this case, the most you can open the iris is f1.8. The second f-stop, 2.8, shows that the optical designers of this lens "cheated" to make it smaller and lighter. To keep the amount of light passing through the lens the same at both wide angle and telephoto, they would have had to make the glass elements much larger. So, the f2.8 means that's the maximum aperture when you zoom in to 42mm. It also means that if you zoom all the way from wide to tight continuously during the shot, there will be a one-stop darkening of the image from beginning to end. Automatic exposure circuits will probably compensate, but remember this when in manual mode.

To find out approximately what your mini DV lens would be if it were a full frame 35mm still lens, multiply by 10 for a 1/4" CCD and multiply by 11 for a 1/3" CCD.

So, the 4.2-42mm on a 1/4" chip camera be similar to a 42mm to 420mm zoom lens in 35mm still format. If your mini DV had a 1/3" chip, it would be roughly equivalent to 48mm to 480mm.

DV Lenses and 35mm Motion Picture Equivalents

I usually multiply a still lens by .8 (8/10) when comparing 35mm still lenses with 35mm motion picture lenses.

So, for those of us cinematographers with limited math skills but 35mm motion picture lens angles of view indellibly etched in our memories, the quick and slightly inaccurate—but close-enough—conversion is to multiply by 8 for a 1/4" CCD and multiply by 9 for a 1/3" CCD.:

Conversion Chart: DV to 35mm

	35mm Motion Picture Format	35mm Still Format
1/4" CCD	multiply by 8	multiply by 10
1/3" CCD	multiply by 9	multiply by 11

Why DV Doesn't Look Like Film

There are a number of reasons why DV does not look like film—not even film transferred to DV. The biggest single reason is depth of field. And one of the immutable laws of optics is that the smaller the image area, the greater the depth of field.

Depth of Field

Video: Studio rig

Depth of field is a measurement of how much of the scene is in focus.

Let's say you're filming a mouse sitting in the middle of a staircase, and let's assume the mouse will hold still for the entire duration of your experiment. Maybe it's a stuffed mouse. You are using a 100m lens at T2.8. You are shooting with a 35mm motion picture camera. You focus on the mouse. The stair steps immediately about and below the mouse will appear sharp.

To get more stair steps in focus, you can change a number of variables. Stop the lens down to T11. The more you close down the iris, the more depth of field. Or you can zoom wider. The wider the lens, the more depth of field. Or you can use a 16mm camera, or a DV camera. The smaller the gathered image area, the greater the depth of field.

Since DV usually uses such small CCDs, the depth of field is enormous. Almost everything is in focus.

"What's wrong with that?" you ask. Nothing. But that's the main difference in look. And it cannot be changed with "film look" conversions or lighting.

One of the distinctive qualities of 35mm motion picture photography is its usually shallow depth of field. In essence, the camera selectively focuses on an area, putting emphasis on it. Backgrounds tend to become "soft." 16mm film has more depth of field, and 8mm even more.

You may be wondering about an exception to the rule: *Citizen Kane*. Everything is in focus. We call it deep focus. Yes, and most of it was shot by Greg Toland with lenses closed down almost to pinholes and so much light that it could have been measured with a thermometer instead of a lightmeter.

Lens Attachments

With the exception of Canon's XL-1 and JVC's DV500U, most MiniDV camcorders are fitted with zoom lenses that are permanently mounted.

If you want to shoot wider or tighter than the lens that comes with the camera, you can purchase wide-angle and telephoto lens adapters. They screw into the front filter thread of the existing lens.

Doublers, or tele-extenders, do just that. They magnify the image two times. They typically come in strengths of 2x and 1.6x

So, if your zoom lens is 4 to 10mm, the doubler makes it the equivalent of 8 to 20mm.

Wide angle attachments typically widen the field of view of the zoom lens. They typically come in .6x, .7x and .8x.

The sunshade that came with your camera probably will not fit. It's a good idea to use a sunshade with the new adapter.

You can purchase these adapters from the manufacturer, or from specialists like Century Precision Optics or Optex.

Century Precision and OpTex

You pay for what you get. If you use a cheap lens adapter, the image might become degraded.

Century Precision Optics (California) and OpTex (London) have been making converters and adapters for motion picture lenses for years, and now have a complete line of accessories for video lenses.

Wide Angle Adapters

.5x, .6x, .7x, .8x, Super Fisheye
No exposure compensation is required with wide angle adapters.

Tele-Extenders

The 1.6x extender attaches to the front of your lens, and does not cause any light loss. The 2x extender is intended for removable lenses, and fits between the camera body and the lens. It "eats" two stops of light.

Diopters

Diopters work like your reading glasses. They allow the lens to focus closer. Single element diopters from Tiffen and other filter companies typically come in strengths of +1/2, +1 and +2. They are relatively inexpensive, but can cause a little chromatic aberration and softening of the image.

Century's Achromatic Diopters use two elements and are optically much better, and of course, cost more. They come in strengths of +1.6, 2, 2.6, 3.5, 4 and 7.

Anamorphic

If you're planning on a theatrical release, an anamorphic adapter will provide a wide-screen aspect ratio by "squeezing" the image horizontally. This image is "unsqueezed" when projected. By recording in the 4:3 mode, you are taking advantage of all the pixels, rather than relying on the camera's built-in 16:9 conversion. Be careful with anamorphic adapters—there may be some vignetting around the edges at wide angle which you will not see in the viewfinder. Check the monitor.

OpTex Anamorphic

Optex PL to XL-1 Lens Mount Adapter

Most professional Arriflex motion cameras have a PL Mount. It has a 54mm diameter, and the flange focal distance (space from the lens seating to the image plane) is 52mm.

There are thousands of PL mount lenses worldwide. To take advantage of them on an XL-1, OpTex has a mechanical (non-optical) adapter.

Since the CCD is smaller than a 35mm frame, your 10mm Zeiss Standard Lens will appear more like a 40mm in 35mm motion picture format.

Canon 1/3" and 1/2" Lenses

18x	12x
9-162mm f1.8/2.5 18x zoom, internal focus YJ18x9B KRS (for 2/3") 6.7-121mm f1.4/1.8 18x zoom, internal focus YH18x6.7 KRS (for 1/2")	6.5-78mm f2/2.6 12x zoom, internal focus YJ12x6.5B KRS (for 2/3") 4.8-58mm f1.5/2 12x zoom, internal focus YH12x4.8KRS (for1/2")
18x with built-in doubler	**12x with built-in doubler**
9-162mm f1.8/2.5 18x zoom 18-324mm f3.6/5 with internal 2x YJ18x9B IRS (for 2/3") 6.7-121mm f1.4/1.8 18x zoom 13.4-242mm f2.8/3.7 with internal 2x YH18x6.7 IRS (for 1/2")	6.5-78mm f2/2.6 12x zoom 13-156mm f4/5.2 with internal 2x YJ12x6.5B IRS (for 2/3") 4.8-58mm f 1.5/2 9.6-116mm f 3/4 with internal 2x YH12x4.8 IRS (for 1/2")

Fujinon Lenses

Fujinon Lenses for 1/2" and 2/3" CCD Cameras

SPECIFICATIONS	S15x6.1 EVM/ ERD	S10x3.5 EVM/ERD	S12x5 RM
FOCAL LENGTH	(1x)6.1-91.5mm (2x)12.2-183mm	(1x)3.5-35mm (2x)7-70mm	5-60mm
ZOOM RATIO	15x	10x	12x
EXTENDER	2x	2x	NO
MAXIMUM RELATIVE APERTURE	1:1.4(6.1-82mm) 1:1.6(91.5mm)	1:1.4(3.5-29mm) 1:1.7(35mm)	1:1.8(5-54mm) 1:2.0(60mm)
MINIMUM OBJECT DISTANCE (M.O.D.)	0.65m	0.3m	0.5m
OBJECT DIMENSIONS AT M.O.D.	6.1mm 639x479mm 91.5mm 43x32mm	3.5mm 618x464mm 35mm 62x46mm	5mm 638x478mm 60mm53x39mm
ANGULAR FIELD OF VIEW	6.1mm 5°22'x42°57' 119mm 4°0'x3°0'	3.5mm 84°52'x68°53' 35mm 10°27'x7°51'	5mm 65°14'x51°17' 60mm 6°06'x4°35'
MACRO	YES	YES	YES
FILTER THREAD	M82x0.75	M127x0.75	M82x0.75
LENGTH	210.3mm	249mm	183mm
WEIGHT (WITHOUT LENS HOOD)	1.4kg/1.5kg	1.85kg/1.92kg	1.2kg
OPERATING SYSTEMS	EVM/ERD	EVM/ERD	RM
NOTES	INTERNAL FOCUS	INTERNAL FOCUS	-

SPECIFICATIONS	S17x6.6 RM	S19x6.5 RM/ERM*	S22x5.8 EVM/ERD*
FOCAL LENGTH	6.6-112mm	6.5-123mm (1x)6.5-123mm* (2x13-246mm*	(1x)5.8-128mm (2x)11.6-256mm
ZOOM RATIO	17x	19x	22x
EXTENDER	NO	NO 2x*	2x
MAXIMUM RELATIVE APERTURE	1:1.4(6.6-90mm) 1:1.9(112mm)	1:1.4(6.5-91mm) 1:1.9(123mm)	1:1.4(5.8-94mm) 1:1.9(128mm)
MINIMUM OBJECT DISTANCE (M.O.D.)	0.9m	0.9m	0.8m
OBJECT DIMENSIONS AT M.O.D.	6.6mm 808x606mm 112mm 48x36mm	6.5mm 835x626mm 123mm 44x33mm	5.8mm 823x617mm 128mm 37x28mm
ANGULAR FIELD OF VIEW	6.6mm 51°44'x39°58' 112mm 3°16'x2°27'	6.5mm 52°25'x40°32' 123mm 3°44'x2°59'	5.8mm 57°46'x44°58' 128mm 2°52'x2°09'
MACRO	YES	YES	YES
FILTER THREAD	M82x0.75	M82x0.75	M95x1
LENGTH	181.8mm	204.1mm 204.1mm*	219.4mm 219.4mm*
WEIGHT (WITHOUT LENS HOOD)	1.25kg	1.35kg 1.45kg*	1.7kg 1.77kg*
OPERATING SYSTEMS	RM	RM/ERM	EVM/ERD
NOTES	INTERNAL FOCUS	INTERNAL FOCUS	INTERNAL FOCUS

Light and Lighting

What is ASA of CCD?

As a Director of Photography, one of the first decisions I make is what kind of film to use. There are many choices: daylight or tungsten, fast or slow, saturated or muted, color or black and white. Low ASA (also known as ISO or EI) film generally reveals less grain, but requires more light.

One of the first things I want to know, when shooting with a DV camcorder, is its "effective" ASA. In other words, how sensitive is the chip? If this were film, how would I set my lightmeter?

Here's a quick chart, calculated using a Spectra IV meter, as explained below. It's not a scientific or mathematical formula—just a useful estimate. There are numerous electronic circuits in a video camera that boost gain, change shutter angle (exposure time) and alter contrast. This chart assumes all that is turned off.

1000 ASA	is	200 Lux	at F11
800 ASA	is	260 Lux	at F11
500 ASA	is	400 Lux	at F11
400 ASA	is	500 Lux	at F11
320 ASA	is	600 Lux	at F11
250 ASA	is	800 Lux	at F11
200 ASA	is	1000 Lux	at F11
160 ASA	is	1200 Lux	at F11
120 ASA	is	1600 Lux	at F11
100 ASA	is	2000 Lux	at F11
64 ASA	is	3300 Lux	at F11
50 ASA	is	4100 Lux	at F11
25 ASA	is	9600 Lux	at F11

Using Lightmeter Instead of Waveform Monitor

Most video people grew up looking at waveform monitors. Most film people were weaned on lightmeters. There are many advantages to using a lightmeter, not the least of which will be the look of utter horror and scorn bestowed upon you by members of the video persuasion who haven't yet read these immortal suggestions. For, no matter how good your eye is, it can easily be fooled. Next time a video engineer argues with you about the infallibility of the human eye, remind him that the whole principle of video and persistence of vision is a total trickery of brain and eye. Further argument can be quelled by looking at a fluorescent tube and asking why we don't see any green.

Having said that, a waveform monitor and scope is a very useful tool. However, we usually don't carry one around on DV shoots. Instead, we'll rely on our fallible eyes and an infallible lightmeter.

Let's say you're doing a DV sequel to *The Magnificent Ambersons.*

```
INT. Ballroom - NIGHT
Charles and his girlfriend are waltzing around the dance
floor.

Cut to Charles, smiling.

Cut to girl.
                    Girl
          Charles, what to you want
          to be when you grow up?


Close on Charles.

                    Charles
          A yachtsman.

The couple dance off into the distance.
```

Assuming we have the rights to do this, and we've found an actor as good as young Orson Welles, our lightmeter might be the tool that can help propel this picture onto the DV film festival circuit.

A lightmeter will help us maintain consistent exposures throughout the show. Cutting back and forth will look terrible if Charles is dark in one scene, and his partner is much brighter in the next.

You can achieve balance by measuring the light falling on their faces, and using manual exposure on the camera.

Waveform monitors are typically used in broadcast and serious video production. But they often slow things down. For DV work, I find them tedious and an impediment to artful lighting. Here's how to avoid using them.

Lux

Just as every film stock has a suggested ASA rating, which is its measured sensitivity to light according to the engineers, video cameras also have defined sensitivity ratings. If you look at the spec sheets, many video camcorders are rated "1000 Lux at F11." What that really means is that the camera has a sensitivity equivalent to 200 ASA at 1/60th second.

How do we know this? Take out your Spectra Pro IV or IVa meter. We like this meter because it allows simple conversions from f/stops to lux.

1. Slide the **F/STOP/ILLUM.** switch to the right, to the **ILLUM** position.

2. Push the **FC/LUX** switch until you see **LUX** displayed on screen. Footcandles and Lux are both measurements of illumination—but since most of the world is metric, it would be foolish to force everyone to think of brightness as numbers of candles flickering one *foot* away. Thus, lux.

3. Take a reading in sunlight or under a bright light, and move the meter around until it displays 1000 Lux.

On a Spectra IV, 1000 Lux will be displayed like this: *x10*
(If the "*x10*" is absent, the small digit at the right is   *LUX 100 0*
fractional, and can be ignored.)

On a Spectra IVa, 1000 Lux will be displayed like this:
(Ignore the last digit).   *LUX 100 00*

4. To convert to something meaningful, slide the **F/STOP/ILLUM** switch to the **F/STOP** position.

5. Set **FPS/TIME** to 30 fps or 1/60 second (they're both equal). NTSC DV is recording at 60 fields per second, 30 frames.

6. Push the **ISO** (ASA) button until F/11 is displayed on the screen.

7. Read your answer: it should be ISO 200.

Adjust these calculations to whatever the lux sensitivity at F11 is.

Zebra Pattern

Few consumer and prosumer DV camcorders tell us Lux at F11 sensitivity. But here's another way to find out your effective ASA.

1. Set the camera's **ZEBRA** Pattern to 70 (70%).

2. Turn on Manual exposure (Iris).

3. Set the manual shutter to 1/60.

4. Be sure there is no ND filtration, and the GAIN is 0.

5. Aim the camera at a Kodak 18% gray card, or a Caucasian face. They both have almost the same amount of light reflectance.

6. Adjust the lens aperture (iris) until you just start seeing zebra stripes on the 18% gray card or the face. Notice what the f-stop is.

7. Pick up your Spectra IVa incident lightmeter. Measure the incident light coming toward the gray card or the face. Aim the globe of the meter toward the camcorder. Do NOT aim the meter toward the card. That would be a reflected reading.

8. Adjust the Spectra meter so its LCD displays 1/60 second and the f-stop you observed on the camera. The variable, desired ASA, will now be revealed. I find the Sony PD150 is equivalent to 400 ASA. The PD100A seems to be 250 ASA. I wish the manufacturers would rate cameras this way.

Lightmeter

Now that you know your ASA, you can check lighting ratios, maintain consistent exposure, and even know when the dreaded electronic gain circuitry is going to kick in. Even though your camera says it can record down to 7 Lux, that doesn't mean it's going to look good. F2 is 357 Lux, F1.4 is 166 Lux at 200 ASA. Anything darker than that is going to become "noisy," which is the video equivalent of grainy.

Neutral Density Filters

Neutral density filters are like sunglasses for your camcorder.

The ND filter switch on a DV camcorder does not use the same terminology as photographic ND filters. It should.

The ND filter on Sony's PD100a causes an 84% reduction of light. This approximates an ND9 filter, which cuts light down by 3 stops.

Sony's DP150 has a 3-position ND switch, labeled **OFF, 1, 2**.

According to Sony specs:

1 allows 1/4 of the light to hit the CCD, which is ND6.

2 lets 1/32 of the light reach the CCD, which is approximately ND3.5

Gain

When using manual gain control, 3 db equals 1/2 stop. Anything above 6 db introduces noise that is considered unacceptable for broadcast.

Lighting

A few years ago we were shooting a fashion commercial with a very high-maintenance model. Between our setups, an even higher-maintenance still photographer was on hand to shoot print ads that would accompany the campaign. We had a plethora of "rags" and ancillary equipment to soften the light. "Rags" are large pieces of fabric stretched onto metal frames. They come in a large assortment of sizes, densities and material. We were using sailboat spinnaker cloth on enormous frames all over the place because the model told us that it had been a rough night before our shoot, and she would appreciate not having any direct light in her eyes. Our lighting was natural, soft, flattering "north light," that blended in the distress even make-up couldn't hide under her eyes.

The scene complete, the star still photographer was summoned. He asked our gaffer (chief lighting technician) to wheel in a 10K (10,000 watt light) and aim it on the model. Sal (the gaffer) turned it on. "Get closer," shouted the still photographer. Sal wheeled it in until it was almost on top of her. It was so hot, her hair almost became incinerated, and so bright that she requested sunglasses. "Perfect!" exclaimed the photographer. "Perfect?" muttered Sal. "It looks like the 6 o'clock news!"

With all fairness to still photographers, a single hot light can sometimes look wonderful. It lights the eyes, fills in shadows, and often "burns out" blemishes when it is over-exposed. So why is the six o'clock news such an object of scorn?

Too much on television is poorly lit. We are treated to a daily spectacle of news *anchors*, with multiple nose shadows, melting under blazing lights. Cut to the live reporter in the field, illuminated by a single, intense halogen bulb mounted just above the camera's lens.

I should add several chapters here on lighting, but that will be the topic of another book. Until then, read Ross Lowel's *Matters of Light and Depth*.

You don't have to spend a fortune on lighting equipment. The credits on your next low-budget opus can read "Grip and Lighting Equipment supplied by Home Depot." Construction work lights cost less than a hundred dollars, and come complete with stands, halogen bulbs and cable. Fluorescent light banks can be improvised from twenty-dollar shop fixtures. "Rags" can be made from bed sheets and shower curtains.

On the other hand, few things can replace the quality added by a well-outfitted professional 5 or 10 ton grip/electric truck.

Matteboxes and Filters

In addition to keeping flares and glare from the sun and studio lights off the lens, matteboxes are designed to accommodate filters that enhance, modify, soften, texturize, shade, color and otherwise add artistic control to what you are shooting. Filters are optical pieces of glass, made round or square, that are attached to the front of the lens.

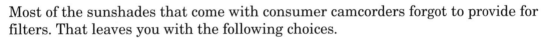

There are essentially three ways to mount filters on a DV camcorder.

The easiest, messiest and most frowned upon method is to simply tape the filter to the front.

Most of the sunshades that come with consumer camcorders forgot to provide for filters. That leaves you with the following choices.

Simplest are round, screw-in filters. They come in as many sizes as there are thread diameters for cameras. This doubtlessly provides eternal employment for the manufacturers of filters, because whenever you use a different camera or lens, you need a different filter. You can purchase step-up or step-down adapter rings.

Or you can buy square filters that fit into a filter tray that slides into the mattebox.

For DV work, lightweight clamp-on matteboxes and filter-holder/ sunshade combinations are available. Some of the best come from Chrosziel, Birns and Sawyer, and CineTech.

Studio and dramatic work suggests a mattebox that slides onto rods that attach below the camera. You can also add a follow focus assembly for keeping the action critically sharp.

Chrosziel Mattebox

Chrosziel makes excellent matteboxes and follow focus units. Other manufacturers of matteboxes and filters include Formatt (distributed by Ste-Man Inc).

Filter Sizes for Camcorders

The charts on the next pages were supplied by my friends at Tiffen, and should help in selecting filters. There may be some errors, so please double check.

CANON	FORMAT	FILTER SIZE
ELURA	Mini DV	27mm
ELURA II	Mini DV	27mm
ELURA ZMC	Mini DV	27mm
GL1	Mini DV	58mm
OPTURA PI	Mini DV	30.5mm
XL1	Mini DV	72mm
ZR10	Mini DV	30.5mm

PANASONIC	FORMAT	FILTER SIZE
AG-DVC10	Mini DV	43mm
AG-EZ1	Mini DV	49mm
AG-EZ30U	Mini DV	43mm
PV-DV100	Mini DV	49mm
PV-DV200	Mini DV	49mm
PV-DV400	Mini DV	49mm
PV-DV600	Mini DV	49mm
PV-DV800	Mini DV	49mm
PV-DV900	Mini DV	43mm
PV-DV950	Mini DV	43mm

SHARP	FORMAT	FILTER SIZE
VL-FD1U	Mini DV	30mm
VL-PD3U	Mini DV	30mm
VL-SD20U	Mini DV	30mm

JVC	FORMAT	FILTER SIZE
GR-DV3	Mini DV	*27mm / 25.5mm
GR-DVF11	Mini DV	40.5mm
GR-DVF21	Mini DV	40.5mm
GR-DVF31	Mini DV	40.5mm
GR-DVL300	Mini DV	37mm
GR-DVL300U	Mini DV	37mm
GR-DVL500	Mini DV	37mm
GR-DVL505U	Mini DV	37mm
GR-DVL805U	Mini DV	37mm
GR-DVL9500	Mini DV	37mm
GR-DVL9800	Mini DV	37mm
GR-DVL9800U	Mini DV	37mm
GR-DVM5	Mini DV	*27mm / 25.5mm
GR-DVM50U	Mini DV	27mm
GR-DVM70	Mini DV	27mm
GR-DVM70U	Mini DV	27mm
GR-DVM80U	Mini DV	27mm
GR-DVM90U	Mini DV	27mm
GR-DVM90U	Mini DV	27mm
* = 27mm lens hood / 25.5mm direct lens mount		

SONY	FORMAT	FILTER SIZE
DCR-PC5	Mini DV	-
DCR-VX1000	MiniDV	52mm
DCR-VX2000	MiniDV	58mm
DSR 200A	DV Cam	52mm
DSR 250	DV Cam	58mm
DSR PD100A	DV Cam	52mm
DSR-PD150	DV Cam	58mm

Tiffen Filters

Sizes

Tiffen Filters come in the following sizes:

Screw-in: 37mm, 40.5mm, 43mm, 46mm, 49mm, 52mm, 55mm, 58mm, 62mm, 67mm, 72mm, 77mm, 82mm, 86mm

Round: series 9, 4 1/2" round

Square: 3" x 3", 4" x 4", 4" x 5.650"

Although there are several other excellent filter manufacturers, my friend Ira Tiffen and his staff helped assemble the following descriptive list.

Effects

In addition to coming in different sizes, each filter "type" comes in varying degrees of strength. In DV, be careful not to go too heavy. What you see is what you get, so look at the filter by holding it up to your eye, and then through the camera on a good monitor. Here are some of the filters available.

Black Pro Mist®: Image softening with less flare than an equivalent white Pro-Mist. Reduces contrast by combining modest lightening of shadows with darkening of highlights.

Circular Polarizer: A polarizer designed for cameras with beam splitters. The beam splitter prism divides the light into separate paths. Beam splatters polarize light. If a conventional (linear) polarizing filter is added to the path of light, the combination of two polarizers will give underexposure to the picture. Many single and 3-chip camcorders require the use of a circular polarizer.

Close-up Lens: Single element diopter lenses let you focus on subjects much closer than the standard lens allows. Great for detail photos of products, flowers and small critters. Available in several diopter strengths.

Color Compensating (CC) Filters: Used to compensate for deficiencies in the color of light sources, but also as a color effect. Available in primary colors - red, blue, green—and in secondary colors—cyan, yellow, magenta. Available in different strengths and may be combined to achieve precise color rendition.

Color Grad® Filter: Half color, half clear, with a smooth transition—no hard line. Creates deep blue skies, with a Blue Color-Grad, while retaining natural foreground color. Creates brilliant sunsets with the Red or Orange Color Grad. Selectively tone down bright areas with the Neutral Density Color Grad. Rotatable for proper alignment within your image. Available in many colors and densities.

Color Grad® Complement Filters: Made in 3 series: Blue for use with Tropic Blue, Cyan, Cool Blue, Grape, Blue and Twilight; Red for use with Plum, Magenta, Cranberry, Pink, Red, Skyfire, and Twilight: and Amber for use with Chocolate, Sepia, Coral, Tangerine, Tobacco, Straw, Antique Suede, Skyfire and Sunset. Available in two grades, Grade 1 provides milder tones for more moderate application; Grade 2 is for more dramatic color statements. Designed to be used in combination with Color Grad filters; the Complement Filter colors the foreground while the Color Grad filter colors the background for color consistency throughout the overall image.

Coral Filters: Warming filters available in a wide range of densities. Used to adjust Kelvin temperature for different times of day. Also used as a warming filter to enhance skintones.

Day-for-Night Filters: Creates a nighttime look while shooting in daylight. Cool Day-for-Night for a blue moonlight look with an addition of a low contrast component. Monochrome Day for Night desaturates color for a natural nighttime look, using color correction in the final rendition (color timing for film production).

Double Fog Filters: Combines a soft fog with a heavy low contrast effect. This allows clearer detail than the standard fog filter, while maintaining a dense fog appearance. Available in several densities.

Enhancing Filter: Made of special didymium glass, creates warm vibrant color by selectively improving saturation of reds and oranges, with a diminished effect on other colors.

Fog Effect Filter: Creates or enhances the effect of a natural fog. Fog filters have the ability to cause lights to flare and "mist" to appear where none previously existed. An even mist density is produced throughout the scene. Available in several densities.

Haze 1: Reduces excessive blue haze caused by UV light by absorbing 71% of UV. Great all-around UV control.

Haze 2: Absorbs all UV light; reduces haze; maintains color and image clarity. Best for high altitude and marine scenes.

Low Contrast Filters: Low Contrast filters cause light to spread from highlight areas to the shadows. Lowers contrast, mutes colors, white areas remain, while blacks become lighter. Allows more detail in dense shadow areas. Ideal for slide duplication work. Available in several densities.

Low Light Ultra Contrast: All the effects of the Ultra Contrast filter, for use in low light situations, especially outdoors at night.

Neutral Density Filter: Used to reduce the amount of light reaching the film with no selective absorption effects on colors. Available in several densities.

Polarizer: Reduces glare and reflections, saturates colors and darkens blue skies. Ideal when photographing water or through glass to reduce reflections. The polarizer can be rotated to determine the amount of reflection to be removed. When photographing scenics, rotate the polarizer to change blue sky densities from light to dark blue. Creates dramatic contrast between blue skies and white clouds.

Pro-Mist® Filter: Used to create a "silky," slightly romantic effect. Smooths out textures, adds slight glow to highlights, removes harsh edges, and slightly reduces contrast and video harshness.

Sepia Filters: Creates a warm brown tone and offers an antique look to your scene. Sepia filters are available in densities 1, 2, and 3. #1 is a light effect, #2 and #3 offer the same denser color, but #3 combines a fog for enhanced effect, producing softness and highlight flare along with the warmer color.

Softnet® Black Filter: Net material laminated between optical clear glass. Creates a soft diffusion affect while causing no halation from highlights. Dark areas remain dark. Available in several densities.

Softnet® White Filter: Net material laminated between optical clear glass. Creates a soft diffusion effect while adding a misty look. Softens contrast by lightening shadows; dark areas appear less dense. Available in several densities.

Soft Contrast Filters: Contrast is reduced by darkening highlights while allowing shadow areas to stay dark; also produces softer, less intense color. Available in several densities.

Soft/FX® Filters: Tiny lenslets embedded in glass; used in portraits to retain overall image clarity while softening unwanted details. Will tone down wrinkles and skin blemishes while leaving the eyes appearing sharp. Available in several densities.

Split-Field Lenses: Essentially a close-up lens cut in half, it allows close-up focusing on one portion of the scene while retaining sharp focus on a more distant background. The ultimate depth-of-field extension lens. To use, focus on the background, and then move in or out the slight distance required to focus on the foreground. With the proper choice of lens focal length and diopter strength, Split-Field lenses can produce a variety of fascinating scenes. Available in several diopter strengths.

Streak Filter: Designed to enhance point highlights by creating a two-point streak effect. Produces an effect similar to a star filter. Improves a scene without affecting contrast. Available in all sizes.

Stripe Filters: Unlike standard Color Grad filters, Stripe filters have a stripe of color in the middle graduating to a clear top and bottom. Used to add a band of color to accentuate a specific portion of a scene; in combination to provide layered color or light attenuation; in combination with standard Color Grads; in combination with other solid filter colors. May be used in slidable rotating mounts that allow for proper alignment vertically, horizontally or diagonally within an image.

Ultra Contrast Filter: Lowers contrast by lightening shadow areas without causing any flare or halo effects from direct bright light sources, reflections or highlights. It uses ambient light to lower contrast evenly throughout the whole scene, even in an image where there are areas of dramatically greater or lesser brightness.

Warm Black Pro-Mist® Filter: Combines the Black Pro-Mist with the 812 filter. Softens image with subtle flare, while adding warmth to the image.

Warm Pro-Mist® Filter: Combines the Pro Mist with the 812 filter. Tones down excessive sharpness, while adding warmth to the scene. Balances contrasting skin tones within one scene.

Warm Soft/FX® Filter: Combines the Soft/FX filter with 812 filter. Softens unwanted details while adding warmth and balance to skintones.

Set Camera to Manual Control

When using filters, be sure to turn off auto-pilot control of the camera. With automatic white-balance and exposure turned on, the camera will try to overcome the effects of the filter.

Tripods and Heads

Almost as important as the camera you choose is the head and tripod it will sit on.

The tripod is a pedestal to which you attach a head. The tripod is adjustable up and down. Three pointed tips at the bottom of each leg assure a firm grip on soft ground as well as the certain wrath of the homeowner whose wooden floor you have just scratched and perforated.

A spreader protects precious floors, and also prevents the embarrassment of watching the camera tumble onto the slippery marble as the legs slip apart. Some spreaders mount halfway up the leg. These require separate "feet" to cover the tips. Some tripods use rubber bushings, threaded onto the tips, that retract when needed.

There are two mounting options on top of the tripod: flat or ball. A ball receptacle makes leveling the camera much easier than individually adjusting the legs. There are three common sizes of ball receptacles for tripods: 75mm, 100mm and 150mm diameter. For DV, 75mm is the most popular.

head

tripod

spreader

A fluid head allows smooth and balanced moves of the camera. The operator can pan, tilt and zoom (assuming the zoom control is attached to the pan handle) with one hand, leaving the other hand free to operate a Dutch head, tweak focus, grab a cell phone or a cup of coffee.

Fluid heads contain a viscous fluid, usually silicone, that dampens and smoothes out motion. Mechanical (friction) heads should be avoided, unless you're just doing a locked-off shot or stop-motion.

The best way to choose a head is to check it out with the intended camera. B&H Photo in New York and Samy's in LA have large demo areas where you can play.

Fluid Heads

After agreeing on the desirability of fluid being better than friction, very few camera operators will agree on the notion of a perfect head. Some operators prefer a stiff feel; I like a loose touch. Some like thick handles, other like thin.

The big names in fluid heads and tripods are Sachtler, Cartoni, Miller, Gitzo, Manfrotto and O'Connor.

Most heads have a safety latch to prevent accidental release. Pull down on the safety latch, and slide the release to the left to unlock the camera. When mounting the camera, always double check that it is securely latched by pulling up on the camera itself.

The sliding top balance plate compensates for cameras that are front or back heavy. To balance your camera, release the pan and tilt locks. Turn the friction dials to 0. Move the balance plate until the camera is level. Then, set the spring tension to counter-balance the weight of the camera, and turn the tension dials to a comfortable level.

I recommend a head that tilts straight up and straight down. It is frustrating to attempt an angle on a jet swooping overhead, only to be thwarted by limited tilt.

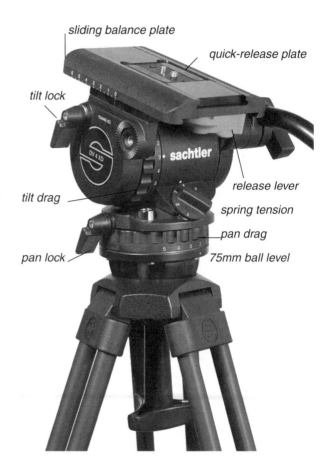

sliding balance plate

quick-release plate

tilt lock

release lever

tilt drag

spring tension

pan drag

pan lock

75mm ball level

Tripods

It's ironic that professional tripods and heads often cost more than the DV camcorder itself. Fortunately, a new line of cheaper DV support systems are appearing. They cost a couple of hundred dollars, and while not quite as smooth or robust as their more expensive siblings, they will certainly get the job done.

Unfortunately for your back, it is usually true that heavier tripods and heads offer more stability and smoother moves.

The main thing is to choose a tripod that isn't a burden to take with you wherever you go. If you're shooting news or documentaries or sports, it should be small and light enough to fit in or on a backpack.

Several models from Gitzo stand out. The Gitzo Mountaineer Compact G1128 is a 4-section carbon fiber tripod, 19 inches long when folded, that weighs a mere 2½ pounds. It has a flat top.

Three other Gitzo carbon fiber tripods, called Mountaineer Mk2, range from 4.5 to 6.75 pounds and can be configured with 75mm or 100mm bowls on top for quick leveling. Aluminum legs cost a few hundred dollars less, but weigh about 1.5 pounds more.

Support Systems

Gitzo's G2380 is a 3 pound head that accommodates cameras from 2 to 11 pounds. Heavier cameras benefit from a beefier, 5 pound head—Gitzo's G1380. Six different springs come with the head to hold cameras from 3 to 22 pounds.

Gitzo is distributed by Bogen Photo in the US. They also distribute Manfrotto tripods and heads. One of the least expensive systems is a Manfrotto 501 Video Head with 3221 Video Tripod.

The Sprinter Tripod from Miller (distributed by Ste-Man in US) simplifies the process of adjusting a two-stage tripod with lever locks positioned next to each other. Multiple stage tripods collapse to smaller sizes, but previously took longer to set up.

Low angle shots are accomplished with "baby legs" and "high hats."

Some tripods can be configured so the legs spread out flat on the floor, thus doing double duty.

Soft, nylon tripod cases are much easier to handle than rigid tubes. However, if you're going to ship the tripod and head by air, be sure to pack your soft case inside a hard one. Carbon fiber and aluminum legs will not survive an unprotected trip beneath a load of Samsonite suitcases.

Baseplates

There are many ways to attach the camera to a tripod head: direct bolt or quick release plate. Each manufacturer has its own size and style, along with its own method of balancing the camera on top.

There are many more styles. Each manufacturer has its own idea of what a quick release plate should look like—which doesn't help when we want to use multiple brands on a multiple camera shoot. "They" should standardize the mounting system. Perhaps it's just a legacy from the film world, where Panavision and ARRI use vastly different methods of attaching camera to head.

Miller Quick-Release Plate

Moving the Camera

Now that we've discussed how to keep the camera steady, we should discuss how to put movement into moving pictures. In the world of production, we rent dollies, remote-control heads, cranes, and all kinds of other paraphernalia to gracefully move the camera during a shot.

You can improvise and get similarly satisfying results. Lighter cameras enable simpler solutions. A skateboard makes an excellent low-angle dolly. Handheld shots sitting in a wheelchair is a time-honored documentary technique. Innovision, Band Pro, OpTex and others make inexpensive remote-control heads that can be operated with joysticks or handles.

Monitors and Decks

One of your most important choices for editing is a really good monitor. You'll be staring at it for hours on end. You'll be using it to make value judgements on focus, color and composition.

1. LCD or CRT. LCD monitors are great, if you can afford one. They are lighter, flatter, cooler (giving off less heat) and can provide comparable, if not superior, color and sharpness. As of this writing, the Apple Cinema Display is one of the best LCD monitors. Sony, Viewsonic and Mitsubishi make most of the CRT monitors popular with editors.

2. Bigger is better. If your computer editing system has just one monitor, I recommend a 21" model. If you're using two monitors, 21" is still best, but 19" or 20" monitors are fine if desktop real estate is limited. Try to get a short-depth monitor. They take up less space front-to-back.

3. Watch out for glare. Two things affect glare: coating and curvature. Some models have better coatings than others. Also, flat-screen models usually have less glare, but sometimes a little more distortion.

4. Placement. Try to avoid having a window behind you. It will reflect in your monitor. If it's unavoidable, get some dark shades.

5. Speakers. Some monitors have built-in speakers. Avoid them like the plague.

6. Controls. The monitor should offer easy adjustment of vertical and horizontal position and size, contrast, brightness, white-balance and color.

Anatomy of a Monitor

CRT (short for Cathode Ray Tube) computer monitors and televisions use similar technology. Take a flashlight and aim it at a wall. Start by the ceiling, and wave the beam back and forth as you "paint" the wall with beams of light down to the floor.

Three "guns" at the back of the monitor "shoot" narrow beams of electrons at the screen. The screen is made of a multitude of little phosphorescent dots, colored red, blue and green. As the beams hit the dots, they glow, giving us a picture.

The speed at which the beams "paint" across the screen is called horizontal frequency. It is a measure of number of lines scanned in one second. Refresh rate is the number of times the entire screen is "painted" each second, measured in times per second, or hertz (Hz). Rates below 65 will appear to flicker, and will probably give you a headache. The higher the better--85 and above is good.

The dots are called pixels. The distance between them is called dot pitch. Resolution is measured by the number of pixels counted horizontally by the number counted vertically times the number of colors. So a 1024 x 768 screen has 786,432 x 3 dots (2,359,296).

Dot pitch is the distance between pixels of the same color. This is usually .20mm to .27mm on good monitors. Smaller is better.

Shadow masks, made of perforated foil, are often used behind the screen to keep the beams aligned with the dots. Sony and Mitsubishi use a matrix of wires, called an aperture grill, instead of the perforated mask. There is much debate about the merits of each, but the aperture grill usually provides a brighter image and finer vertical resolution.

Decks

Many users play back their DV tapes with the camcorder. Although this saves money and works, it can shorten the life of the camera. If you plan to do a lot of editing, a professional deck with timecode and RS-422 serial control provides more accurate tape transport, better quality and faster shuttling.

Probably the least expensive DVCAM/Mini DV Recorder/Player with RS-422 control is the Sony DSR-40, at a list price of $5,100.

Decks provide analog to digital converters. If you want a stand-alone A to D box, there is Sony's DVMC-DA2 as well as other brands.

Sony's smallest deck (DSRV-10) is useful for expeditions and remote documentaries. You can also use it on the airplane getting there to watch pre-recorded movies.

It has a 5.5" LCD monitor, and weighs 2.2 pounds.

It has an i.LINK (DV IN/OUT) connector, and accepts Mini DV and Mini DVCAM cassettes.

There is no RS-422 deck control; however, there is a LANC connection.

List price $2,800.

Sony's DSR-11 is a low cost NTSC and PAL deck. It will not, however convert one format to the other. It accepts both mini and standard size cassettes, DV and DVCAM.

List: $2,600.

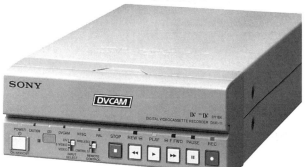

The Sony DSR-1600 is one of the least exprensive DV/ DVCAM recorder/ players with full RS-422 control. That's important for batch digitizing, precise edits, and dubbing from other timecode sources.

List $6,650.

Going up the price ladder, more features get added to Sony's DSR-1800 and DSR-2000.

Dubbing to BetaSP UVW-1800

Sometimes I dub my DV tapes to BetaSP, using a Sony UVW-1800 videocassette recorder. Here are some pointers on how to avoid the dreaded black sync bar going across the picture.

1. Plug the S-Video connector into the S-Video Input on the back of the UVW-1800.

2. Plug the yellow video RCA jack into the VIDEO REF input connector on the UVW-1800 (you need an RCA to BNC adapter).

3. Be sure to set the VIDEO IN switch on the UVW-1800 front panel to S-VIDEO.

What we're doing is feeding S-Video into the UVW-1800. But we need a sync signal, and we're getting it from the composite video signal.

If you don't want to use S-Video, here's the same procedure for composite:

1. Plug the yellow video RCA jack into the VIDEO input connector on the UVW-1800.

2. Run a short BNC cable from the second BNC VIDEO input connector (it is essentially serving as an output) to the top left BNC REF. VIDEO connector.

3. Slide the VIDEO termination switch to OFF.

4. Slide the REF VIDEO termination switch to ON, unless you're hooking something else up to reference video.

Hostile Environments

I spent three months on the Juneau Icefields of Alaska with a camera and three changes of clothing (one for each month). We laughingly referred to any location without room to pitch a tent as a hostile environment. I have a jaded neighbor in New York who thinks whenever he leaves the city he's camping out. It's all a matter of degree.

The new generation of lightweight and small DV camera equipment is wonderful for expedition and location shooting. They easily fit in your pack without taking up precious room otherwise needed for extra underwear or food. With care, you can keep the camera running in all kinds of weather.

Caring for Your Camcorder

The camcorders do not require lubrication. You should not use grease anywhere. Try to keep them out of dusty, moist or salt air as much as possible. Use rain covers, plastic bags or garbage bags in these "hostile" environments.

Around salt water and humid areas, wipe the external sufaces of the camera with CRC 5-56 or LPS 1 (not LPS 3). These lubricants are not greasy or slippery (WD-40 is). Use a cotton rag on large surfaces. Use a foam swab, Kimwipe or lens tissue for screw heads and hard-to-get places. Use a small amount—a little goes a long way. Apply to the rag first. Do NOT spray the camera. Do not use inside the tape transport area, or around the glass lens elements. Do not use on the battery or on electrical connections. Here, you will need an electrical contact restorer, such as CONTACT RE-NU or CRC 2-26.

Most cameras will run from 32° Fahrenheit to +110° Fahrenheit, and most will do better than that.

In very hot climates—desert, sand, tropics—put a Space Blanket, white barney or T-shirt on the camera to reflect the sun's heat.

In very cold conditions, a black cloth or black side of a space blanket will absorb sunlight. A heater barney made of neoprene or foam will extend the temperature range. When it's really cold, stuff a small hand warmer inside. Wearing a belt battery under your parka will extend battery life. An electric sock, popular with ice fishermen and skiers, will also work to heat the camera body.

The zoom lenses become excessively stiff in Arctic cold conditions. You may want to have them winterized by an authorized service shop. They remove grease and use a lighter lubricant.

In very sticky, humid conditions, the tape can stick to the head when it is stopped. Try not to keep the camera in pause for long periods, and eject tapes at the end of the day. NEVER lubricate this area with anything other than head cleaner.

Use head cleaner daily. Tapes with built-in head cleaners are helpful.

Lens Cleaning

There is really only one good way to clean a lens or camera optical surface. Blow plain air with a hand operated air syringe. (Dust-Off is more convenient, but will leave a chemical residue which smears.)

If the dust is gritty, gently brush it off with a fine camel's hair brush which you have reserved for lens use only.

If the lens is smeared, dirty or finger-printed, squirt one or two drops of lens fluid (Pancro is recommended) on a crumpled lens tissue. Wipe the lens in a circular motion. Dry the lens immediately with a dry piece of lens tissue. Also wipe in a circular motion—but don't scrub. If the lens is really dirty, you will have to repeat this process a number of times until the residue disappears.

Microfiber cloths like Luminex are also excellent for cleaning lenses. But they should not be used to scrub away stubborn smears instead of lens fluid. Also, the microfiber cloths should be washed often.

Low-Tech Rain Covers

Perhaps in response to the observation that most crews are better protected in their penultimate Patagonia high-tech, multi-colored, breathable, waterproof, windproof, windowed, toggled, tabbed and Velcro-vented raingear than their cameras, several well-designed rain covers have emerged from rental houses, from Camera Essentials in Hollywood, Ewa-Marine in Germany, and Scubacam in London.

After it rains, don't forget to dry the covers out. Mildew is not a pleasant odor.

If you need a disposable cover, there is a clear, cheap, garbage-bag rain cover. Having scoured the janitorial supply catalogs of the world, I recommend Extra Heavy Duty 4 mil Clear Chiswick Poly Bags, which are sold in lots of a thousand. They are available in a multitude of sizes costing less than a dollar a bag. Cut a hole for the lens, and attach the bag over the mattebox with a Velcro strap.

Cut another hole for the eyepiece, and use a rubber band to hold it in place. Bunch up the unused part of the bag with a clip. Of course, you can always use a lowly, ordinary garbage bag. But Chiswick's clear alternative lets you see what is inside, and for a modest extra fee, they will add your name or logo.

High-Tech Rain Covers

The one rule of rain covers is that one cover will rarely be acceptable for all configurations of a camera: handheld, on tripod, on a car mount, underslung on a remote head. You will very often need several variations.

Scubacam and Ewa-Marine Mini DV camera rain covers are higher-tech than the garbage bags we usually use, and easier to use. A provision in the design gives the operator fully unhindered viewing of an on-board monitor, while still being able to use the conventional viewfinder.

Ewa-Marine rain covers have an optical glass port to cover the front element of the lens. The cover is made of PVC that remains flexible from 14° to 158° F.

On the Scubacam covers, the viewfinder is secured by a drawstring that pulls tightly over the viewfinder eyecup. An adjustable lens strap holds the cover over the lens hood of the camera. A clear viewing panel is located over the main body of the camera to enable the operator to see the camera functions. A two inch elongated tube behind the video door allows the operator to access the lens for focus control.

Rain covers from Camera Essentials are clear plastic.

Sun/Dust Covers

A camera can get as hot as the interior of your car on a scorching, summer day, which, if you read the small print on most video cassettes, the manufacturer warns against. Don't leave the camcorder inside your trunk or hot vehicle. Scubacam and Camera Essentials have a line of sun and dust covers made of silver, reflective 4 oz. nylon. Space blankets or old, white T-shirts, clipped together with plastic spring clips, will work in a pinch.

Scubacam SurfAce

Scubacam makes a splash (repeat: Splash)
housing of 1/8" (2.5mm) natural yellow
latex, which is advertised to be waterproof
to 22' (7 meters) when sealed with its
heavy duty watertight zipper. It can be
handheld or mounted on a tripod. A 30'
long umbilical cord contains two power
cables, remote on/off and video cables
which attach to the camera with
waterproof external connectors.

Scubacam for GL-1

The front and rear ports are fixed to an
internal shoe. The camera is mounted onto
an adjustable quick release plate on this shoe. This allows the camera to be
positioned within the housing depending on the lens used. It should be positioned
as close to the front port as possible, to reduce refraction and eliminate vignetting.

An auxiliary 2.9" color monitor is viewed through the rear port. This is connected
to the camera via an internal A/V lead. The monitor is powered by its own battery
pack, giving a 4-hour constant run time. The monitor can be turned on and off
externally. Available in either NTSC or PAL. Access to the "standby" switch and
the "Tape run" button is from outside the housing. The zoom rocker can also be
operated through the wall of the housing.

The Scubacam mini DVCAM housing is
designed to fit most styles of Mini DV
camcorders. When the zipper is fully
closed, the unit can be submerged to a
maximum depth of 7 meters. Do not leave
the unit unattended at any time while
underwater.

Caution: Before every use, carry out a
visual inspection to determine if there is
any damage to the housing. To check,
seal the unit without the camcorder
inside, and submerge it in water, remove
and inspect for leaks.

There are also Scubacam models for
larger shoulder-resting DVCAM/
DVCPRO cameras manufactured by
Phillips, Sony, Ikegami and Panasonic.

Scubacam for XL-1

EWA-Marine

Ewa-Marine makes a similar splash housing for most DV camcorders. The advertised depth is 5 meters (about 15 feet). Again, I would suggest the emphasis is more on splash, and less on underwater.

Underwater Housings

For serious protection of your investment underwater, your DV camera should be used inside a rigid underwater housing. Some of the respected names in the field are:

Amphibico (www.amphibico.com)
Seacam (www.seacamsys.com)
Gates (www.gateshousings.com)
Ikelite (www.ikelite.com)
Oceanimages (www.oceanimagesinc.com)

Shooting Action

Para*Mount camera helmets from Skydance Photography are designed for skydiving, but can also be used for skiing, mountain biking, running, and other action sports. There are several different models that provide a lightweight and secure platform for your camera. The Stealth model's dual camera mounts (two cameras, no waiting, strong neck muscles) are molded into the fiberglass shell.

The Para*Mount Velocity (pictured above) is available as a helmet only, or can be upgraded to fully "camera-ready" with a variety of camera platforms and other accessories. The helmet is made of rigid fiberglass, and will not obstruct your vision. The helmet liner is interchangeable, allowing the helmet to be re-sized from Small to XX-Large in seconds.

Accessories for Skydance Velocity Helmet

Tinted Boresight

A transparent amber sight with a center-spot makes it easy to aim on the center of your subject, without obstructing your field of view. You'll appreciate this when using the helmet to do a POV shot following a bunch of freestyle skiers racing through the trees.

Camera Cover

This protective neoprene cover fits your video camera like a glove. It is easy to put on and is designed to help protect the camera from dust, condensation, cold weather, lens fog and damage from riser slap and abrasion. The thermal properties of neoprene insulate your camera from rapid temperature changes which cause condensation, cold weather shutdown and lens fog. Available for Sony PC1, PC7, PC10 & PC100.

Velocity Side Mount Platform

The side mount video platform is designed to accept most Sony, JVC, and similar digital camcorders. The video platform is contoured to the shape of the helmet which reduces the chance of snagging on a tree branch or parachute line. The mount adjusts up or down from 0 to 30 degrees, in either direction. The mount can also be rotated 180 degrees, letting you shoot backwards or upside down.

Velocity Top Mount Platform

To mount the camera on top, this 3" wide (side to side) x 6" long (front to back) platform easily attaches to any Velocity helmet. The hinged top design allows for quick access to the camera tripod mount screw to secure or remove the camera. The top mount platform features a twin-point helmet attachment and variable pitch for adjusting the camera's angle.

Aerials

Many people balk at the idea of jumping out of perfectly fine airplanes. They would prefer to film aerials from the comfort of a bouncy, noisy, stomach-churning helicopter.

Small camcorders with stabilization devices built in are perfect for this. There are a few tricks that will help.

Try not to shoot through the window. Open the window or remove the door.

Keep the camera inside the chopper, out of the slipstream.

You can make a cheap helicopter rig with a few spare pieces of climbing equipment.

To take the weight off your hands, and to isolate vibration, rest the camera on a pillow, piece of foam or inflatable kid's toy placed on your lap. You'll be amazed how much easier it will be, and steadier too.

Keep a light touch on the camera to keep it free of your body's vibration. Keep the zooming and pans to a minimum, and let the helicopter make the moves. A pilot-to-you intercom is helpful, along with warm, windproof clothing if the door is off.

Make sure the sunshade is firmly threaded on, and don't leave any loose pieces of equipment or tape on the seat.

If you're leaning out an open door, wear an extra safety harness.

Cases and Shipping

It is best, though not always practical, to hand carry the camcorder with you wherever you go. Not only will you avoid the wear and tear of shipping, but you'll also avoid the sinking feeling of being the only person left at baggage claim still watching an empty conveyor belt. But be warned: airlines sometimes arbitrarily refuse to let you carry the camera on board if it is "big." So, take the empty camera body case with you. Ship the tripods, lights and accessories, and carry what you need to shoot.

Soft-sided shoulder bags and backpacks that fit under airline seats are great. A large, padded shoulder bag with adjustable foam-lined compartments can carry the camcorder, accessory lenses, filters, batteries, charger and tape. Having these items with you all the time saves time and footwork. Tenba, Lowe, KATA, Portabrace, Tamrac and Tough Traveler are popular brands of camera shoulder bags.

If your style is more corporate, you'll be happy with attaché size waterproof cases by Pelican #1550 (19" x 14" x 7.75"), Pelican 1450 (15" x 10.5" x 6'), Tundra SK821 (20.9" x 12.9" x 8.4"), or Tundra SK518 (17.8" x 12.8" x 5.1"). Aluminum Halliburton cases look great until you ding them the first time. Furthermore, they are not waterproof.

Monitors, lenses and fragile accessories should be shipped in cases with generous padding to protect the equipment from the rigors of airline handling and dropping from cargo hold to runway. Thermodyne ABS Cases, which are totally waterproof, lightweight and resilient, come in many sizes, including a popular configuration of 24" x 18" x 14".

Fiberglass-covered plywood cases made by A&J and Calzone are heavier, not waterproof, but more durable. "Rigidised" aluminum cases are lighter and popular in Europe, since they only seem to be made in England and are never spelled with a "z".

It's a good idea to have three inches of foam surrounding all pieces of equipment.

Tripod Case

I don't like round tripod cases. They roll around and waste space. Most lightweight tripod systems will fit in one TEK Series Rolling Tripod Case from Tamrac. It is a foam padded "soft case," and has a couple of skateboard wheels. Nalpak and A&J make good octagonal cases.

Expeditions

Lowe makes good expedition packs for far-off places. For ski and mountaineering shoots, smaller day packs with padded compartments are helpful. For extreme conditions, you can substitute clothing and expedition gear for the foam.

To get to location, you can ship the equipment in the packs. The packs should, however, be protected by a rigid case. A waterproof Thermodyne will protect the pack from crushing and flooding. And you never know, you might be able to use the Thermodyne as a life raft.

Cutting Cases

You can't avoid custom fitting the foam inside your cases.

Buy an electric knife to cut the foam. Lubricate the blades with silicone from time to time. For hard-to-reach areas, use an X-Acto knife with a 2" blade (#26).

Use 2 inch thick foam for the first layer, then some 1 inch layers, then 1/4 inch, and finally 1/2 inch. Cut layer by layer, working your way down. Outline the equipment directly onto the foam with a marker. Don't bother using templates.

Glue the layers together with Contact Cement or 3M Foam and Fabric Spray Adhesive #74 for soft foams, and Barge Cement for hard foams.

Taping Cases

To protect the latches and ensure cases stay shut, always run some gaffers tape over the latches and over the two halves of the case.

Mark the destination address on the tape in case the equipment is lost.

It also helps to write down the flight number and destination airport should the airline tag be ripped off.

Gaffers tape now comes in numerous colors for easy identification.

Choosing a DV Camcorder

Choosing a DV Camcorder

DV Camcorder Jargon

Or, How to Translate all Those Labels

When you go out shopping for a DV camcorder, you'll see more trademarks, logos, technical terms, letters, numbers and stickers plastered on the posters, brochures and cameras than a NASCAR racing car. Each manufacturer has its own jargon, not to mention proprietary features, to try to elevate its products above the competition. Competition is good. Here's how to decipher it all.

Canon Mini DV Camcorders

Progressive Scan CCD: CCD image sensor produces a full-frame video image 60 times per second. However, each frame is repeated twice. In contrast, the conventional interlace CCD produces only half a full frame, known as a field, in the same time. Progressive Scan CCD provides sharper images of fast moving subjects.

RGB Primary Color Filter: Separates the image into individual red, green, and blue color components. It is not a 3-CCD system, however.

Normal Movie Mode: Canon's name for full motion video.

Digital Photo Mode: Canon's name for digital still capture. By pressing the photo button, captures VGA resolution (640 x 480) still images with audio onto the video tape for six seconds each. Up to 700 still pictures can be recorded on a single mini DV cassette at SP speed. Video and still pictures can be combined on the same cassette. You can also record still images to the MultiMedia Card. Megapixel cameras record in higher resolutions, as indicated.

Digital Motor Drive: Canon's name for progressive scan recording of 30 full frame still images per second continuously.

Zoom: All the cameras have optical zooms, and all have electronic circuitry to digitally magnify the picture even more—sometimes up to 300x. I have not included statistics on the digital zoom, because I feel the picture becomes blocky and degraded. However, if you're using the camera for surveillance or telemetry, that's another story.

PCM Digital Stereo Audio: Choice of 16 bit (one set of stereo tracks, better quality than CD) or 12 bit (two sets of stereo tracks). Use 16 bit when you can.

i.Link (IEEE-1394, FireWire) DV Receptacle: available on all Canon DV camcorders.

MultiMedia Card: Canon's "MultiMediaCard" (Flash Memory) lets you store and transfer still images to a PC (with a PCMCIA adapter). Canon's Elura 2MC, ZR25 MC, and ZR30 MC come with an 8 Mb card. "MC" after the name indicates the camera has MMC capability.

Analog Input: An analog video signal can be recorded onto the mini DV cassette.

Image Stabilizer : Optical or electronic, as indicated. Optical is better.

5 Mode Program AE (**Auto Exposure**): Automatic exposure settings for Sports, Portrait, Backlight, Sand & Snow, Low Light.

Control L (Lanc): Serial connection for edit controllers and other accessories. Also useful for external control of zoom lens, remote on-off and other functions.

Digital & Special Effects: Not listed in the specs of camcorders in this book. Save them for the editing room.

JVC

The following features, terms and jargon apply to JVC mini DV camcorders:

Spline Interpolation: On some of the higher-end JVC cameras, "spline interpolation" technology smoothes out jagged edges sometimes seen as an artifact in DV. Also, during playback, you can zoom in on part of an image and magnify it up to 10 times. Probably not a wild selling point for aspiring filmmakers, but certainly a bonus for military and security types.

Digital Still Camera: Most JVC camcorders have a still mode. The best can capture photo quality still images up to 1600 x 1200, which can be printed out as a 320 dpi 5" x 4" print.

Dual Shooting Mode: Lets you shoot video and stills simultaneously. Push the still photo button while taping, and the image is also recorded onto a Memory Card at 640 x 480.

Power: Some cameras turn on as soon as you pull out the viewfinder or open the LCD monitor. A good idea.

Image Stabilization: JVC cameras use digital stabilization.

Info-Shoe: JVC name for hot shoe that accommodates eye light, flash and microphones.

Panasonic

WideSight 3.5" wide angle color LCD Monitor viewing screen uses polysilicon materials to help keep the picture clear when viewed from practically any angle, and rotates 270°. Built-in speaker.

Sony

The copyrighters have been working overtime at Sony thinking up a plethora of trademarks and proprietary names. All to good purpose, however, since Sony consistently comes up with interesting and innovative ideas. Some of the terms that follow are not unique to Sony, and will be found on other brands.

16:9: Wide mode allows you to record and playback in a "widescreen" aspect ratio.

Index Titler: Titles (22 characters), 8 pre-set titles, 2 sizes, 9 positions.

AccuPower Meter: Continuously displays the amount of battery time remaining in minutes in the viewfinder or LCD.

Advanced Titler: Preset & custom titles (in English, French, Portuguese, Spanish, and Chinese).

Advanced HAD CCD: CCD that reduces noise in the video signal. It improves the signal-to-noise ratio by up to 6dB.

Analog to Digital Conversion with Pass Through: Analog inputs with a built-in analog to digital converter will convert analog video and audio to a digital signal that can be recorded onto tape or passed-through the i.Link interface to a compatible computer.

Analog Recording: Input converts and records analog video source to DV.

Aspherical Lens: Reduces optical distortion, and provides better corner to corner focus and color.

Carl Zeiss Lens: Glass lenses with a lens coating that reduces glare and flares, with good resolution and contrast.

Cassette Memory: found in select Sony mini DV cassettes. Add or change titles at any time.

Control L (Lanc): A serial connection for external zoom controls, edit controllers and other camera or tape functions. Allows precise control during editing.

Digital Effects: Provides 6 digital options, which you'll rarely use—Old Movie, Luminance Key, Flash Motion, Still, Slow Shutter, and Trail.

Digital Program Editing: Allows you to edit the tape in-camera using the i.Link (iEEE-1394) interface by setting in and out points for up to 20 cuts. I can't imagine why you would want to do this when you have all kinds of non-linear editing options. This is clearly a left-over from a news camera fantasy.

Digital Still Camera (DSC): Allows you to capture VGA (640 x 480) JPEG digital still images, and store them onto Memory Sticks or DV tape.

Edit Protocol: Control-L (Lanc).

Edit Search: Allows you to review the last several seconds of video without leaving the record mode.

i.Link: Sony's name for DV FireWire Interface (IEEE-1394). Available on all Sony DV camcorders

InfoLithium Battery with AccuPower: The lithium batteries can be recharged at any time without developing memory effect, and are light weight. AccuPower shows how much charge is left.

Interval Recording: Timelapse recording of video in preset intervals that range from every 30 sec, 1, 5, 10 minutes for selectable lengths of .5, 1, 1.5 or 2 seconds.

LCD Monitor: Active matrix LCD screen swivels up to 270 degrees and can be adjusted to "mirror" mode for self-portraits or so the talent can watch themselves.

LaserLink: Wireless Transmitter System for connection between camcorder and television for playback of video. Operates up to 16 feet away with the optional LaserLink receiver IFT-R10A or IFT-R20.

Manual Functions: In addition to the automatic functions, some cameras have various manual adjustments—Zoom, Focus, Iris, Shutter speed, Gain, AE (Auto Exposure)Shift, White Balance, Custom Preset (Color Level, Sharpness, White Balance Shift, AGC Limit), ND Filters (1/4 and 1/32), Spotlight Button, Audio Recording Level.

Mega Pixel CCD: A CCD capable of rendering over a million pixels (eg: 1,070,000 pixels). Provides better detail in video, with 520 lines of resolution. But it's really useful when capturing still images at 1152 x 864 and better resolution.

Mini DVCAM and mini DV Recording: With the DSR-PD150 you have the capability to record DVCAM or DV format, on the Mini tape size. The DVCAM format records a highly reliable professional video and audio. For audio, an audio lock mode is used. In the DV format you can record in SP mode only.

PCM Stereo Audio: Pulse Code Modulation (PCM) recording provides 96db dynamic range. Sony DV camcorders have two recording modes: 12 and 16 bit audio. 12 bit creates two sets of stereo tracks, and 16 bit mode offers one pair of stereo tracks. Use 16 bit.

Photo Mode: Uses Sony's Adaptive Frame Interpolation (field-doubling). Compare with Progressive Scan Still Mode. Store up to 700 still photos on a 60 minute cassette in the LP Mode.

Picture Effects: 8 Picture Effects, in case the 6 Digital Effects don't satisfy you—Black & White, Sepia, Negative Art, Solarization, Pastel, Slim, Stretch, and Mosaic. Don't be tempted by gratuitous effects. A grateful audience will thank you.

Precision Black & White Viewfinder: Black and white viewfinder provides 500 lines horizontal resolution; more on high end cameras. This enables easier manual focussing.

Precision Color Viewfinder: Most are around 180,000 pixels, with up to 400 lines of resolution.

Program AE: Features a 7-mode Programmed Exposure for a variety of lighting conditions: Portrait, Beach and Ski, Sports Lesson, Landscape, Backlight, Sunset and Moon.

Progressive Scan CCD: Progressive Scan CCDs capture a complete frame of video rather than interlacing two separate fields to produce a video frame. This eliminates the stair stepping effect that is sometimes seen in standard interlaced systems when capturing still images. The images will be sharp and clear with excellent definition.

Super Laser Link: Optional IFT-R20 wireless receiver connects to your TV so that the camcorder can play back without cables from up to 26 feet away.

Super SteadyShot: Sony's name for optical image stabilization. The system uses motion sensors to compensate for camera "shake" without degrading picture quality. Also eliminates high frequency vibration.

Timecode Preset: The timecode can be set to any number in Hour/Minute/Second/Frame format. The timecode mode can be selected between "rec-run" or "free run." User bits can also be set. This is only on the big-gun cameras, not on anything from the PD150 on down.

XLR Audio Inputs: This camcorder features dual XLR audio inputs for connecting professional microphones. The input level can be selected from Mic/Line/Mic Attenuator positions. 48 V DC power can be supplied. Input 1 audio can be recorded on either CH1, or CH1 and CH2 audio tracks (selected by switch).

Why Don't They...

My daughter always asks "why don't they..." or declares "they should..." about almost everything in the world around her that she finds poorly designed for an eight year old.

Why don't they make sinks adjustable in height?

Why don't airplanes have giant parachutes?

Why don't they require all car and truck bumpers be at the same level?

Why don't they make the weather man pay us when he is wrong?

She's absolutely right. And while THEY are at it, why don't they design a DV camera that is ergonomically as easy to use as a 35mm still camera or even a 16mm movie camera?

What are the engineers thinking? They probably don't try to use their cameras outdoors in cold weather with gloves on. They haven't tried to manually adjust the audio level quickly—a process that sometimes requires ten different steps in a complicated menu structure.

Here is our list of suggestions to the nice folks designing the next generation of DV cameras:

1. All electronic menus should be subcontracted to whoever does the electronic menus for Nokia cell phones. They're the only ones who get it.

2. Resist the urge to have all the controls electronic. Analog dials are often easier to use. Look at the Nikon F4 or F5 for inspiration. And make sure we can turn the dials with gloves on.

3. Audio level controls must be manual dials.

4. Zoom lenses should look like still camera and motion picture camera lenses, with separate barrels for focus, zoom and iris. They should be calibrated with scales showing distance, focal length and f-stop. The barrels should have end stops—they should not keep spinning round and round.

5. The Canon XL1 is the only small DV camera to accept interchangeable lenses. Sony's engineers don't think the public really wants this, nor would they pay for the additional cost of lens mounts and additional hardware. Nonsense.

6. Zoom lenses should all have a quick-disconnect for the electric zoom motor, so you can manually zoom smoothly. And Preston Cinema Systems should make their wildly propular Microforce Zoom Control available to all DV cameras.

7. The zoom lens is not a handle. If you hold the camera by the lens, eventually the mount is going to bend, and you're going to start going out of focus. The legacy of twenty years of poor ENG news camera design has carried over to DV. Almost every shoulder-resting camera on the market has that silly handgrip attached to the lens. It's there because it is cheaper to make and simpler to build. But look at film cameras for the last hundred years. The handgrip goes on the camera body.

8. 1/2 inch chips should be more widely used on small DV cameras in the future. There is a huge inventory of interesting 16mm film lenses, and they cover the 1/2 inch chip perfectly.

The 16mm film gate measures 10.3mm wide x 7.5mm high. Super16 is 12.3mm wide x 7.5mm high. Draw a square of those dimensions on a piece of paper using a metric ruler, and then dig out your inches ruler and measure diagonally across the rectangle you've just drawn.

9. While we're at it, changing the world, let's measure video chips in metric units, not fractions of an inch.

10. And while we're still on the subject of lenses, professional and HD cameras should use 1 inch chips. That way, they could use all the 35mm motion picture camera lenses in the world without modification.

The 35mm full gate is 23.5mm wide x 17.5mm high (.980" x .732"). Draw that out on paper, and measure across the diagonal to see it's about one inch.

How to Choose a DV Camcorder

There must be over a hundred different DV camcorders. Just look at the websites of Sony, Canon, JVC, Panasonic, or one of the retailers, like B&H Photo or J&R. The choices are almost as numerous as restaurants in New York, but like those restaurants, just a few stand out.

A shopping list of some of the models follows, along with some recommendations.

I think the best web site and source of information on camcorder, at the moment, is B&H Photo Video in New York, which can be found at www.bhphotovideo.com. They have more complete information and specifications than most of the manufacturers.

Consumer Report

What did the broadcast executive buy his wife? I recommended Sony's PC-110. At the moment, I feel it represents the best combination of small size, simple operation and great pictures. For the home user, that's my choice. The Canon Elura 2MC comes in second.

For beginning film students, Sony's PD100a or PD150 get my vote.

For advanced film students, it's hard to beat the picture quality of Sony's PD150. However, interchangeable lenses and low cost make the following good choices: Canon's XL-1, JVC's GY-DV500U or Panasonic's AG-DVC200.

For the prosumer, independent or documentary filmmaker, it would be a Sony PD100a for lots of handheld work or a Sony PD150 when audio is more critical.

Corporate, event and wedding photographers should be happy with Sony's DSR-250, Panasonic's AG-DVC10, or JVC's GY-500U.

DV Camcorder Shopping List

Unless otherwise noted, all the following are NTSC mini DV Camcorders, using ¼" (6mm) mini DV tape.

Prices are only for ballpark comparisons, and are sometimes list price, sometimes street price, and by no means totally accurate.

Canon

Canon's Elura 2MC and Elura 2 are Canon's smallest "juicy-juice" size camcorders. The only difference is that the MC has a Memory Card to store stills. Both have a 30 frames-per-second "Digital Motor Drive," and a 10x zoom. These two models compete with Sony's PC-5, 110 and other small, vertical , pocket-size cameras.

Canon ELURA 2MC

- CCD: 1/4" Progressive Scan CCD 680,000 Pixels (360,000 Effective Pixels), With RGB Color Filter
- Zoom: 10 x Optical, 3.5-35mm f/1.6-2.6
- Filter Size: 27mm
- Stabilizer: Electronic
- Minimum focus: 3 ft 3 3 /8 in. (1 m); 3 /8 in (1 cm) at wide angle
- Max shutter: 1 /2,000 sec
- Min Lux: 7.5 lx w/ Low Light program
- Recommended illumination: More than 100 lux
- Viewfinder: 0.44" Color (113,000 Pixels)
- LCD Monitor: 2.5" (With 200,000 Pixels)
- Manual Controls: Focus, Exposure, White Balance, Shutter Speed
- Power: 4.3 Watts, 7.4 Volts (Battery)
- Dims (W/H/D): 1 7/8" x 4 1/8" x 3 3/8" (48 x 106 x 86mm)
- Weight: 13 3/4 oz (390 g)
- Memory Card
- Other: 5 Mode Program AE, 16:9 Wide Screen, Analog Line IN
- "Digital Motor Drive" 30 frames per second stills
- Street $1100

Canon ELURA 2

- same as Elura2 MC, but without Memory Card
- Street $1000

Canon OPTURA Pi

Slightly larger than the Canon Elura. Horizontal style. Bigger zoom range (12x). Bigger LCD Screen (3.5"). Color Viewfinder. Optical Image Stabilizer. Progresive Scan. "Digital Motor Drive" provides 30 stills per second.

- CCD: 1/4" Progressive Scan 380,000 Pixels (360,000 Effective) with RGB Primary Color Filter
- Zoom: 12 x Optical, 4.1-49.2mm f/1.6-2.5
- Minimum focus: 3 ft 3 3 /8 in. (1 m), 3 /8 in (1 cm) on maximum wide angle
- Filter Size: 30.5mm
- Stabilizer: Optical Image Stabilizer
- Lux: 2.5 lux
- Recommended illumination: More than 100 lux
- Viewfinder: Color, 0.44-inch, 113,000 Pixels
- LCD screen: 3.5", 200,000 pixels
- Viewfinder Info Zoom, Image Stabilizer, 16:9 Wide Mode, Focus, White Balance, Audio Dub, SP/LP, Date/Time,
- Manual Controls: Focus, Exposure, White Balance, Preset Shutter Speed 1/60-1/100-1/250-1/500-1/1000-1/2000-1/4000
- Accessory Shoe: Hot Shoe For Light And Stereo Mic
- Power: 7.4 V DC (Battery), 4.7 W (viewfinder), 5.5 W (LCD screen)
- Dimensions (W/H/D) 2.7" x 3.4" x 5.8" (68 x 87 x 148mm)
- Weight: 1.4 lbs (650 g)
- Other: 5 Mode Program AE, Analog & Digital Input, 16:9 Wide Mode, SP/LP
- Street $1050

Canon ZR20, ZR25 MC and ZR30 MC

Canon's ZR30 MC, ZR25 MC, and ZR20 have a traditional "handycam" shape. They all share a 10x optical zoom, electronic image stabilization, full-motion video or stills. The ZR25 MC adds a Memory Card and a progressive scan CCD. The ZR30 MC adds an Accessory Shoe for microphone or video light, the VCR buttons light up, and it adds some slow speeds.

This line of camcorders is positioned as an entry-level DV camcorder under $1,000.

- color viewfinder
- 2.5" LCD viewscreen
- 10x optical zoom
- electronic image stabilizer
- built-in stereo microphone
- digital photo mode
- IEEE 1394 digital video in/out
- analog in/out
- programmed autoexposure
- AE shift

Canon GL1

20x zoom and 30 fps
"Frame Movie Mode"
(similar to "digital motor
drive"). High quality 20x
Zoom. Color Viewfinder
2.5" LCD Screen. Optical
Image Stabilizer.

The GL1 uses 3 CCDs, and
is postioned one step below
the venerable XL1. The
GL1 does not have
interchangeable lenses.

Canon uses a proprietary
Pixel Shift technology to
increase resolution.The
green CCD is moved the
equivalent distance of 1/2
pixel from the red and blue
CCD. The green signal is
then sampled more
frequently. The lens is
quite good; fluorite-coating
reduces flares.

- CCD: 3 CCD 1/4" 270,000 pixels (250,000 effective pixels)
- Lens: F/1.6-2.9 to F11, 20x zoom, 4.2-84mm (35mm still equiv: 39.5-790mm)
- Minimum focus: 3ft 3 3/8 inches (1 m), 3/8 inch (1 cm) on maximum wide angle
- Maximum shutter speed: 1/15,000 sec.
- Minimum illumination: 6 lux
- Recommended illumination: More than 100 lx
- Filter diameter: 58 mm
- Viewfinder: 0.55-inch, color LCD (approx. 180,000 pixels)
- LCD screen: 2.5 inches measured diagonally (6.4 cm), 122,000 pixels (approx.)
- Microphone: Stereo electret condenser microphone
- Manual focus ring, aperture; shutter speeds fr 1/60 sec to 1/15,000 sec; white balance
- Zebra pattern
- Power: 7.2 V DC, 6.7 W (viewfinder), 7.4 W (LCD screen)
- Audio: PCM digital, 16 bit (48kHz/2ch), 12 bit (32kHz/4ch)
- Dimensions: 4 5/8 x 5 3/8 x 10 3/4 inches (117 x 135 x 272 mm)
- Weight: 2 lb 12 1/8 oz (1.25 kg)
- List $2699 / Street $2100

Canon XL1

One of the top three in the DV popularity contest.

Main strengths are interchangeable lenses, three 1/3" CCDs, optical image stabilization, many manual controls for lenses, choice of color or black and white viewfinder.

The optical stabilization system is especially good at removing low frequency movements like breathing, handheld shake and bounce.

The main drawback is that the XL1 is front-heavy. The built-in fold-out shoulder pad helps, but you still have to push up on the handgrip. The XL1 does not sit on your shoulder like a friendly house cat or an Aaton 16mm camera.

The camera does not have an on-board LCD monitor. You can add an aftermarket one, which will add to the already substantial size of this camera. Canon also makes a black and white viewfinder, which is better for checking focus.

The MA-100 shoulder pad incorporates XLR audio connectors for audio input only. It does not supply +48v phantom power.

XL-1 Lenses

When you purchase the XL1, it comes standard with a 16x zoom 5.5-88mm f1.6–2.6 lens (35mm still format equivalent: 39mm to 633mm.)

The 3x zoom 3.4-10.2mm f1.8 lens is the equivalent of a 24 to 72mm zoom in 35mm still format.

Lens accessories include a 1.6x tele extender, an EF adapter to mount most of Canon's EOS still lenses, and matteboxes from Optex. Optex makes a Nikon lens adapter that accepts most Nikon still lenses, as well as a PL adapter for motion picture lenses. The lenses become fully manual, and their original focal lengths are multiplied by 8 to 10 times. Theoretically, you could follow the space shuttle with a 17,280mm lens. Atmospheric haze might be a problem.

Optex has modified the Fujinon 1/3" 14x 5.5-77mm f1.4 manual zoom lens to use the XL mount. This is the lens to get. It has full manual focusing with real index marks.

To mount a lens, align the red dot on the camera body with the red dot on the lens, then turn the lens clockwise until it clicks and locks into place.

To remove the lens, slide and hold the **LENS RELEASE** button and turn the lens counter-clockwise until it stops. Then, remove the lens from the camera body.

Optex/Fujinon Manual Zoom Lens

XL1 Manual Controls

XL1 manual controls include focus, iris, shutter speed, white balance and audio level. This is one of the few small camcorders that actually has easy-to-use knobs to adjust audio input.

You can go on full autopilot by turning the power dial to the green **Easy Recording** position which will absolutely override all manual controls.

Canon XL1 specs

- CCD: 3 CCD 1/3" Pixel Shift 270,000 pixels (250,000 effective)
- Lens mount: XL interchangeable lens system
- Lens: Standard: 16x zoom 5.5-88mm f/1.6-2.6 to f16
- Maximum shutter speed: 1/15,000 second
- 3 slow shutter speeds (1/8, 1/15 and 1/30 sec) for "blurred motion look"
- Minimum illumination: 2 lux (w/ XL 5.5-88mm lens at 1/8 second shutter)
- Recommended illumination: More than 100 lux
- Filter diameter: 72mm (XL lens)
- Viewfinder: 0.7-inch, color LCD (approx. 180,000 pixels). Black & White finder optional.
- Microphone: Stereo electret condenser, 3.5mm stereo mini-jack
- Records DV Time Code (Drop-Frame) and data code - Date, Time, Shutter Speed and Exposure information (remains hidden until selected for display.)
- Zebra pattern and Color Bar generator
- Power: 7.2 V DC; 9.5 W (Approx).
- Audio: PCM digital, 16 bit (48kHz/2ch), 12 bit (32 kHz/4 ch simultaneous)
- Audio input gain controls: One of the few mini DV cameras with knobs to manually control audio input levels, along with audio level meters.
- Dimensions: 8 3/4 x 8 7/16 x 16 5/16 in (223mm x 214mm x 415mm)
- Weight (not including lens and battery pack): 3 lbs 11 15/16 oz approx. (1.7 kg) (fully loaded): 6 lbs 4 7/8 oz approx. (2.86 kg)
- List: $4,699 / Street: $3,690

  Lenses
- D510320201 (14XXL1) 14x Manual Zoom Lens
- D510300201 (3XXL1) 3x Wide Zoom Lens
- D560080201 (1.6XXL1) 1.6x Extender
- D560070201 (EFAXL1) EF Adapter for XL Mount

JVC

Ultra Compact

These are the successors to the cameras first introduced by JVC about five years ago that began the revolution in tiny digital camcorders that fit in your pocket.

GR-DVM80U

Juicey-juice box style, color viewfinder, 2.5" LCD screen

- CCD: 1/4" Progressive Scan CCD, 680,000 Pixels
- Zoom 10x 3.8-38mm f1.8-2.4
- Filter Size 37mm
- Digital Image Stabilizer
- Color .55" CRT Viewfinder
- LCD Monitor 2.5" 112,000 pixels
- Manual Controls Focus, Exposure, White Balance, And Iris Lock
- Dimensions (W/H/D) 2 1/16" x 4 15/16" x 3 7/8"
- Weight 1.2 lbs (g)
- List $1,299 / Street $800

GR-DVM90U

Similar to DVM80, with 4Mb Memory Card, Flash, digital stills VGA (640X 480 pixels) and XGA (1024X 768 pixels) sizes.

- CCD: 1/4" Progressive Scan CCD, 680,000 Pixels
- Zoom 10x 3.8-38mm f1.8
- Filter Size 27mm
- Digital Image Stabilizer
- Built-in flash
- 8 Mb Memory Card
- Color .44" CRT Viewfinder
- LCD Monitor 2.5" 112,000 pixels
- Manual Controls Focus, Exposure, White Balance, and Iris Lock
- Dimensions (W/H/D) 2 1/16" x 5" x 3 4/5" (51 x 125 x 97mm)
- Weight 1.1 lbs (510 g)
- List $1,399 / Street $980

JVC "Handycam" Style

GR-DVL300U

10x Zoom, B/W Viewfinder, 2.5" LCD Screen,

- CCD: 1/4" Interlace CCD, 680,000 Pixels
- Zoom 10x 3.6-36mm f1.8; Filter Size 37mm
- Digital Image Stabilizer
- Viewfinder B/W
- LCD Monitor 2.5"
- Manual Focus, Exposure, White Balance, and Iris Lock
- Built In Light
- Dimensions (W/H/D) 3 3/16" x 3 13/16" x 6 5/16" (80 x 96 x 159mm)
- Weight 1.3 lbs (580 g)
- List $999

GR-DVL505U

10x Zoom, B/W Viewfinder, 3" LCD Screen, 2Mb Memory for Stills Storage

- CCD: 1/4" Interlace CCD, 680,000 Pixels
- Zoom 10x 3.6-36mm f1.8; Filter Size 37mm
- Digital Image Stabilizer
- Viewfinder B/W
- LCD Monitor 3"
- Manual Controls Focus, Exposure, White Balance, And Iris Lock
- Built In Light
- Dimensions (W/H/D) 3 3/16" x 3 1/16" x 6 5/16" (80 x 96 x 159mm)
- Weight 1.3 lbs (580 g)
- List $1,099

GR-DVL805U

10x Zoom, Color Viewfinder, 3.5" LCD Screen, Digital Image Stabilizer, 2Mb Memory for Stills

- CCD: 1/4" Interlace CCD, 680,000 Pixels
- Zoom 10x 3.6-36mm f1.8; Filter Size 37mm
- Digital Image Stabilizer
- Color .44" CRT Viewfinder
- LCD Monitor 3.5"
- Manual Controls Focus, Exposure, White Balance, And Iris Lock
- Built In Light
- Dimensions (W/H/D) 3 3/16" x 3 1/16" x 6 5/16" (80 x 96 x 159mm)
- Weight 1.3 lbs (580 g)
- List $1,099

JVC GR-DV2000U

A medium-sized camcorder with lots of bells and whistles. Records DV and Megapixel 1600 x 1200 digital stills. Progressive Scan 680,000 pixel single CCD achieves 520 lines horizontal by 480 lines vertical resolution. Pixel Shift Technology. Dual Cam feature with a removable SD Memory Card/ MultiMediaCard (16MB MMC card included) lets you shoot video and stills at the same time. USB output to download stills to computer.

GR-DV2000U Specs

- CCD: 1.92 Mega-Pixel, Video Actual Pixels 690k, Still Actual 1.92 Megapixel
- 520 lines horizontal by 480 lines vertical resolution. Progressive Scan.
- Digital still pictures with resolution of 1600 X 1200 (1.92 Megapixel)
- Dual Cam with removable SD Memory Card / MultiMediaCard (16MB)
- Dual shooting mode to shoot video and stills (640 x 480) at the same time uninterrupted
- Digital still output via USB cable or card
- Info-Shoe for Auto Light, Video Flash and Stereo Zoom Mic
- Analog input
- Hyper High Speed Recording and Pro-Slow Playback for viewing slow motion
- 3.5" LCD view screen
- Zoom 10x with spline interpolation technology, Lens 3.8-38mm f1.8
- Filter Size 52mm
- Digital Image Stabilizer
- Viewfinder Color (with 110,000 Pixels)
- LCD Monitor 3.5" (With 200,000 Pixels)
- Line In Recording Digital & Analog
- Inputs: IEEE-1394, Audio/Video, S-Video, USB, Edit and DC Input.
- Outputs IEEE-1394, Audio/Video, S-Video
- Power Consumption 4.4 Watts, DC 7.2 Volts
- Dimensions (W/H/D) 2.9" x 3.5" x 7.1" (74 x 90 x 178mm)
- Weight 1.4 lbs 660 g (1.7 lbs 740 g With Battery and Tape)
- List $2,199

- Batteries
  BN-V416U 2 Hour Battery, BN-V428U 4 Hour Battery
- Lenses
  GL-V0752 Wide Angle Adapter, GL-V1452 Telephoto Adapter
- CU-MMC08 8MB, CU-MMC16 16MB Multimedia Card
- MZ-V3 Stereo Zoom Microphone (For Hot Shoe)

Panasonic

Panasonic Consumer mini DV Camcorders, from Matsushita, come in models and prices for just about anyone. The dazzling array of choices is driven by product features. Start with a basic model, which has a price point usually well below the competition. Then add features and add to the price. The trick is knowing which things you really want, and which ones you can avoid.

It's like buying a refrigerator. You go to the showroom thinking you just need a box with some doors that keeps the beer cold. But then you see the automatic icemaker, and the built-in cold water dispenser. Next, you can't live without side-by-side doors and the filter that protects you from tainted water to whose bio-hazards even intrepid digital cameramen are not immune. And then you hear about Dual Digital Electronic Image Stabilization, which stabilizes the image being played back, after it has already been recorded. (After!)

Panasonic Comparison Chart

MODEL NO.	PV-DV100	PV-DV200	PV-DV400	PV-DV600	PV-DV800	PV-DV950
3 CCD System						X
Hi-Definition Zoom	18x	18x	18x	18x	18x	12x
Color LCD Monitor	2.5 in.	2.5 in.	3.0 in.	3.0 in.	3.5 in.	2.5 in.
WIDESIGHT- 3.5" Color LCD Monitor					X	
Color Viewfinder			X	X	X	X
i.LINK™ (IEEE 1394 PC Interface	X	X	X	X	X	X
CARD LINK (MultiMediaCard)		X	X	X	X	
Electronic Image Stabilization (Record & Play)	X	X	X	X	X	EIS
PhotoShot™ Built-in Digital Still Camera	X	X	X	X	X	X
Image Size (Normal / Fine)	320x240/ 640x480	320x240/ 640x480	320x240/ 640x480	320x240/ 640x480	320x240/ 640x480	
Image Capacity (Normal / Fine)		approx. 240 / 60	approx. 240 / 60	approx. 240 / 60	approx. 240 / 60	
IR Filter On/Off (0 Lux)			X	X	X	
Analog In				X	X	
High Speed Shutter (1/60 - 1/8,000)	X	X	X	X	X	X
Unit Size (HxWxD in inches)	4.25x3.37x7.5	4.25x3.37x7.5	4.25x3.37x7.5	4.25x3.37x7.5	4.25x3.37x7.5	4.12x3.12x7.5
Weight (lbs.)	1.54	1.57	1.5	1.52	1.48	1.5

Panasonic PV-DV100

Black & White Viewfinder. 2.5" LCD.
18x zoom, inexpensive Panasonic Mini
DV camcorder.

- PHOTOVU LINK to transfer stills from MiniDV tape via RS-232C Serial cable
- PhotoShot™ Still Camera mode
- DUAL Digital Electronic Image Stabilization (Record and Playback)
- 5-Mode Program AE (Auto Exposure)
- PCM Stereo (12-bit/16-bit)
- Book Mark Search to find end of tape
- CCD 1/4" 460,000 Pixels
- 5 Lux
- Viewfinder B/W
- LCD Monitor 2.5"
- PCM Stereo 12 bit-32 KHz, 16 bit-48 KHz
- Zoom 18 x
- Filter Size 49mm
- Manual Focus, Preset White Balance Indoor/Outdoor, Shutter 1/60-1/8000
- Line In Recording via FireWire 1394-IEEE Only
- Dimensions (W/H/D) 3.4" x 4.3" x 7.4" (85 x 107.5 x 188mm)
- Weight 1.54 lbs (0.7 kg)
- List $799; Street $590

Panasonic PV-DV101

20x zoom

- 2.5" LCD Monitor
- PHOTOVU LINK
- PhotoShot™ Still Mode
- 20x Zoom
- 680,000 pixel 1/4" CCD
- DUAL Digital Electronic Image Stabilization (Record and Playback)
- Picture-In-Picture places a still image in lower right corner during recording
- 5-Mode Program AE (Auto Exposure)
- PCM Stereo (12-bit/16-bit)
- List $899; Street $630

Panasonic PV-DV200

8MB Memory Card, 18x zoom

* i.LINK™ (IEEE 1394 PC Interface) lets you use the industry standard IEEE1394 interface1
* PHOTOVU LINK
* CARD LINK with included 8MB removable MultiMediaCard
* PhotoShot™ Still
* 18x Zoom
* DUAL Digital Electronic Image Stabilization
* 5-Mode Program AE
* PCM Stereo (12-bit/16-bit)
* List $999; Street $620

Panasonic PV-DV201

20x zoom
* PhotoShot™ Still Camera
* SD Card Slot (For use with MultiMedia Card™ or SD Memory Card)
* 680,000 pixel CCD
* Movie Messenger to transfer motion or still image files from Palmcorder to PC via USB cable or IEEE 1394 interface.
* DUAL Digital Electronic Image Stabilization
* 20x Zoom Lens 3.6-72mm /f1:1.6
* Filter Size 43mm
* Image Stabilizer: Electronic Image
* 5 lux
* Viewfinder 0.4" B/W
* LCD Monitor 2.5"
* Manual Controls Focus, Preset White Balance Indoor/Outdoor Setting, Preset Shutter Speed 1/60-1/8000
* List $799; Street $699

Panasonic PV-DV400

Color Viewfinder, 3" LCD, 18x zoom

- CCD 1/4" 460,000 Pixels
- PCM Stereo 12 bit-32 KHz, 16 bit-48 KHz
- 18 x Zoom Lens 3.9-70.2mm f 1.6
- Filter Size 49mm
- Image Stabilizer: Dual Digital Electronic
- 5 Lux (IR Filter Like Night Shot)
- Color Viewfinder 114,000 Pixels
- LCD Monitor 3.0"
- Manual Focus, Preset White Balance Indoor/Outdoor Setting, Preset Shutter Speed 1/60-1/8000,
- Line In Recording via FireWire 1394-IEEE Only
- Dimensions (W/H/D) 3.4" x 4.3" x 7.4" (85 x 107.5 x 188mm)
- Weight 1.5 lbs (0.7 kg)
- List $999; Street $679

Panasonic PV-DV401

3.0" LCD Screen, Color Viewfinder,
0 Lux IR Filter, Mic Input, 20x zoom

- CCD 680,000 Pixels
- PCM Stereo 12 bit-32 KHz, 16 bit-48 KHz
- 20 x ZoomLens 3.6-72mm f1.6
- Filter Size 43mm
- Dual Digital Electronic Image Stabilization
- 5 lux (0 lux with MagicVu Infrared)
- 0.44" Color Viewfinder with 114,000 Pixels
- Viewfinder Info Battery/Tape Remaining, Zoom, Picture Effects, SP/LP, Date/Time, Time Code, Program AE, Image Stabilizer.
- LCD Monitor 3.0"
- Manual Focus, Preset White Balance Indoor/Outdoor Setting, Preset Shutter Speed 1/60-1/8000
- Line In Recording
- IEEE-1394 FireWire
- Outputs: S-Video, A/V Mini (Cable with 3 RCA), USB
- Accessory Hot Shoe
- Power DC 7.2 Volts, 18 Watts
- Dimensions (W/H/D) 3.3" x 4.2" x 6.5"
- Weight 1.5 lbs
- List $999, Street $759

Panasonic PV-DV 601

3" Color LCD Monitor, Analog-In,
Manual Focus Ring, Built-In Light.

- CCD 680,000 Pixels
- PCM Stereo 12 bit-32 KHz, 16 bit-48 KHz
- Zoom 20x Lens 3.6-72mm f1.6
- Filter Size 43mm
- Dual Digital Image Stabilization
- 5 lux (0 lux with MagicVu)
- Viewfinder 0.44" Color Viewfinder with 114,000 Pixels
- LCD Monitor 3.0"
- Manual Focus Ring, Preset White Balance Indoor/Outdoor Setting, Preset Shutter Speed 1/60-1/8000
- Inputs: IEEE-1394 FireWire (4 Pin), Line In Recording, Analog & Digital
- Outputs: S-Video, A/V Mini, USB
- Power: DC 7.2 Volts, 18 Watts
- Dimensions (W/H/D) 3.3" x 4.2" x 6.5"
- Weight 1.5 lbs
- Other: Picture In Picture, Headphone Jack, Accessory Hot Shoe, Built In Light
- List $1099; Street $899

Panasonic PV-DV800

3.5" LCD Viewing Screen

- CCD 1/4" 460,000 Pixels
- PCM Stereo 12 bit-32 KHz, 16 bit-48 KHz
- Zoom 18 x Lens 3.9-70.2mm f 1.6
- Filter Size 49mm
- Dual Digital Electronic Image Stabilization
- 5 Lux (IR Filter)
- Viewfinder Color (With 114,000 Pixels)
- LCD Monitor 3.5"
- Manual Focus, Preset White Balance Indoor/Outdoor Setting, Preset Shutter Speed 1/60-1/8000
- Line In Analog And Digital (IEEE-1394)
- Dimensions (W/H/D) 3.4" x 4.3" x 7.4" (85 x 107.5 x 188mm)
- Weight 1.52 lbs (0.7 kg)
- Other: Photo Mode 320 x 240 or 640 x 480 Resolution Stills On Tape/ Media Card; 5 Mode Program AE, Backlight, Mic. Input, Headphone Jack, (Mini) Accessory Hot Shoe For Eye Light (PV-DLT9)
- List $1399

Panasonic PV-DV901

List: $1,799
Mini DV Camcorder with Mega Pixel
CCD and 3.0" Diagonal Color LCD
Monitor

- PHOTOVU LINK with driver software to transfer still images on the MiniDV tape via serial cable
- CARD LINK to transfer still images captured on the included 16MB removable Memory Card
- SD Card Slot for use with MultiMedia Card or SD Memory Card
- 16MB SD Memory Card Included
- PhotoShot Built-in Digital Still Camera (up to 1200 x 900 High Resolution Still Images)
- 10x Zoom
- Color Viewfinder
- Digital Electronic Image Stabilization
- Analog in
- Manual Focus Ring
- 5-Mode Program AE (Auto Exposure)
- PCM Stereo (12-bit/16-bit)
- SD USB Reader/Writer Included

Panasonic PV-DV950

- 3 CCD chips 270,000 pixels
- IEEE 1394
- 12x Zoom Lens 4-48mm /F1.6
- Filter Size 43mm
- Color Viewfinder (160K pixels)
- Color LCD Monitor 180,000 pixels
- PhotoShot™ Digital Stills
- Manual Focus Ring
- Shutter from 1/60 to 1/8000 sec.
- Iris Control with 16 steps from f1.7 to f16
- AE (Auto Exposure) Lock
- Gain Control in five steps from 0 to 12db to meet your video requirements
- 5-Mode Program AE
- Digital Electronic Image Stabilization
- S-Video Output
- PCM Stereo (12-bit/16-bit)
- Power: Battery 7.2
- Dimensions (W/H/D) 3 1/8" x 4 1/8" x 71/2" (80 x 105 x 189mm)
- Weight 1.5 lbs (0.69 kg)
- List $2,499; Street $1,899

Panasonic PV-DV951

- 3 CCD (1.6 million pixels)
- i.LINK™ (IEEE 1394)
- PHOTOVU LINK
- CARD LINK
- 16 MB SD Memory Card Included
- SD Card Slot
- PhotoShot™ Digital Still Mode (up to 1488x1128)
- 10x Zoom
- Color Viewfinder
- Digital Electronic Image Stabilization
- Analog in
- Manual Focus Ring
- 5-Mode Program AE (Auto Exposure)
- PCM Stereo (12-bit/16-bit)
- List: $2,699; Street $1,999

Sony

Sony Palm-sized Camcorders

Sony DCR-PC5 Mini DV Camcorder

The smallest of the Juicy-Juice style Mini DV Camcorders. 10x (Optical) Carl Zeiss Zoom Lens, Color Viewfinder, 2.5" Touch Panel LCD Screen, Super Steady Shot

- CCD: 1/4" 680,000 Pixels
- 10 x Carl Zeiss Lens; Filter Size 30mm
- Optical Image Stabilizer
- 5 lux (Nightshot 0 lux Infrared System)
- Color Viewfinder with 180k Pixels
- 2.5" Touchscreen LCD Monitor with 200,000 Pixels
- Manual Focus, Exposure, White Balance
- Line In Recording: IEEE-1394, S Video, composite Video+Audio (Mini Plug)
- Mic. Input: Mini Stereo
- Headphone Jack: Mini Stereo
- Accessory Shoe: not hot—not powered
- Power 13 watts
- Weight 1 lbs (450 g)
- Dimensions (W/H/D) 2 1/8" x 4" x 3 7/8" (54 x 101 x 97mm)
- Other: Record Digital Still Images On Memory Stick VGA 640x480 as JPEG File, 7 Mode Program AE, Backlight, 16:9 Wide Mode, PC Serial Cable Connection
- List Price $1,499
- Optional Accessories
- Batteries
  NPF-S11, NPF-S21, NPF-S31 InfoLithium Battery
- Battery Chargers
  AC-VQ11AC Power/Battery Charger
  DC-VF10 DC Power/Battery Charger
  DCCL-50 DC Power Adapter (For Camcorders)
- Memory Sticks
  MSA-8A 8MB; MSA-16A 16MB; MSA-32A 32MB; MSA-64A 64MB; MSA-128A 128MB
- Lens Accessories
  VCL-0630S 0.6 x Wide Angle Lens
  VCL-2030S 2x Telephoto Lens

Sony DCR-PC100

Fits in your jacket pocket, takes great pictures, and doesn't look threateningly like a serious video camera, even though it is.

There was a DVCAM version of this style, the DSR-PD1, but it has been discontinued.

The image pickup is a 1/4" CCD rated at 1,070,000 Pixels, over 500 lines of horizontal video resolution, and is manufactured for reduced noise (in the video signal) and improved signal-to-noise ratio by up to 6db (2x better than a standard CCD). It is particularly effective when shooting in dark situations.

In Stills Mode, the CCD captures images at 1152 x 864 and can store them on tape or on a removable Memory Stick. A 4MB Memory Stick comes with the camera.

The lens is 4.2-42mm Zeiss Vario-Sonnar, which is equivalent to a 48-480mm in 35mm format.

The 2.5" Swing-Out LCD Display (200k Pixels) is very useful, but not great in bright sunlight.

The optional NP-FM90 battery lets you record up to 6 1/2 hours on one charge.

Rechargeable Lithium Ion batteries do not have the "memory effect" of Nicads, meaning you can charge them before full discharges. You can see a display of the battery time remaining in minutes, in the viewfinder or on the LCD screen.

Optical image stabilization eliminates high frequency shake and vibration by using motion sensors, without degrading the video image.

Night Vision permits shooting up to ten feet away in total darkness (0 Lux) using a built-in infrared system. Applying a slower shutter speed increases picture brightness.

There is a wireless connection between the camcorder and television that operates up to 16 feet away with an optional LaserLink receiver.

Accessory Shoe on top of the Sony PC100 provides power and on/off switching to accessories.

8 Picture Effects: Black & White, Sepia, Negative Art, Solarization, Pastel, Slim, Stretch, and Mosaic.

6 Digital Effects: Old Movie, Luminance Key, Flash Motion, Still, Slow Shutter, and Trail.

Analog Recording Inputs convert and record analog (NTSC or PAL) video to DV.

Mechanical Shutter System is variable for sharpening high speed subjects or special effects such as motion blur.

Scanning is interlaced.

Sony PC-100 Specs

- 1/4" Mega-Pixel CCD (1070k Pixels)
  Video Actual Pixels 690k, Still Actual Pixels 1,000k. Advanced HAD CCD
- Zoom 10x Carl Zeiss Vario-Sonnar Lens, 4.2-42mm f1.8-2.2 (35mm Equiv 48-480mm)
- Filter Size 37mm
- Optical Image Stabilizer
- 7 Lux (Nightshot 0 Lux Infrared System)
- Color Viewfinder With 180k Pixels
- Progressive-Shutter System
- 2.5" LCD Monitor With 200,000 Pixels
- Manual Focus (Ring), Exposure (Dial) 24 Steps, White Balance In Menu Hold/Indoor/Outdoor Settings
- Line In Recording: Digital IEEE-1394, S-Video or analog Audio/Video Input (Mini Plug).
- Memory Mode to capture still images on a memory stick
- Accessory Intelligent Hot Shoe
- Power Consumption 3.9 Watts,
- Dimensions (W/H/D) 2.5" x 5" x 4 7/8"
- Weight 1 lbs 3 oz
- List $1799; Street $1399

Sony PC-100 Additional Info

- Mega Pixel/Advanced "HAD" CCD provides 1,152 x 864 still images.
- 16:9 Wide Mode,
- Laser Link
- Backlight control
- 7 Program Auto Exposure with shutter speeds from 1/4 to 1/4000
- Mic. Input (Stereo Mini Plug)
- Headphone Jack   (Stereo Mini Plug)

Optional Accessories

- Batteries
  NPF-M50, NPF-M70,
  NPF-91 InfoLithium Battery

- Battery Chargers
  BCV-M50 For M Series Batteries
  ACV-Q800 Ac Power/Battery Charger with Display
  DCCL-50 DC Power Adapter (For Camcorders)
  DCV-Q800 DC Power/Battery Charger with Display

- Memory Sticks
  MSA-8A 8MB, MSA-16A 16MB, MSA-32A 32MB, MSA-64A 64MB, MSA-128A 128MB

- Lens Accessories
      VF-R37K Filter Kit
      VCL-0637H 0.6 Wide Angle Lens
      VCL-R2037 2x Telephoto Lens
      VCL-HG0737 High Grade WA
      VCL-HG2037 High Grade 2x

- Intelligent Shoe Accessories:
      ECM-HS1 Zoom Microphone
      HVL-IRH Night Shot Light
      HVL-FDH3 3 Watt Video Light/
      Flash for Photo Mode
      HVL-S3D 3 Watt Video Light
      Laser Link Receiver IFT-R10A

Sony DCR-PC110

10x (Optical) Carl Zeiss Zoom Lens.
Mega Pixel CCD. Color Viewfinder.
2.5" LCD Screen. Super Steady Shot
Super Laser Link. Automatic pop-up
flash for stills. MPEG Movie on
Memory Stick. USB Port.

- CCD: 1/4" Mega-Pixel CCD (1,070,000 Pixels) Video Actual Pixels 690K, Still Actual Pixels 1,000K.
- Progressive Shutter System
- Audio: PCM Digital Stereo, 12 bit-32 KHz, or 16 bit-48 KHz
- Zoom: 10x Carl Zeiss Vario-Sonnar Zoom Lens, 4.2-42mm f1.8-2.2 (35mm equiv. 48-480mm)
- Filter Size: 37mm
- Image Stabilizer: Optical Super Steady Shot (Optical)
- Lux: 7 lux (Super Nightshot 0 lux Infrared System)
- Viewfinder: Color Viewfinder with 180,000 Pixels
- LCD Monitor: 2.5" LCD with 200,000 Pixels
- Manual Focus, Exposure
- Inputs: IEEE-1394 4 Pin, S Video Composite Video + Audio
- Outputs: IEEE-1394, S-Video, A/V Mini Jack
- USB Port
- Memory Mode Allows You To Capture Still Images On A Memory Stick
- Mic. Input: Mini Plug
- Headphone Jack: Mini Plug
- Accessory Shoe Intelligent Hot Shoe
- Built In Flash for stills, not for video
- Power: 3.6 watts
- Dimensions: (W/H/D) 2.4" x 4.8" x 4.8" (60 x 122 x 122mm)
- Weight: 1 lbs 4 oz (590 g)
- Other: 16:9 Wide Mode, Backlight, Shutter Speed 1/4-1/4000 in AE Mode.
- List Price: $1,999

Optional Accessories for Sony DCR-PC110

- Batteries
  NPF-M50 InfoLithium Battery
  NPF-M70 InfoLithium Battery
  NPF-91 InfoLithium Battery

- Battery Chargers
  BCV-M50 For M Series Batteries
  ACV-Q800 Ac Power/Battery Charger with Display
  DCCL-50 DC Power Adapter (For Camcorders)
  DCV-Q800 DC Power/Battery Charger with Display

- Memory Sticks
  MSA-8A 8MB of memory
  MSA-16A 16MB of memory
  MSA-32A 32MB of memory
  MSA-64A 64MB of memory
  MSA-128A 128MB of memory

- Lens Accessories
  VF-R37K Filter Kit
  VCL-0637H 0.6 Wide Angle Lens
  VCL-R2037 2x Telephoto Lens
  VCL-HG0737 High Grade Wide Angle
  VCL-HG2037 High Grade 2x Telephoto Lens

- Laser Link Receiver IFT-R20 up to 26 feet, or IFT-R10A up to 16 feet

- Intelligent Shoe Accessories
      ECM-HS1 Zoom Microphone
      HVL-IRH Night Shot Light
      HVL-FDH3 3 Watt Video Light/Flash for Photo Mode
      HVL-S3D 3 Watt Video Light

Sony DCR-TRV11

Single CCD, Mini DV Camcorder with
10x Optical Carl Zeiss Zoom Lens,
Color Viewfinder, 3.5" LCD Screen,
Super Steady Shot, Laser Link.
List Price $1,299.00

- CCD: 1/4" 680,000 Pixels (Effective Pixels 340,000) Advanced HAD CCD
- Audio: PCM Digital Stereo 12 bit 32 KHz/4ch, 16 bit 48 kHz/2ch
- Zoom: 10x Carl Zeiss Lens, 3.3-33mm f1.7-2.2 (35mm equivalent = 42-420mm)
- Filter Size: 30mm
- Image Stabilizer: Optical (Super Steady Shot)
- Lux: 5 lux (Super Nightshot 0 lux)
- Viewfinder: Advanced Color Viewfinder (113,000 pixels)
- LCD Monitor: 3.5" (184,000 Pixels)
- Manual Controls: Focus, Exposure, White Balance Indoor/Outdoor,
- Edit Protocol : Control-L (Lanc)
- A/V Dubbing: Audio Dub In 12 bit Mode
- Line In Recording : IEEE-1394, S Video, or analog through Audio/Video Input
- Special Effects: 8 Modes (Slim, Stretch, Mosaic, Solarization, Monotone, Sepia, Negative Art, Pastel)
- Digital Effects: 6 Modes (Still, Flash Motion, Luminance Key, Slow Shutter, Trail, Old Movie
- Fader: 5 Mode: Black, Overlap, Monotone, Bounce, Mosaic)
- Titler: 8 Preset & 2 Custom Titles
- Mic. Input: Mini Stereo
- Headphone Jack: Mini Stereo
- Laser Link: Super Laser Link with Optional IFT-R20
- Accessory Shoe : Intelligent Hot Shoe
- Power Consumption: 3.6 watts, 100-240 V 50/60 Hz
- Dimensions (W/H/D): 2.8" x 3.7" x 6.4"
- Weight: 1 lbs 5 oz

Sony DCR-TRV20

High-end, single 1.07 Megapixel CCD, 520 lines of video resolution. Carl Zeiss 4.2-42mm (10x) /f1.8-2.8 lens. 0 Lux Infrared System, ¼ - 1/4000 shutter, Memory Stick. List price $1,699. Street price $1,300.

What does it have that the TRV11 doesn't? Mega-Pixel CCD, higher resolution viewfinder (with 180,000 pixels vs. 113,000 pixels), higher resolution 3.5" LCD viewing screen (with 246,000 pixels vs. 3.5" with 184,000 pixels), 37mm Filter Size (vs. 30mm Filter Size).

The Mega Pixel CCD (1,070,000 pixels) is useful for capturing still images on Memory Stick at 1152 x 864 resolution—which provides bigger and sharper print-outs.

- CCD: ¼" Mega-Pixel CCD (1070k Pixels) Video Actual Pixels 690k, Still Actual Pixels 1,000k, "HAD" CCD
- Audio: PCM Digital Stereo 12 bit 32 kHz/4ch, 16 bit 48 kHz/2ch
- Zoom: 10x Carl Zeiss Lens, 4.2-42mm / f1.8-2.8 (35mm equivalent 48-480mm)
- Filter Size: 37mm
- Image Stabilizer:Optical, Super Steady Shot
- Lux: 7 lux (Nightshot 0 lux Infrared System)
- Viewfinder: Color Viewfinder with 180k Pixels
- LCD Monitor: 3.5" LCD with 246,000 Pixels
- Manual Controls: Focus (ring), Exposure dial with 24 Steps
- White Balance: Hold/Indoor/Outdoor Settings
- Edit Protocol: Control-L (Lanc)
- Audio Dub: Audio Dub in 12 bit Mode
- Line In: IEEE-1394, Analog, S Video, Audio-Video Input (Mini Input)
- Digital Stills (DSC):
- Special Effects: B/W, Sepia, Negative Art, Solarization, Pastel, Slim, Stretch, Mosaic.
- Digital Effects: Old Movie, Luminance Key, Flash Motion, Still, Slow Shutter, Trail.
- Fader

- Titler: 8 Preset & 2 Custom Titler
- Mic. Input: Stereo Mini
- Headphone Jack: Stereo Mini
- Laser Link: Super Laser Link with Optional IFT-R20
- Accessory Shoe: Intelligent Hot Shoe
- Power Consumption: 3.7 watts, 100-240 V 50/60 Hz
- Dimensions (W/H/D): 2.8" x 3.6" x 6.7"
- Weight: 1 lbs 7 oz
- Other: Mega Pixel/Advanced "HAD" CCD Technology Provides A 1152 x 864 Still Image Resolution (Better than XGA 1024 x 768 Resolution Or VGA 640 x 480 Res). 16:9 Wide Mode, Backlight, 7 Program AE with Shutter Speed 1/4-1/4000 in AE Mode

Optional Accessories

- Batteries
  NPF-M50 InfoLithium Battery
  NPF-M70 InfoLithium Battery
  NPF-M91 InfoLithium Battery

- Battery Chargers
  BCV-M50 For M Series Batteries
  ACV-Q800 AC Power/Battery Charger with Display
  DCCL-50 DC Power Adapter (For Camcorders)
  DCV-Q800 DC Power/Battery Charger with Display

- Memory Sticks
  MSA-8A 8MB
  MSA-16A 16MB
  MSA-32A 32MB
  MSA-64A 64MB
  MSA-128A 128MB

- Lens Accessories
  VF-R37K Filter Kit
  VCL-0637H 0.6 Wide Angle Lens
  VCL-R2037 2x Telephoto Lens
  VCL-HG0737 High Grade Wide Angle
  VCL-HG2037 High Grade 2x Telephoto Lens

- Laser Link Receiver IFT-R20 up to 26 feet, or IFT-R10A up to 16 feet.

- Intelligent Shoe Accessories
  ECM-HS1 Zoom Microphone
  HVL-IRH Night Shot Light
  HVL-FDH3 3 Watt Video Light/Flash for Photo Mode
  HVL-S3D 3 Watt Video Light

Sony DCR-TRV900

Three-chip version of Sony's TRV11 and 20 (and earlier models TRV8, 9 and 10, now discontinued). Rival of Canon GL1. Three ¼" 380k pixel CCDs, 12X optical zoom, optical image stabilization system, five-mode program auto exposure and a progressive scan mode, color viewfinder, 3.5" LCD screen.

Still photo mode for 640x480 stills on tape, PC card or Memory Stick. List Price $2299. Street price $1650.

A floppy drive (supplied) plugs into the rear PCMCIA slot, allowing you to download stills to a 3 1/2" floppy disc. Purchasing an optional PCMCIA Memory Stick adapter will record the same images to the faster, smaller flash media.

- CCD: 3 CCD, 1/4" / 380,000 Pixels (Progressive Scan CCD)
- Audio: PCM Digital Stereo, 12 Bit-32 kHz, Or 16 Bit-48 kHz
- Zoom: 12 x Optical, 48 x Digital
- Lens: 4.3-51.6mm /f1.6-2.8, (35mm stills equiv = 41.3 - 496mm)
- Filter Size: 52mm
- Optical Image Stabilizer
- Lux : 4 Lux
- Viewfinder: Color (180,000 Pixels)
- Viewfinder Info: Focus, Cassette IC Memory, Remaining Batt, Zoom, Gain Exposure,Digital/Picture Effect, Prog. Scan, 16:9, White Balance, Prog. Ae, Shutter Speed, Steady Shot, Tape Remaining, Audio Mode, Audio Meter, Nd Filter, Data File, Time Code, Self Timer, Back Light
- LCD Monitor: 3½"

Sony DCR-TRV900 Specs, cont'd

- Manual Controls: Focus (Ring), Exposure (Dial), Shutter 1/4-1/10,000, Iris, Gain, White Balance, Mic Level Control,
- Edit Protocol : Control-L (Lanc)
- A/V Dubbing: (Audio Dub In 12 Bit)
- Line In Recording
- In/Output: Digital IEE-1394 Fire Wire Interface, S-Video, Analog Video (RCA receptacle)
- Digital Effects: Still, Flash Motion, Luminance Key, Slow Shutter, Trail, Old Movie, "Time-Lapse",Single Frame Recording
- Picture Effects: Slim, Stretch, Solarization, Monotone, Sepia, Negative, 9-Pictures "Contact Sheet"
- Fade: Black, Monotone, Overlap,
- Titler : Custom & 8 Preset Titles, with Cassette IC Memory Chip
- Laser Link
- Mic. Input: Mini Stereo
- Headphone Jack : Mini Stereo
- Accessory Shoe: Intelligent Hot Shoe
- Power Consumption: 4.1 Watts. 5.2 W with LCD screen
- Dimensions (W/H/D): 3 2/3" x 4" x 7 1/2" (93 x 103 x 193 mm)
- Weight: 1 lbs 15 Oz (890 g)
- Floppy Disk Adapter
- Memory Card
- Slide Show Mode
- Zebra Pattern
- Color Bar Generator
- Digital Noise Reduction (DNR)
- 5 Mode Program AE
- Laser Link
- Stills at 640 x 480 (VGA), JPEG File Format
- Images On Memory Media: Super Fine 19-23, Fine 38-45, Standard 63-75
- Interval Frame Recording

Sony DSR-PD100A

Sony Broadcast & Professional Division version of TRV900, with same features, plus: uses mini DVCAM or mini DV Cassettes (records and plays both fromats), one XLR audio input with 48v phantom powering, SMPTE timecode.

One of the smallest DVCAM format camcorders, 4:3/16:9 aspect ratios; Three ¼-inch 380,000 pixel CCDs; Scanning modes: 480 progressive (480p—for Stills) or interlaced (for Video). Built-in PCMCIA slot and Memory Stick adapter. Timecode with Drop Frame and Non Drop Frame.

- CCD: 3 CCD, ¼" / 380,000 Pixels (Effective 360,000) Progressive Scan CCD For Still Images, Interlace Scan for video
- Audio : PCM Digital Stereo, 12 Bit-32 kHz, or 16 Bit-48 kHz
- Zoom: 12 x Optical, 48 x Digital
- Lens: 4.3-51.6mm /f1.6-2.8, (35mm Still Equivalent = 41.3 - 496mm)
- Filter Size : 52mm
- Image Stabilizer: Super Steady Shot (Optical)
- Lux : 4 Lux
- Viewfinder: Color (180,000 Pixels)
- Viewfinder Info: Focus, Cassette IC Memory, Remaining Battery, Zoom, Gain Exposure, Digital/Picture Effect, Progressive Scan, 16:9, White Balance, Prog. AE, Shutter Speed, Steady Shot, Tape Remaining, Audio Mode, Audio Meter, ND Filter, Data File, Time Code, Self Timer, Back Light
- LCD Monitor: 3½"
- Manual Controls: Focus (Ring), Exposure (Dial), Shutter 1/4-1/10,000, Iris, Gain, White Balance, Mic Level Control
- Edit Protocol: Control-L (Lanc)
- A/V Dubbing: (Audio Dub In 12 bit)
- In/Output: Digital IEEE-1394 FireWire, S-Video, Analog Video (RCA receptacle)
- Digital Effects: Still, Flash Motion, Luminance Key, Slow Shutter, Trail, Old Movie
- Picture Effects: Slim, Stretch, Solarization, Monotone, Sepia, Neg, 9 Picture Composite
- Fader: Black, Monotone, Overlap
- Titler: Custom & 8 Preset Titles, with Cassette Memory Chip
- Mic. Input: Mini, and XLR with 48v phantom power—mounts to hot shoe
- Headphone Jack: Stereo Mini
- Accessory Shoe: Intelligent Hot Shoe
- Power Consumption : 4.1 W, W/ Lcd 5.2 W 100/240 V 50/60 Hz

- Dimensions (WHD): 3 2/3" x 4" x 7 1/2" (93 x 103 x 198 mm)
- Weight: 1 lb. 15 oz (890 g)
- List price $2,825

- Other
  Analog Input, IEEE 1394 Fire Wire, Floppy Disk Adapter Memory Card, PCMCIA Slot, Audio Dub, Memory For Still Image Capture, Slide Show Mode, Zebra Pattern, Color Bar Generator, Digital Noise Reduction (DNR), 5 Mode Program AE, Stills at 640 x 480 (VGA), JPEG File Format, Number of Images on Memory Media, Super Fine 19-23, Fine 38-45, Standard 63-75

Sony DSR-PD100A Accessories

- HVL-FDH2 Video Flash
- MSA-8A MemoryStick (up to 150 images)
- ECM-670 directional mini shotgun microphone
- CAC-12 microphone holder, attaches to XLR adapter
- EC-0.5C2 microphone cable
- NPF-950B battery
- NPF-330 battery
- AD80005 PC PCMCIA port adapter
- HVLFDH2 - Light with Flash
- MSA8A - 8MB Memory Stick
- AD80005 - PCMCIA port adapter for PC
- CAC12 - Microphone Holder for DXC and BVP Series Cameras
- EC05C2 - Microphone Cable
- ECM670 - Short Shotgun Microphone

Sony DCR-VX1000

One of the two camcorders that started the DV revolution in 1996 (Canon's XL-1 is the other). Lots of used ones, popular in schools. Minuses: no analog input, no LCD viewing screen, 32 kHz audio only (lower quality), no XLR input. Pluses: good zoom lens, three CCD chips, "Super Steadyshot" stabilization, and timecode.

Some users complain of audio hiss when using manual gain control.

- CCD: 3 x 1/3" CCDs, 410,000 Pixels each chip
- Audio: PCM Stereo Digital (12 Bit-32kHz Rec, 16 Bit-44.1/48kHz Playback)
- Zoom: 10x Optical, 20x Digital
- Lens: 6.1-61mm / F1.6.2.1
- Filter Size: 52mm
- Image Stabilizer: Optical
- Lux: 4 Lux
- Viewfinder: Color .7"
- Viewfinder Info: Manual Focus, N.D. Filter, White Balance, Zoom, Program Ae, Audio Rec Level, Steady Shot, Time Code, Custom Preseting, Stby, Self Timer, Audio Mode, Photo Mode, Cassette Memory, Remaining Tape, Remaining Battery
- LCD Monitor: No
- Still Photo Mode: No
- Manual Controls: Focus (By Ring), Iris, Gain (20 Step), Shutter, (16 Step), White Balance, Audio Level Control
- Date & Time:
- Time Code:
- Edit Protocol: Control-L
- A/V Dubbing: No
- Line In Recording: Digital Only, IEEE-1394 Firewire Connector
- Special Effects: Overlap
- Fader: To Black
- Titler: No
- Mic. Input: (Mini Stereo)
- Headphone Jack:
- Accessory Shoe:
- Built In Light: No
- Power Consumption: 7.2v, 9.5w
- Dimensions (HWD): 4.3 X 5.6 X 12.8"
- Weight: 3lbs 4oz.
- Other: Variable Speed Optical Zoom, 3-Mode Program Auto Exposure, Zebra Pattern, Color Bars, Interval & Frame Recording, Photo Mode, Data Code, Slow Shutter 5 Sec Rec, Built In N.D. Filter, DV I/O IEEE-1394 FireWire
- Original list price $3999. Still available new at many dealers, street price $2295.

Sony DCR-VX2000

The successor to Sony's VX1000 has a 6-72mm (12x) zoom lens, Mini DVCAM, three 1/3" 380,000 pixel CCDs, Optical image stabilization, 2.5" color LCD flip-out viewing screen, color viewfinder, progressive scan mode, five-mode auto exposure plus full manual control. 16x9 mode.

What does the VX2000 have that the VX1000 doesn't? HAD CCD with 3 x 380k Pixels (vs older technology CCD 410k x3); Progressive Scan CCD; 12/16 bit Audio (vs.12 bit); 2.5" LCD Viewing Screen; 12x Zoom (vs. 10x); Manual Zoom; Analog Input; 16x9; 2 Neutral Density Filters (vs. 1); Built In Titler; Digital Still with Memory Stick; External Battery with ability to use larger Batteries; Accessory Hot Shoe.

- CCD: 3 x 1/3" CCD 380,000 Pixels (340,000 Effective Pixels) HAD CCD Technology, Progressive Scan CCD
- Audio: PCM Digital Stereo 12 bit 32 kHz/4ch, 16 bit 48 kHz/2ch
- Zoom Lens: 12x Aspherical Zoom Lens 6.0-72.0mm f/1.6-2.4
- Filter Size: 58mm
- Image Stabilizer: Optical Super Steady Shot
- Lux : 4 lux
- Viewfinder: Color Viewfinder with 180k Pixels
- LCD Monitor: 2.5" LCD with 200,000 Pixels
- Manual Controls: Focus (ring), Exposure, White Balance, Zoom (ring), Shutter Speed (1/4-1/10,000), Iris, Mic. Level
- Edit Protocol : Control-L (Lanc)
- A/V Dubbing: Audio Dub in 12 bit Mode
- Line In Recording: Digital IEEE-1394, & "Analog" S Video or Through Audio Video Input.
- Special Effects : 6 Mode: Slim, Stretch, Solarization, Monotone, Sepia, and Negative Art.
- Digital Effects: 5 Mode: Old Movie, Luminance Key, Flash Motion, Still, and Trail
- Fader : Black, Overlap, Wipe, Monotone, and Random Dot
- Digital Still Camera (DSC): PCMCIA and Memory Stick
- Titler : 8 Preset & 2 Custom Titler
- Mic. Input: Mini Stereo
- Headphone Jack: Mini Stereo
- List Price $2899.00. Street price $2600.
- Intelligent Hot Shoe
- Power Consumption: 7.2 watts, Ac 110-240 50/60 Hz
- Dimensions (W/H/D): 4 5/8" x 5 3/4" x 13 1/2"
- Weight : 3 lbs 1 oz

Sony DCR-VX2000 Additional Specs

- Color Bar Generator, 2 Position
  Neutral Density Filter
- Interval Record Time (Time Lapse)
  30 seconds/1/5/10 Minute Record
  Time .5/1/1.5/2 seconds, 5 Mode
  Program AE, 16:9 Wide Mode,
  Zebra pattern 100%/70%

Optional Accessories
- Batteries
  - NPF-550 , NPF-750,
  - NPF-960 InfoLithium Battery

- Battery Chargers
  - BCV-615 Portable Charger
  - ACV-Q800 AC Power/Battery
    Charger with Display
  - DCCL-50 DC Power Adapter

(For Camcorders)
  - DCV-Q800 DC Power/Battery
Charger with Display

- Memory Sticks
  - MSA-8A 8MB
  - MSA-16A 16MB
  - MSA-32A 32MB
  - MSA-64A 64MB
  - MSA-128A 128MB

- Lens Accessories
  - VCL-HG0758 0.7 Wide Angle
  - VCL-HG1758 Telephoto

- Hot Shoe Accessories
  - ECM-HS1 Zoom Microphone
  - HVL-FDH3 3 Watt Video Light/Flash for Photo Mode
  - HVL-S3D 3 Watt Video Light

Sony PD-150

Honey, they shrank the news camera. Sony Broadcast & Professional Company's DSR-PD150 looks like a miniature news camera shrunk down to a Handycam.

It shares many of the same features as Sony's consumer division DCR-VX2000, but can use both Mini DVCAM and Mini DV Cassettes, has SMPTE timecode, and two XLR audio inputs with 48v phantom powering.

Unlike the DCR-VX2000, the viewfinder is black and white—which is sharper, and easier to judge focus than the color viewfinder of the VX2000. The audio hiss problem of the VX2000 and early PD150 cameras has been fixed. The 2.5" color LCD viewing screen is smaller than the PD100's 3.5 inch screen, but the 500 line black and white finder is sharper compared with the color viewfinder of the PD100.

The DVCAM DSR-PD150 costs about $800 more than the consumer version DCR-VX2000.

Why are we paying $1000 more for this camera? The PD150 provides user settable SMPTE timecode, XLR audio input, choice of recording and playing back on DVCAM or Mini DV and a sharp black and white viewfinder.

This is about as good as it gets for ultra-portable DVCAM. The main difference between this camera and the larger DSR-200a/300/500 professional cameras is that the bigger brothers use interchangeable lens and have 1/2" or 2/3" chips.

PD-150 Overview

The lens is mechanically one of the smoothest of any small camcorder. Manual focus is an easy switch from AUTO, and the black and white finder helps a lot.

There are two balanced XLR receptacles at the front of the camera, and switchable 48 volt phantom power for both channels.

The shotgun microphone looks serious, and its directional quality provides better sound than most.

The handle on top is very helpful for carrying and low-angle shots.

The DSR-PD150 has three 1/3-inch CCDs with 380,000 pixels (effectively 340,000 pixels), while the DSR-PD150P (PAL) has three 1/3-inch CCDs with 450,000 pixels (effectively 400,000 pixels).

These CCDs are capable of both interlace scan for motion and progressive scan for stills.

12x Zoom Lens

Sony optics 12x lens with a 58 mm filter diameter, for 530 lines of horizontal resolution. Unfortunately, the lens is not interchangeable—it is permanently mounted to the camera body, which of course, saves size and weight.

Optical Image Stabilizer

The DSR-PD150 has an optical image stabilizer in which the horizontal and vertical movements are detected independently by electronic sensors. A prism system located in the front of the lens adjusts and optically compensates for unsteadiness, while maintaining image quality.

180,000 Dot LCD Precision Black &White Viewfinder

The black and white viewfinder provides 500 lines of horizontal resolution—more than 20% greater than current color viewfinders. This helps manual focusing.

200,000 Dot LCD Monitor

The DSR-PD150 has a high-resolution color LCD monitor for viewing the recording picture, or checking the playback picture on location.With its large screen, it is helpful in setting the menu or audio recording level, as well as monitoring the camera and audio status while mounted on a tripod.

PD-150 — 2 ch XLR Audio Input

There are two XLR receptacles (on the camera right side in front of the carrying handle) for audio input and connecting professional microphones. The input level can be selected from Mic/Line/Mic Attenuator positions. 48 V DC power can be supplied. INPUT 1 audio can be recorded on either CH1, or CH1 and CH2 audio tracks (selected by switch). One monaural microphone is supplied with the unit.

16-bit/12-bit PCM Digital Sound and Audio Dub Capability

The DSR-PD150 records two channels of audio with the 48kHz/16-bit or 32kHz/12-bit mode. On a pre-recorded tape with two channels recorded in the 32kHz/12-bit mode, it can dub additional two channels through the external mic input (XLR connectors or RCA pin jacks, DVCAM tape only).

DVCAM/DV Recording

The DSR-PD150 uses the DVCAM format. For professional audio editing, an audio lock mode is used. It is also capable of recording and playing back DV format tapes (SP mode only), which is chosen from the menu.

Manual Functions

In addition to the automatic functions,the DSR-PD150 has various functions for manual adjustment.

- Zoom
- Focus
- Iris
- Shutter speed
- Gain
- AE (Auto Exposure) Shift
- White Balance
- Custom Preset (Color Level, Sharpness,White Balance Shift, AGC)
- ND Filters (1/4 and 1/32)
- Spotlight Button (for example, someone on stage under a spotlight)
- Backlight Button
- Digital Effects: Still,Flash Motion,Luminance Key, Trail, Old Movie
- Audio Recording Level: Separate or Linked adjustment of CH1 and CH2
- Zebra Patterns (100% or 70%)

PD-150 —Timecode Preset

The timecode can be preset using any number in Hour/Minute/Second/Frame format, and offers the choice of "record-run" or "free run." User bits can also be set. This is a big bonus for such a little camera, allowing you to identify each tape. In contrast, the PD100a can only reset timecode to 0.

Power

The power consumption of the DSR-PD150 is 4.7 W (with viewfinder). With the optional NP-F960 battery pack, it can record for up to eight hours.

Title Function

When using a cassette with Cassette Memory, the titles can be set and recorded in the Cassette Memory. This information is not superimposed on the video signal, but is displayed during playback. It can be used as an index later. The DSR-PD150 also has a Tape Title function that displays a title on the tape during the first five seconds of recording.

Fader

There are five fading modes: Black Fade (IN/OUT), Monotone Fade (fade from Black & White to color), Overlap (last image becomes a still image and overlaps onto the new scene), Wipe and Dot.

Digital Still Camera Functions with Memory Stick

A Memory Stick can be inserted directly into the DSR-PD150.

Memory Photo

The camera can be switched to the progressive scan mode for capturing still images. VGA-sized (640x480) JPEG files are recorded on the Memory Stick in one of three image quality modes.

PD-150 — Battery Life

Continuous Recording Time, indoors at 25 °C

Battery	with Viewfinder	with LCD Monitor on
NP-F330 (supplied)	60 min.	50 min.
NP-F550	130 min.	110 min.
NP-F750	265 min.	230 min.
NP-F960	480 min	420 min.

Keying

Images stored on a Memory Stick can be keyed over camera images.

M.CHROM (Memory Chromakey): The blue area of a still image on the Memory Stick can be replaced with a picture from the camera.

LUMI (Memory Luminancekey): The bright part of a still image on the Memory Stick can be replaced by an image from the camera.

C.CHROM (Camera Chromakey): A moving picture from the camera can be superimposed on a still image from the Memory Stick.When shooting a picture with a blue background, the area of the moving picture will be taken out and the still picture will be shown.

M.Overlap (Memory Overlap): The still image on the Memory Stick can be faded into a moving picture.

Still Images on Memory Stick: Quantity and Quality

	Super Fine compression 1/3	Fine compression 1/6	Standard compression 1/10
Memory Stick Capacity			
4MB	20 images	40 images	60 images
8MB	40 images	81 images	122 images
16MB	82 images	164 images	246 images
32MB	164 images	329 images	494 images
64MB	329 images	659 images	988 images

PD-150 — Controls

- Zoom
- Focus
- Iris
- Shutter speed
- Gain
- AE (Auto Exposure) Shift
- White Balance
- Custom Preset
- Color Level, Sharpness, White Balance
- AGC Limit
- ND Filters (1/4 and 1/32)
- Spotlight Button (for shooting performances lit by spotlights)
- Backlight Button (compensates when subject is lit from behind)
- Digital Effects (Still, Flash Motion, Luminance Key, Trail, Old Movie)
- Audio Recording Level (Separate or Linked adjustment of CH1 and CH2)
- Zebra Patterns (100% or 70%)
- Guide Frame (Vertical and Horizontal alignment of the subject to guide frame)

Specs

- Three 380k pixels 1/3" CCDs (360,000 pixels effective)
- Two scanning modes: 480 progressive (for still) or interlaced (for video).
- SuperSteadyShot™ and Autofocus
- 12X optical zoom
- 530 lines of horizontal resolution
- 2 lux minimum illumination
- Auto or manual exposure
- 480p VGA 640 x 480 progressive scan still image capture
- Tape photo mode for recording still images to tape
- Still mode recording to MemoryStick
- 4 MB MemoryStick™ included stores up to 60 JPEG images
- Directional shotgun (mono) directional electret microphone included
- Two independent XLR audio inputs with independent audio level control, line/mic select and phantom power are provided
- 2 built-in XLR inputs.
- Slot for a flash memory card or MemoryStick for still image storage.
- Up to 988 JPEG pictures can be stored in one 64 MB MemoryStick. The stored images can be mixed or keyed to the live image allowing logo insertion and/or mix effects.
- 12x Zoom lens with Manual/Electric zoom, Manual/Autofocus, Manual/Auto Iris controls, and electronic image stabilization
- Software package for logo generation and included USB port adapter
- 16:9/4:3 aspect ratio switchable. 4:3 native
- 16 bit/12 bit PCM audio for two or four channel audio modes
- I.LINK (IEEE 1394 compliant) input and output
- Color 2.5" swing-out reversible 200,000 dot LCD panel display

- Image Device: prism mounted 3-chip 1/3 inch, Interline-Transfer (IT) 380,000 CCDs
- Lens: 12X variable speed zoom F6.0 to 72.0mm, F1.6 at 2.4mm
- Filter diameter: 58mm
- Picture Elements: 360,000 pixels effective 380,000 pixels total
- 2 Built-in Filters: ND1: 1/4 and ND2: 1/32
- Shutter Speed: 1/4 to 1/10000 sec
- Connectors: S-Video, A/V, Audio In, i.LINK, LANC, Headphone stereo mini
- Minimum Illumination: 2 lux
- Viewfinder: 180,000 dot B & W, 500 lines
- Audio: rec. 48 KHz 16 bit, 32 KHz 12 bit
- LCD Panel: TFT 200,000 dots
- Format: DV/DVCAM recording (SP mode), DVCAM/DV playback (SP mode)
- Memory Card Slot: Memory Stick up to 64B
- Power consumption: 4.7 watts REC with viewfinder ON only
- Operating temperature: 0 deg C to +40 deg C
- Image Device: prism mounted 3-chip 1/3inch, Interline-Transfer (IT)
- Scanning System 2:1 interlaced, 525 lines, 60 fields/sec. for video
- 480p for still images
- Horizontal Frequency: 15.734 kHz
- Vertical Frequency 59.94 Hz
- Sync System: Internal
- Connectors: S-Video, A/V, Audio In, i.Link, LANC, Headphone stereo mini
- Minimum Illumination: 2 lux
- Audio rec: 48KHz/16 bit, 32KHz 12 bit
- Speaker: built in dynamic
- Format: DV/DVCAM recording (SP mode), DVCAM /DV playback (SP mode)
- Memory card slot: MemoryStick up to 64B
- Format: Mini DVCAM with 530 Lines of Resolution / Mini DV (SP Mode)
- CCD: 3 x 1/3" CCD 380,000 Pixels(340,000 Effective Pixels)
- Audio: PCM Digital Stereo 12 bit 32 kHz/4ch, 16 bit 48 kHz/2ch
- Zoom: 12 x Optical, 24 or 48 x Digital (Manual Zoom Ring)
- Lens: Aspherical Lens 6.0-72.0mm f/1.6-2.4
- Filter Size: 58mm
- Image Stabilizer: Optical Super Steady Shot
- Viewfinder: 0.4" B/W Viewfinder 180,000 pixels provides 500 Lines
- LCD Monitor: 2.5" Precision LCD with 200,000 Pixels
- Manual Controls: Focus(ring) , Exposure, White Balance, Zoom (ring), Shutter Speed (1/4-1/10,000), Iris, Gain, Audio, ND Filter 1/4 and 1/32), Zebra Patterns (100% or 70%)
- Edit Protocol: Control-L (Lanc)
- A/V Dubbing: Audio Dub in 12 bit Mode
- Line In Recording: Digital IEEE-1394, S Video, Analog Composite
- Special Effects: 6 Mode: Slim, Stretch, Solarization, Monotone, Sepia, and Negative Art
- Digital Effects: 5 Mode: Old Movie, Luminance Key, Flash Motion, Still, and Trail
- Fader: Black, Overlap, Wipe, Monotone, and Random Dot
- Digital Still Cam: Allows You To Capture Still Images On A Memory Stick
- Titler: 8 Preset & 2 Custom

- Microphone Inputs : Dual XLR Mic Input
- Headphone Jack: Stereo Mini
- Accessory Shoe: Cold Shoe
- Power Consumption: 7.2 watts, Ac 110-240 50/60 Hz
- Dimensions (W/H/D): 5" x 7 1/8" x 13.5" (125 x 180 x 342mm) without Mic.
  5 1/8" x 7 1/8" x 16" (128 x 180 x 405mm) with Mic.
- Weight: 3.5 lbs (1.5 kg)

Other
- Color Bar Generator,
- 2 Position Neutral Density Filter
- Interval Recorder (Time Lapse) 30 seconds/1/5/10 Minute Record Time .5/1/1.5/2 sec
- 5 Mode Program AE
- 16:9 Wide Mode
- Preset Time Code

- Accessories
  ECM670PAC - Microphone Package (Optional Accessories)
  MSAC-FD2M FLOPPY DISC ADAPTER (Optional Accessories)
  MSAC-PC2 MEMORY CARD ADAPTER (Optional Accessories)
  NPF-960 BATTERY (Optional Accessories)
  AC-L10 (Required Accessories)
  DVCAM OR DV TAPE (Required Accessories)
  NPF-960 (Required Accessories)
  A/V CABLE (Supplied Accessories)
  AC-L10 AC ADAPTER (Supplied Accessories)
  DIRECTIONAL MONO MICROPHONE ECM-NV1 (Supplied Accessories)
  DK CABLE (Supplied Accessories)
  LARGE EYECUP, LENS HOOD, LENS CAP (Supplied Accessories)
  PICTURE GEAR 4.1 LITE AND USB DRIVER (Supplied Accessories)
  RMT-811 REMOTE COMMANDER (Supplied Accessories)
- List price $4000

Big Guns

JVC

JVC GY-DV500U

Now we get to the camcorders that are about the size of a cereal box on its side. The JVC 500 is a very economical professional shoulder-resting camera, about half the size of conventional BetaSP and DigiBeta big guns. It is rapidly gaining popularity for

news, documentary and corporate users because it has all the familiar features of much more expensive cameras. It uses interchangeable lenses with a bayonet lens mount, three ½ inch chips, capable of low light shooting down to .75 lux.

Die-cast magnesium body. Full Auto Shooting (FAS) mode for point-and-shoot operation (you still have to zoom and focus). Full Auto Shooting sets the camera to the Auto Iris Mode, even if the lens is in the manual position.

Accu-Focus activates the electronic shutter for approximately ten seconds, forcing open the lens diaphragm. When the lens is wide open, it is easier to check critical focus. Rmember, most of the good lenses are not auto focus.

JVC Variable Scan allows flicker-free shooting of computer monitors. Shutter speeds can be set from 1/60.5 to 1/196.7 of a second in 255 increments to precisely match the scan rate of the monitor.

JVC GY-DV500U Specs

- CCD: 3 x 1/2" CCD, 380,000 pixels
- 750 TV lines equivalent horizontal resolution (768 H x 494 V)
- 14-bit DSP digital signal processing
- Uses mini DV format
- 5 kg (11 lbs.)
- Three 1/2" 380,000-pixel CCDs
- Advanced circuitry virtually eliminates vertical smear when shooting bright lights, as well as lag and image burn
- F1.4 prism optical system
- Lolux mode at 0.75 lux illumination (better than what you can see with your eyes)
- IEEE 1394 (DV) input/output
- RS-232C serial port
- Standard professional 1/2" bayonet lens mount, accepts Panasonic, JVC, Fujinon and Canon lenses, among others
- PCM sound: two 16-bit 48-kHz channels or two 12-bit 32-kHz channels with a dynamic range of more than 85 dB
- Viewfinder displays various events, camera setting recorder operation, and selected setup parameters

- Super Scene Finder (SSF) lets you log scenes automatically or manually in the field, and mark which scenes are good. This speeds up the transfer process and saves disk space, because you can batch digitize only those scenes needed for editing. Scene data is written directly onto the MiniDV cassette. Up to 134 scenes can be marked per cassette.
- Scene data from last 3 cassettes held in camcorder memory, allowing data to be added to cassette at a later time automatically
- Menu dial to navigate through viewfinder menu, as well as set shutter speed
- Full auto shooting for one-touch automatic operation
- Continuous auto black (CAB)
- Full auto white
- Automatic level control (ALC) for continuous automatic control of gain
- Back tally lamp for letting talent behind the camcorder know you are shooting
- Accu-focus mode for aid in focusing
- Back-lit LCD display for VTR menu and status indications
- Tape/battery remaining indicator
- Variable scan view for shooting computer screens
- Sync lock mode for multi-camera shooting (genlock)

JVC GY-DV500U Specs

- Black stretch/compress for enhancing or suppressing shadow areas
- Adjustable gamma
- SMPTE timecode reader/generator
- SMPTE type color bars
- Lens Mount: 1/2" bayonet
- Filters: 3200k, 5600k
- Gain: -3, 0, 6, 9, 12, 18 dB, variable gain in ALC and LOLUX
- Video Output: Composite (BNC), S-Video type 4 pin
- Professional XLR Audio with phantom mic power, Audio 1 and 2
- Audio Input (Audio 1, Audio 2): 2x XLR
- Line Output (Line 1, Line 2): unbalanced (RCA)
- IEEE1394: 4 pin
- RS-232C: Mini DIN 6 pin
- Power: XLR 4-pin DC 10.5 V to 17 V
- Dimensions: (WxHxD) Body only: 10 7/8 x 9 11/16 x 5 1/8" (275 x 245 x 130 mm)
- Weight: 11 lbs. (including viewfinder, battery, microphone, and tape)
  5 kg. (including viewfinder, battery, microphone, and tape)
- Optional Accessories:
  VF-P400U: 4" Viewfinder
  SAK-400: 4" Viewfinder Mount
  BH-P27U: Battery Holder for NB-G1U or NP-1B Batteries
  AA-P250U: AC Power Adapter/Single position Charger for NB-G1U
  AA-G10U: AC Power Adapter/Four position Charger for NB-G1U
  NB-G1U: Ni-Cd Battery (2.2Ah)
  NP-1B: Ni-Cd Battery (2.3Ah)

- List $4,635.00, without lens
- List $5995 (Street $5199) with 14:1 zoom lens

JVC GY-DV700W

If you're going to be shooting a dramatic show on DV, the eyepiece extender of this camera facilitates smoother moves on a fluid head.

The 3x 2/3" CCD chips render better images, and accept a wider range of lenses. The CCDs are manufactured as true 16:9 format chips. Shooting in widescreen mode will not yield a lower resolution picture than 4:3, which happens on conventional cameras where the 16:9 image is just using a masked, and smaller, picture area.

The Chrosziel Mattebox and follow focus are familiar to film shooters. Having an assistant "pull" focus on moving subjects is the best way to ensure perfectly sharp images. The mattebox accepts professional size filters—usually 4"x4" or 4"x5.650" (Panavision size).

Because it accepts SMPTE timecode in and out, you can jam sync it with a DAT recorder and digital slate.

The F11 at 2,000 Lux rating gives it an equivalent ASA rating of 100. Uses MiniDV cassettes only.

- Dimensions (WxHxD): 11 7/16 x 9 11/16 x 5 1/8" (290 x 245 x 130mm)
- Weight: 3kg 6.6lbs
- CCD: 3x 2/3" CCD's (Effective Pixels 480k, 980(H) x 494(V) lines)
- Lens Mount: 2/3" Bayonet
- Switchable 4:3, 16:9 format
- Dual-pipeline 14-bit Cine-DSP
- Three 2/3-inch 16:9 CCDs (480,000 pixels x3)
- F11 at 2,000 lux (min. illumination 0.75 lux)
- B4 lens mount compatible with Prime HD lenses, and standard 2/3" lenses
- 16:9 switchable
- IEEE 1394 digital in/out
- Uses standard MiniDV cassettes
- SMPTE timecode in/out
- List price $9800, without accessories

Panasonic Broadcast & Television

DV Proline

Panasonic AG-DVC10

Panasonic AG-DVC10 is a MiniDV Camcorder disguised as a big-gun shoulder-resting camera that has been bent in the middle. It is probably aimed at the corporate, training and wedding markets. It accepts Anton Bauer batteries and eye-lights. 12x Zoom, Color Viewfinder, 3-CCD. Unlike Canon's XL-1, the lens is not removable; like the XL-1 there is no LCD viewing screen. Happily, the handgrip is firmly attached to the body instead of the lens.

- CCD: 3 x 1/4" CCDs (270,000 Pixels)
- PCM Stereo Digital, 12 bit-32kHz 4-channel, 16 bit-48kHz 2-channel
- 12 x Zoom with Macro, Lens 4-48mm, f1.6
- Filter Size 43mm
- Electronic Image Stabilizer
- 5 lux
- Viewfinder 0.5" Color
- No LCD Monitor
- Manual Focus, Iris, White Balance, Shutter Speed 1/60-1/8000 (14 steps), Gain Selection 0/3/6/9/12 dB, Mic Level
- Line In IEEE-1394 FireWire 4-Pin
- Audio/Video Out: 1x A/V RCA, 1x S-Video
- Power DC 7.2 Volts, Ac 18 Watts
- Dimensions (W/H/D) 7 1/8" x 8 13/16" x 16 3/4" (181 x 224 x 426mm)
- Weight 4.85 lbs (2.2 kg)
- Other: Program AE Mode, Zebra Pattern, Wide Mode, Photo Mode, ND Filter, Index Search, Built In Speaker. Mic. Input (Mini), Headphone Jack, (Mini)
- List $2,595.00

Panasonic AG-DVC200

DV and miniDV Camcorder.
3 x ½" 410,000 Pixel CCDs.
Records on large DV tape, in
addition to MiniDV.
Over 4 hours of recording on
one large DV Tape. Good for
news, business and
education. Interchangeable
1/2" image area bayonet
mount lenses.

Built-in color bar generator,
Anton/Bauer Battery mount
1.5" b&w viewfinder. Color
playback capability.

- CCD ½" 410,000 pixel 3-CCD
- Lens: ½" image area Bayonet Mount
- Optical Filters ND/CC combination, 4 position
- Minimum Luminance 0.5 lux
- Horizontal Resolution 800 lines
- S/N Ratio 62 dB
- Viewfinder 1.5" Monochrome
- Maximum Recording Time 270 min. SP
- Tape Speed SP - 18.812 mm/sec.
- Input/Output: IEEE 1394 4-pin, Mic In XLR x 1, Video Out BNC x 1, S-Video Out 4-pin
- Audio Out RCA x 2 (L/R)
- Headphones Stereo 3.5 mm x 1
- Weight 11 lbs.
- Power 12 VDC (10.5 to 17 V), 18 watts
- 16-bit, 48kHz digital audio, balanced XLR mic/line inputs with 48 volt phantom power, and auto and manual audio gain control
- List $5495 without lens

Panasonic DVCPRO

TV news stations have been buying this camera with good reason. It looks like a serious camera, but costs less than $10,000.

Panasonic AJ-D400 DVCPRO

- CCD: 3 x ½" 410,000-Pixel FITs
- 1/2" image area bayonet lens mount 2-Lux Shooting Illumination
- Full Black-and-White or Color Playback
- 48 kHz sampling, 16-bit recording, two-channel PCM digital audio
- Shockless AWB Control ensures smooth adjustment of white balance
- Synchro Scan Electronic Shutter (six settings: 1/100 to 1/2000-sec.) reduces flicker when shooting CRT displays
- 1.5" b&w Viewfinder
- Anton/Bauer Gold Mount Plate (installed)
- Power: DC12V (11 V to 17 V), 23 W
- Weight: 12.87 lbs. (5.85 kg) (including lens, viewfinder, tape, and battery pack)
- Minimum Illumination: 2 lux (F1.4, +30 dB gain)
- Shutter Speeds: 1/100, 1/120, 1/250, 1/500, 1/1000, 1/2000-sec.
- Syncro Scan: 1/30.4 to 1/57.4-sec., 1/61.7 to 1/250-sec. (variable)
- Optical Filter: 3200K, 5600K+1/4ND, 5600K, 5600K+1/16ND
- S/N Ratio: 62 dB (standard)
- Horizontal Resolution: 750 lines (center)
- Vertical Resolution: 450 lines/500 lines (Super-V)
- Registration: Less than .03% (all zones, without lens)
- Viewfinder: CRT 1.5" monochrome
- Horizontal Resolution: 600 TV lines (Center)
- Tape Speed: 33.820 mm/s
- Tape: 1/4-inch Metal Particle Tape
- Cassette Size: (AJ-P66M) 97.5 x 64.5 x 14.6 mm
- Recording/Playback Time 66 min. with AJ-P66M cassette
- FF/REW Time: Around 3 min. using AJ-P66M
- Audio Sampling Frequency: 48 KHz
- Frequency Response: 20 Hz to 20kHz, +1.0/-1.0 dB
- Distortion: Less than 0.1% (at 1 kHz, reference level)
- Genlock In: BNC x 1, 1.0 Vp-p 75 Omega
- Mic In: XLR (CH1/CH2), balanced,
- Audio In: XLR (CH1/CH2), balanced, 10kOmega
- Timecode In: (option) 0.5 to 18 Vp-p, high impedance
- Camera Out: BNC x
- Video Out: BNC
- Audio Out: XLR (CH1/CH2/MIX selectable)
- Earphone: Stereo mini jack
- DC Out: 4-pin, DC 11V to 17V, Max. 0.1A
- Suggested List Price: $9,375

Panasonic AJ-D610WA DVCPRO

Key features include switchable aspect ratio between 16:9 and 4:3, Super-Iris for one-button backlighting.

3-2/3" CCDs, Synchro-Scan from 1/60.8 to 1/250 sec. for shooting computer monitors or electronic readouts.

Camera set-ups can be saved on a removable PCMCIA Memory card, allowing access to user-designed camera settings for given scenes, or matching multiple cameras.

- Power 12 VDC (11 V to 17 V), 24 Watts
- Weight 6.6 kg (14.5 lbs.)
- CCD: 3x 2/3" CCDs, 520,000 pixels
- Minimum Illumination 0.5 lux (F1.4, +36 dB gain)
- Shutter Speed 1/100, 1/120, 1/250, 1/500, 1/1000, 1/2000-sec.
- Synchro Scan 1/60.8 to 1/250-sec. (variable)
- Optical Filter 3200 K, 5600 K+1/8ND, 5600 K, 5600 K+1/64ND
- S/N Ratio 63 dB (standard)
- Lens Mount 2/3" bayonet mount
- Mic In XLR balanced,
- Audio In XLR (CH1/CH2), balanced,
- Genlock In/Video Return BNC
- Time Code In BNC
- Camera Out BNC
- Video Out BNC
- Audio Out XLR (Channnel 1/Channel 2/MIX selectable) balanced, low impedance
- Earphone Stereo mini jack (x 1)
- Timecode Out BNC
- DC Out 4-pin, 11 VDC to 17 V, 100 mA
- Suggested List Price: $14,500.00

Panasonic AJ-D700A DVCPRO

- 3-CCD 1/2" FIT 410,000 pixels
- 2 Lux minimum illumination
- SMPTE timecode reader/generator
- Under 13 lbs., under 24 W
- PCMCIA memory set-up card
- One touch camera status report
- Syncro scan electronic shutter
- Anton Bauer Gold Mount attached
- High resolution 1.5" viewfinder
- Suggested List Price: $15,700.00

Panasonic AJ-D810A DVCPRO

- High-sensitivity 2/3" IT-3-CCD
- 2-Channel PCM audio system and cue audio recording
- "SUPER GAIN" enables 0.2-Lux shooting illumination
- "SUPER IRIS" for one-button backlight
- Scene file on PCMCIA SRAM card
- Synchro scan electronic shutter
- Auto white and auto black balance
- Color bar and audio reference signal output
- One-touch camera status report function
- One-touch rec review function
- Built-in SMPTE time code generator/reader and TC IN/TC OUT connectors (BNC)
- Analog video input (BNC) and audio line input (XLR x 2CH)
- Large, high-resolution 1.5" EVF
- Built-in gen-lock function
- Phantom power supply (48-VDC phantom mic)
- Built-in monitor speaker
- Suggested List Price: $18,750.00

Panasonic AJ-D910WA DVCPRO/DVCPRO50

Switchable from 16:9 to 4:3, and between DVCPro25 and DVCPro50 (the faster, better 4:2:2 format).

- Three 2/3" high sensitivity IT CCDs
- 2/3-inch CCDs are compatible with existing 2/3-inch lenses
- 16:9 / 4:3 and DVCPRO/ DVCPRO50 switchable
- 33 minutes record time (66 minutes in DVCPRO)
- Uses industry-standard PCMCIA scene memory card (Optional)
- Synchro Scan: 1/60.3 ~ 1/253.4 sec. for shooting PC screens
- 10-bit digital signal processing
- Optional field production system stores shot logging data in camera memory and records it on tape during the eject cycle. Information can be read by Panasonic's newsBYTE 4X transfer DVCPRO NLE system.
- High gain mode selectable up to 46dB
- Signal-to-noise ratio of 63dB and minimum illumination of 0.2 lux
- Power consumption: less than 28 watts
- Weighs 15 pounds in full-operating condition
- Built-in color bar generator with tone and ID
- Optional 26-pin VTR interface
- Dual filter wheel
- Record video/genlock input connector
- List Price: $24,200.00

Sony Professional

Sony DSR-250

The DSR-250 is the least expensive shoulder-resting camcorder from Sony's Broadcast and Professional Division. For a little more than the price of a PD150, and not much heavier, you can have the comfort of a camera that snuggles on your shoulder all day for well-balanced handheld shooting. It accepts both Mini DVCAM and MiniDV cassettes, and the larger Standard sizes. This makes it a perfect camera for wedding videographers, event, educational and corporate users. It's perfect for schools to record graduations, school plays and sports events.

The DSR-250 has a built-in 2.5" color 200K dot (880 x 228 pixel) LCD that flips out from the rear operator's side. This is a welcome addition rarely found on professional camcorders. The 1.5" black and white viewfinder has 600 lines of horizontal resolution. The viewfinder and the monitor can operate at the same time, which can be helpful, for example, alternately checking focus in the viewfinder and operating a low angle handheld shot. Additionally, the operator can use the viewfinder while the audio person watches the frame line, or the producer watches the shot on the LCD screen. Menu settings and audio levels can be superimposed on the LCD viewing screen.

There are three 1/3" CCDs with 380,000 pixels providing interlace scan for moving video, and progressive scan for stills. The chips have a 4:3 shape, so shooting 16:9 will use a smaller, masked picture area. The lens is a fixed 12x zoom, with Super Steady Shot to optically stabilize the image. The DSR-250 captures still images as JPEG files on a Memory Stick at 640 x480 resolution.

SMPTE timecode can be reset to Hours/Minutes/Seconds/Frames, in Record-Run or Free-Run. Free-Run timecode is often used on multiple camera setups, where each camera is jam-synced to a master clock, so each camera is recording the same timecode time of day. This helps the editor find corresponding angles of the same scene.

The DSR-250 uses the Sony BP-L40, BP-L60, and BP-L90 Lithium-Ion batteries that mount directly to the back of the camcorder. A single BP-L90 will power the camcorder for about nine hours. Anton Bauer batteries can be attached with the optional QR-DSR Gold Mount.

DSR250 Specs

- 3 1/3" CCDs with 380,000 pixels, interlace for video; progressive for stills
- Lens 12:1 Variable Speed
- Filter size: 58mm
- Focus Auto/Manual/Infinity/One push auto
- White Balance Auto/One-push/Outdoor (5800K)/Indoor (3200K)
- Shutter Speed 1/4, 1/8, 1/15, 1/30, 1/60, 1/90, 1/100, 1/125, 1/180, 1/250, 1/350, 1/500, 1/725, 1/1000, 1/1500, 1/2000, 1/3000, 1/4000, 1/6000, 1/10000 sec
- Exposure Auto, Manual
- Minimum Illumination 2 lux
- Horizontal Resolution 530 horizontal lines
- Audio Signal Record: 48 kHz/16 bit, 32 kHz/12 bit
  Playback: 48 kHz/16 bit, 32 kHz/12 bit, 32 kHz/16 bit, 44.1 kHz/16 bit
- LCD Monitor TFT active matrix, 2.5" (880x228)
- Custom Presets: Color Level, Sharpness, WB, AGC
- Digital Effects: Still, Flash Motion, Luminance Key, Trail, Old Movie
- Audio Record Level: Ch 1, Ch 2, Mix
- Zebra: 100%, 70%

Sony DSR250 Manual controls:

- Zoom: optical 12:1, digital 24:1 or 48:1
- Focus: switchable to auto
- Iris: with lens ring
- Shutter Speed: 1/4 to 1/10,000 sec
- Gain: H,M,L
- White Balance: Preset, A, B
- ND Filter: 1/4 & 1/32
- List price $5900.00

I/O Connections

- Analog Video Inputs Composite (RCA) x 1, Y/C (S-video) x 1
- Analog Video Outputs Composite (RCA) x 1, Y/C (S-video) x 1
- Digital Video I/O i-Link (IEEE1394 - 6 pin)
- Audio I/O RCA x 2 (Line level), XLR (3-pin female) x 2 (Mic/Line/Mic with +48V power)
- Lanc Control (L-control) Stereo mini-mini jack
- Power DC 12V (11 to 17V), 10.5 Watts with viewfinder, 12.1 Watts with viewfinder and LCD
- Dimensions 241.7 x 251.2 x 508.8mm (WxHxD) 9 5/8 x 10 x 20 1/8" (WxHxD)
- Weight 4.4kg 9lb 11oz

Accessories

- BP-L40 Lithium-Ion Battery
- BP-L60 Lithium-Ion Battery
- BP-L90 Lithium-Ion Battery
- BC-L50 Battery Charger
- AC-DN2 AC Adaptor
- QR-DSR Anton Bauer Gold Mount
- HyTRON 50 Anton Bauer NiMH 50 Watt/Hour Battery
- D-2401 Anton Bauer Charger/AC Adaptor
- UL-26 Anton Bauer On Camera Light
- MSA-8A 8MB Memory Stick
- MSA-16A 16MB Memory Stick
- MSA-32A 32MB Memory Stick
- MSA-64A 64MB Memory Stick
- MSAC-PC2 PC card adaptor for Memory Stick
- MSAC-FD2M Floppy Disk Adaptor for Memory Stick
- VCL-HG1758 Tele Conversion Lens 1.7X
- VCL-HG0758 Wide Conversion Lens 0.7X
- VF-58PK Filter Kit
- VMC-IL4615 1.5m 4-pin to 6-pin i.Link cable
- VMC-IL6615 1.5m 6-pin to 6-pin i.Link cable

Sony DSR-300

The DSR300 is the next step up from
the DSR250, providing removable
lenses and more features. It's a 1/2"
DVCAM/DV camera that accepts
Mini and Standard cassettes.

The camera incorporates a jog dial
that controls the viewfinder menu.
To select the desired menu item, set
the value with a one-fingered turn of
the jog dial.

Unlike the 250, the DSR300 does not
have a flip-out LCD screen. However,
an on-board monitor can easily be
connected to the BNC monitor output
connector.

Sony's DynaLatitude Function adjusts the contrast of the pixels, and the Skin
Detail Function controls the area of detail by using a cursor on the viewfinder
screen and then pushing the Skin Set button. Black Stretch/Compress Function
variably adjusts contrast in the black area of the picture.

EZ Focus opens the lens iris for critical focus. When the iris is opened, the shutter
speed is automatically increased to maintain correct exposure. EZ Focus turns off
while recording. There is also the EZ Mode autopilot control, which can be
customized to user settings. Clear Scan is used to shoot computer monitors by
selecting one of 183 shutter speeds that match the scanning frequency of the
computer display.

Specs
- CCD: 3x 1/2" CCDs
- Built In Filters:
  1: 3200K/3000K (switchable)
  2: 5600K +1/8ND
  3: 5600K
  4: 5600K +1/64ND
- Lens Mount: 1/2" Bayonet Mount
- Horizontal Resolution: 800 Lines, Vertical Resolution 400 Lines
- Minimum illumination: 0.5 Lux at f/1.4, Hyper gain (30dB+DPR)

- Sensitivity: F11 at 2000 Lux
- Gain Selector: -3 dB, 0 dB, + 3 dB, + 6 dB, + 9 dB, + 12 dB, + 18 dB, + 18 dB +DPR, + 24 dB, + 24 dB +DPR, Hyper Gain (30 db+DPR)
- Shutter Speeds: 1/100, 1/250, 1/500, 1/1000, 1/2000 sec.
- S/N Ratio: 62 dB
- Power: DC 12 Volts (11-17v)
- Power Consumtion: 22.1 with viewfinder
- Battery Run Time: BP-L40 battery 80 min, BP-L60A 180 min, BP-L90A 290 min
- Weight 12 lbs 9 oz (with Viewfinder, Lens, Mic,and BP-L40 battery,)
- Audio Frequency Response: 48kHz: 20Hz to 20kHz. 32kHz: 20Hz to 14.5kHz
- Dynamic Range: More than 80 dB
- Inputs: Genlock Video Input BNC, Time Code Input: BNC
- Mic Input: XLR 3-Pin
- External Audio Input: CH-1/2: XLR 3-pin Female
- Outputs i-Link (IEEE1394)
  26-pin: (Composite, Component, S-Video)
- Composite Video Out: BNC
  S-Video Output: 4-pin
  Monitor Output: BNC
- Time Code Output: BNC
- Audio Output CH-1/2: RCA Others DC In: 4-pin XLR Male
- DC Out: 4-pin XLR Female
- Earphone: Mini-Jack
- Light Out: 2-pin Female
- List $9,900.00

- **Optional Accessories**
  RM-VJ1: Remote Mic/LCD & Camcorder Cntrl
  WRR-855A64: Portable UHF Synthesized Tuner (Ch 64)
  WRR-855A66: Portable UHF Synthesized Tuner (Ch 66)
  WRR-855A: Portable Plug-in Diversity Receiver
  CA-WR855: Case for WRR-855A Receiver
  CAC-12: Microphone Holder
  AC-DN2APAC: AC Power Supply/Charger
  BC-1WD: Battery Charger (NP1 Type)
  BC-L100: 4 Position Lith-Ion Battery Charger (BPL Type)
  BC-L50: 2 Position Lith-Ion Battery Charger (BPL Type)
  BPL-40: Lith-Ion 40 Watt/Hour Battery
  BPL-60A: Lith-Ion 60 Watt/Hour Battery
  BPL-90A: Lith-Ion 90 Watt/Hour Battery
  NP-1B: 2.3 amp Ni-Cad Battery
  AC-550: AC Adaptor
  CMA-8A: AC Adaptor
  DXF-51: 5" Studio Viewfinder

Sony DSR-500WSL

Sony Professional's DSR-500WS camcorder is intended for news, event and high-end corporate users. The three 2/3" CCDs are shaped in a "native" 16:9 format, so shooting widescreen is not the compromise of conventional 4:3 chips which mask out part of the picture area. With 16:9 chips, shooting 4:3 is the format that actually uses fewer pixels. The camera accepts DVCAM and DV cassettes in both Mini and Standard sizes.

The camera will be familiar to professionals who have shot BetaSP, DigiBeta or HD. The camera uses interchangeable lenses. SMPTE timecode can be re-set and jam-synced.

An "Enhanced Skin Tone Detail Correction" reduces wrinkles in skin areas by electronically controlling saturation and hue of skin area only. A good makeup person is still recommended.

The status of camera settings can be automatically recorded onto DVCAM cassette tape while shooting, and can be reviewed during playback. "EZ Mode" is for autopilot over-ride for fast shooting without setup.

- CCD: 3 x 2/3" 16:9 (switchable to 4:3)
- Lens Mount: Sony 2/3" Bayonet Mount
- Built In Filters: 3200K
  5600K + 1/8 ND
  5600K
  5600K + 1/64 ND
- Zebra 1 setting: 70 to 90 IRE control
- Zebra 2 setting: more than 100% video
- Sensitivity: F11 @ 2000 Lux
- Minimum Illumination: 0.5 Lux with F1.4 + Gain 30dB
  0.8 Lux with F1.8 + Gain 30dB
- Gain Selection: -3dB, 0dB, +3dB, 6+dB, +9dB, +12dB, +18dB, +24dB, +30 dB
- Horizontal Resolution: 700 Lines in 16:9 format (Equivalent to 900 lines when using 4:3 CCDs with the same pixel count in 4:3 aspect ratio)
- Horizontal Resolution: 700 Lines in 4:3 format
- Signal To Noise Ratio: 63dB VTR
- Uses mini and standard DV or DVCAM tapes
- Analog Video Output: Composite (BNC x 1)
  Y/C S-Video (Din 4 pin S-Video x 1)
  Monitor Out Composite (BNC x 1)
- Digital Video Output: i.Link (6 pin IEEE1394 DV type)
- Analog Input: Composite (BNC x 1 with optional DSBK501 Pool Feed Board)
- Audio Output: Earphone (Mini Plug)
- Audio Input: Ch 1/Ch 2 (XLR 3-pin Female x 2)

- Connections: Remote 1 (10 pin)
  Remote 2 (Mini Plug)
  Time Code In (BNC)
  Time Code Out (BNC)
  DC Output for Anton Bauer UL-2 Light
- Power Requirements: DC 12V (11 to 17V)
- Power Consumption: 27.1 Watts (With Viewfinder)
- Dimensions: 4 7/8" x 7 5/8" x 11 1/8" (body only)
- Weight: Approx. 13.9 lbs. (With VF, Mic, Battery, and Lens)
- List $16,800

- Optional Accessories:
  RCP-TX7 Remote Control Panel
  RM-M7G Handy Remote Control Panel
  RM-VJ1 Remote Control Unit
  CA-WR855 Camera Adaptor For WRR-855A
  WRR-855A UHF Synthesized Tuner
  DSBK-301A Index Picture Board
  DSBK-501 Analog Composite Input Board
  CAC-12 Microphone Holder
  DXF-51 5" B/W Viewfinder (Service part number A-8274-968-A Is Required To Attach)
  LCR-1 Rain Cover
  2/3" Bayonet Style Lens
- Power Accessories:

AC:
AC-550 AC Adaptor
CMA-8A AC Power Adaptor
AC-DN1 On Board AC Adaptor (for operation under 38W)
AC-DN2A AC Adaptor (for operation under 150W)

DC:
BC-L50 Battery Charger (for Sony Li-ion batteries)
BC-L100 Battery Charger (for Sony Li-ion batteries)
BP-L40 Wedge Mount Style Li-ion Battery
BP-L60 Wedge Mount Style Li-ion Battery
BP-L90 Wedge Mount Style Li-ion Battery
NP-1B Nicad Style Battery (requires DC-L1 battery case)
BP-90A Nicad Style Battery (requires DC-L90 battery case)
QRDSR Anton Bauer Gold Mount (required to use Anton Bauer Nicad or NiMH batteries)

Studio Rigs: JVC and Panasonic

Appendix

Appendix

Suppliers by Name and Address

A & C Ltd   (Powerpod)
83 Headstone Road
Harrow, Middx HA1 2PQ England
0181-427-5168   fax: 0181-861-2469
www.powerpod.co.ukinfo@powerpod.co.uk
(US Distr: Isaia & Co.)

A & J Manufacturing Co.
11121 Hindry Avenue
Los Angeles, CA 90009
(213) 678-3053800-537-4000
fax: 310-216-2694
www.ajcases.com

Adobe Systems Inc.
345 Park Avenue
San Jose, California 95110-2704 USA
408-536-6000
www.adobe.com

Alfred Chrosziel Film-Technik GMBH
Regerstr. 27
D-8000 Munich 90 Germany
phone: 089-448 03 39 fax: 089-447 08 61

American Society of Cinematographers
1782 North Orange Drive
Hollywood, CA 90028
(213) 876-5080
www.cinematographer.com

Amphibico (underwater housings)
459 Deslauriers
Montreal, Quebec, Canada H4N 1W2
Phone: (514) 333-8666 Fax: (514) 333-1339
info@amphibico.com
www.amphibico.com

Angenieux Corporation of America
7700 North Kendall Drive
Suite 303
Miami, FL 33156
(305) 595-1144

Anton/Bauer
One Controls Drive
Shelton, CT 06484
(203) 929-1100

Apple Computer, Inc.
1 Infinite Loop
Cupertino, CA 95014
408-996-1010
www.apple.com

Aquaseal Watersport Silicone
Food Grade, available in Scuba Stores
McNett Outdoor
Bellingham, WA 98227

Automated Media Systems
(Expedition Lithium Batteries)
8 Holton St.
Allston, MA 02134
617-787-4313
www.automatedmedia.com

Avid Technology, Inc.
Metropolitan Technology Park
1 Park West
Tewksbury, MA 01876
800-949-AVID
www.avid.com

BDS Rigidised Cases
(formerly SamCine Cases)
39-41 Lonsdale Road
Kilburn, London NW6 6RA Great Britain
tel: 071 624 2134 fax: 071 624 1331
(and)
Units 18-20, Westbrook Road
Trafford ark Manchester M17 1AY Great Britain
tel: 061 873 8181 fax: 061 876 6599

Beachtek (audio mixers and
accessories)
416-690-9457
www.beachtek.com

Bel-Air Plastics Inc.   (cases)
9938 Hayward Way
South El Monte, CA 91733
(818) 575-8765

Birns & Sawyer
1026 North Highland Avenue
Hollywood, CA 90038
(213) 466-8211   fax (213) 466-7049
www.birnsandsawyer.com

Calzone Case Co.
225 Black Rock Ave.
Bridgeport, CT   06605
(203) 367-5766   800-243-5152
fax: (203) 336-4406

Canon USA
1 Canon Pl
Lake Success NY 11042
1-800-OK-CANON
www.canondv.com

Canopus Corporation
711 Charcot Avenue
San Jose, CA 95131
408-954-4500
www.canopuscorp.com

Cartoni USA
2755 Alamo Street, suite 103
Simi Valley, CA 93065
805-520-6086800-845-6619

Cartoni S.p.A.
Via Giuseppe Mirri
13-00159 Rome, Italy
39.06.4382002fax: 39.06.43588293
www.cartoni.com

Century Precision Optics
11049 Magnolia Blvd
North Hollywood, CA 91601
(818) 766-3715800-228-1254
fax: (818) 505-9865

Christie Electric, Corp.
18120 South Broadway
Gardena, CA 90248
(310) 715-1402   Fax: (310) 618-8368

Chiswick Trading, Inc.   (plastic bags)
31 Union Ave
Sudbury, MA 01776
800-225-8708   fax: (617) 443-8091

Chrosziel
(see Alfred Chrosziel Film Technik)

Cinetech
Karl Horn
719 Arroyo Ave / Unit C
San Fernando, CA 91340
365-0799 fax: (818) 365-8531

CP Rigidised Cases
Worton Hall Industrial Estate
Worton Rd, Isleworth
Middlesex TW7 6ER England
tel: 44-81-568-1881fax: 44-81-568-1141

Coolzoom (remote zoom controls)
Cool Contraptions
25819 Anderson Lane
Stevenson Ranch, CA 91381
fax: 661-288-1808www.coolzoom.com

Coptervision (Model Helicopter)
7625 Hayvenhurst Ave. #36
Van Nuys, CA 91460
310-472-6462   fax: 310-471-4801
www.coptervision.com

Cooke Optics Ltd. (Lenses)
P.O. Box 36, New Star Road   Thurmaston Lane
Leicester LE4 7JQ England
44-116-276-4510fax: 44-116-246-3151
USA: 973-335-4460fax: 973-335-4560

Edmund Scientific Co.
101 E. Gloucester Pike
Barrington, NJ 08007
(609) 573-6250   fax: (609) 573-6295

Edmunds, Larry Bookshop
6658 Hollywood Blvd.
Hollywood, CA 90028
(213) 463-3273

Focal Press
781-904-2500   www.focalpress.com

Focus Optics (lens repairs)
18730 Oxnard St., unit 216
Tarzana, CA 91356
818-757-1007   800-234-LENS
fax: 818 757-1029focusoptic@aol.com

Hale Color Consultants(gray scales)
1505 Phoenix Road
Phoenix, MD 21131
(301) 472-4850   (800) 777-1225

Harrison & Harrison Optical Eng.
677 North Plano St.
Porterville, CA   93257
(209) 782-0121   fax: (209) 782-0824

Ikelite (underwater housings and equipment)
50 West 33rd. Street
Indianapolis, IN 46208
317-923-4523
Fax: 317-924-7988
ikelite@ikelite.com

Jensen Tools Inc.
7815 S. 46 Street
Phoenix, AZ 85044
(602) 968-6231 or 968-6251

JVC Company of America
1700 Valley Road
Wayne, NJ 07470
(800) 526-5308
Parts Orders (Continental USA)
Toll-free phone 1-800-882-2345
Customer Relations 1-800-252-5722
Authorized Service Locator 1-800-537-5722

Kaleidoscope Hot Head
128 Wembley Park Drive
Wembley, Middlesex, England
01-902-1262

Kish Optics
4653 Lankershim Blvd.
North Hollywood, CA 91602
818-506-5800   fax: 818-506-5856

Lemsford Metal WorksLemsford Rigidised Cases
Mill Works - Lemsford
Welwyn Garden City
Herts. AL8 7TW England
0707-323725 or 0707-322461
fax: 0707-373059

Lentequip Inc.
181 Carlaw Avenue, Ste. 250
Toronto, Ontario Canada M4M 2S1
416-406-2442 fax: 416-406-2443
www.lentequip.com

Light & Motion Industries (underwater housings)
300 Cannery Row
Monterey, CA 93940
831-645-1525 (phone) 831-375-2517 (fax)
sales@lmindustries.com
support@lmindustries.com
www.uwimaging.com/

Markertek Video Supply (foam Swabs)
145 Ulster Ave
Saugerties, NY 12477
(800) 522-2025   fax: (914) 246-1757

Matrox Electronic Systems
1055 St. Regis Blvd
Dorval, Quebec Canada, H9P 2T4
800-361-4903
www.matrox.com

Matsushita (Panasonic Consumer
Division, Video Cameras)
201-348-7000
One Panasonic Way
Secaucus, NJ 07094
www.panasonic.com

Media 100 USA
290 Donald Lynch Blvd.
Marlboro, MA 01752
phone: 508-460-1600
www.media100.com

Media 100 Software Division
15951 Los Gatos Blvd., Ste. 1
Los Gatos, CA 95032
phone: 408-356-7373

Miller-Stephenson MS-943 Safe Zone Degreaser
(replacement for tri-chlor)
George Washington Highway
Danby, CT 06810
203-743-4447   818-896-4714

Nalpak (Magliners, Accessories)
1937-C Friendship Drive
El Cajon, CA 92020
tel: (619) 258-1200 fax: (619) 258-0925

NRG Research Inc.(battery vest)
840 Rogue River Hwy.
Building 144
Grants Pass, OR 97527
503-479-9433

O'Connor Engineering Laboratories
100 Kalmus Drive
Costa Mesa, Ca 92626
(714) 979-3993fax: 714-957-8138
www.ocon.com

Optex
22-26 Victoria Road
New Barnet, Herts EN4 9PF England
+434 (0) 181 441 2199
Fax: +44 181 449 3646
www.optexint.com

Panasonic (see Matsushita)

Pancro Mirrors Inc.
12734 Branford St unit #7
Los Angeles, CA 91331-4230
tel: 818-834-2926fax: 818-834-2027
Pancro Lens Fluid
www.pancro.com

Pelican Products
23215 Early Ave.
Torrance, CA 90505
310-326-4700
www.pelican.com

Pinnacle Systems Inc.
280 North Bernardo Ave.
Mountain View, CA 94043
800-474-6622
www.pinnaclesys.com

ProMax Systems (DV systems—Mac and PC)
16 Technology Drive
Suite 106
Irvine, CA 92618
800-977-6629
www.promax.com

Pro Power(NiMH Batteries)
912 South Glenoaks Blvd
Burbank, CA 91502
800-577-67691544

Rank Taylor Hobson Ltd. see: Cooke

Sachtler AG
Gutenbergstrasse 5   D-85716
Unterschleissheim Munich, Germany
Tel. 49-89-321-58-223 or -00 Fax. 49-89-321-58-227

Sachtler Corporation of America
55 N. Main Street
Freeport, NY 11520
(516) 867-4900
and
3316 W. Victory Blvd.
Burbank, CA 91505
(818) 845-4446

Scubacam Ltd
Marine House
Adj. 1 Reynolds Road
Chiswick, London W4 5AR
Tel: +(44) 181-987 8681Fax: +(44) 181-987 8922
www.scubacam.co.uk
US Dealer: Isaia and Co.

Seacam Subsea Systems (underwater housings)
Tel: 714.848.6919 Fax: 714.848.6919
16101 Windemeir Ln.
Huntington Beach, CA 92647-3446 U.S.A
sales@seacamsys.com
www.seacamsys.com

Sharp Camcorders
1-800-237-4277
www.sharp-usa.com

Skydance Photography (helmets)

Steve Wood
P.O. Box 131503
Roseville, MN 55113
Phone: (651)488-0115
Fax: (651)488-0414
sdphoto@aol.com
http://www.pia.com/skydance

Sony Broadcast and Professional Co
Sony Electronics Inc.
1 Sony Drive
Park Ridge, NJ 07656-8003
(201) 930-1000
www.sony.com

Sony Electronics, Inc.
(consumer camcorders)
800 222-7669
www.sony.com

Studio 1 Productions (XLR audio input adapters)
800-788-0068
www.studio1productions.com
3956 Town Center Blvd PMB 159,
Orlando, FL. 32837
407-812-1225
www.studio1productions.com

Tao Systems RS-422 Control Box
To Control DV decks with Avid, Media 100 and
Premiere
www.taosys.com/
888-826-2620

Tiffen Manufacturing Corp.
90 Oser Ave.
Hauppauge, NY   11788
(516) 273-2500

Transvideo (LCD TFT Monitors)
10700 Ventura Blvd. #2A
North Hollywood, CA 91604
818-985-4903fax: 818-985-4921
www.transvideointl.com
France: +33 (0) 2 3232 2761
           fax: +33 (0) 2 3260 1479

Tyler Camera Systems
14218 Aetna Street
Van Nuys, CA 91401
(818) 989-4420

Velcro USA, Inc.
Manchester, NH 03108

Wide screen software(SunPath software)
7838 Saint Clair Ave
N. Hollywood, CA 91605
tel: 818-765-6037
fax: 818. 764. 3639
sunPath sun position software for Mac and PC
widescreen@pobox.com
http://pobox.com/~widescreen

ZGC Inc.(Cooke lenses, Optex in US)
264 Morris Avenue
Mountain Lakes, NJ 07046
973-335-4460
fax: 201-335-4560l
Cooke, Optex, lenses

Tape to Film Facilities (Partial List)

Black Logic
(division of Tape House)
305 East 46 Street
New York, NY 10017
212-557-2929
www.blacklogic.com

Cineric, Inc. (Solitaire Cine III FLX)
630 Ninth Avenue, Suite 508
New York, NY 10036
212.586.4822
www.cineric.com

Colour Film Services Ltd
10 Wadsworth Road
Perivale
Greenford, Middlesex
UB6 7JX England
Telephone: + 44 (0)20 8998 2731
www.colourfilmservices.co.uk

DuArt Film & Video
245 West 55 Street
New York, NY 10019
245 W. 55th St. NY, NY 10019
212.757.4580
800.52.DuART
www.duart.com

DVFilm
2317 Spring Wagon Ln
Austin, Texas 78728
512-252-2343
http://www.dvfilm.com

Four Media Corporation (4MC)
2820 West Olive Avenue
Burbank, California 91505-4455
Sales 818-840-7119
818 985 7566
800 423 2652 Toll Free
www.4MC.com

Sony Pictures High Definition Center
(HD to Film)
Culver City, California
35mm Only
310 280 7433 Tel
310 280 4389 Fax
www.sphdc.com

SWISS EFFECTS
Thurgauerstr. 40
CH-8050 Zurich
Tel. ++41 / 1 / 307 10 10
Fax. ++41 / 1 / 307 10 19
www.swisseffects.ch
Paris ++33 / 6 / 07 10 42 82
New York ++1 / 212 / 727 36 95

Web Resources

www.2-pop.com/boards/board.html?cameras.cgi
www.2-pop.com

www.dvformat.com
www.digitalmedianet.com
www.pcconnection.com

www.pcphotomag.com

Test patterns and color bars (Mac
only) www.synthetic-ap.com/

Credits

Above all, I would like to thank Noemi and Marlena Fauer, wonderful wife and terrific daughter—for all their help and patience.

I would like to extend special thanks to all the people who helped me with this book, generously sharing time and expertise.

At Focal Press: Marie Lee, who instigated all of this; Lilly Roberts, editor—who was always polite even after I missed the deadline; Christine Degon, marketing manager, who quickly had publicity postcards printed to make up for the missed NAB 2001 release date; Maura Kelly, production editor, for her usual excellent job; and Sherri Dietrich for the punctilious proofreading and punctuation correction.

Manuscript content was checked by Jim Pfeiffer and Howard Phillips. Howard has been one of my greatest sources of DV information over the year, with his almost-daily update on DV developments, French cinema technology, restaurant reviews, film history, and valuable introductions to industry notables. I look forward to reading a book on film history by Howard.

The wealth of information on Sony equipment would not have been possible without my friend Ed Grebow, President of Sony Broadcast and Professional Company, who paved the way and introduced me to many incredibly helpful people. Special thanks to Bob Christie for all the work, demo equipment and technical help. And thanks to Leslie Shearn, Alec Shapiro, Carol Whisker, and John Travers of Kollins Communications for Sony photos.

Lots of photos were needed for this book. They would not be here without:

Rosemary Flynn and Gretchen Griswold of Sony Electronics (consumer DV camcorders).

Bill Kupferle of Panasonic Broadcast and Television Systems Company Marketing Department—for photos and technical information.

Tom McKay of Varizoom. Mike Virgintino of Canon USA.

At AVID: Howard Phillips, Michael Phillips, Charlie Russell, Alan Hoff, Alan Stewart. Michael Phillips, author of *Digital Filmmaking*—helped me understand nonlinear editing, 24p, and Avid. See his website: www.24p.com for more.

Paulien Ruijssenaars, Director of Public Relations, Pinnacle Systems, Inc.

Steve Wood, Skydance Photography—for information and pictures of his Velocity Helmets.

Tom McKay of Varizoom.

Jessica Olsen of JVC Company of America.

Bill Meurer and Peter Anway at Birns and Sawyer.

At Digital Origin / Media 100: Jeff Bierly, Mike Micheletti.

Optex and ZGC pictures were supplied by Barbara Lowry of ZGC, Inc.

Bob Carr from Sachtler Corp of America

Film processing and budgeting help came from Charles Herzfeld of Technicolor.

An enormous amount of information came from Patrick Lindenmaier, DP and representative of Swiss Effects, who is one of the true luminaries of the DV world. Help on DV to film also came from Alfie Schloss of Black Logic in New York.

Greg Gilpatrick was the Final Cut Pro guru.

In preparing this book, I have used the following sources:

Books

American Cinematographer Manual. ASC Press

Arriflex 16SR Book. Jon Fauer. Focal Press. 1999

Arriflex 35 Book. Jon Fauer. Focal Press. 1999

The Book of Movie Photography. David Cheshire; Dorling Kindersley/Knopf 1979

Magazines

DV. www.dv.com

PC Photo Magazine, Digital Camera & Photo Buyers Guide. Werner Publishing Corp

Res. www.res.com

Videography. www.videography.com

American Cinematographer. www.cinematographer.com

Macworld. www.macworld.com

Mac Design. www.macdesignonline.com

Film & Video. www.filmandvideomagazine.com

"Future of Digital Entertainment." *Scientific American.* November 2000. www.sciam.com

Internet and Other

Internet Sources on Firewire

"FireWire." Bertel Schmitt, Alexei Gerulaitis. www.dvcentral.org/Firewire.html

"Firewire." www.apple.com

"Rallying Around the IEEE 1394." Terence Dyke, Paul Smolen. http://eagle.onr.com/aea/media/tvtech34.html

"MacInTouch FireWire Guide." www.macintouch.com

Adaptec website: www.adaptec.com

Internet Sources for DV Camcorders

B&H Photo/Video. New York store and mailorder. The best shopping guide. www.bhphotovideo.com

J&R Music World. NY store and mailorder. http://jandrmusicworld.com

Samy's Camera. LA store and mailorder. www.samys.com

PC and Mac Connection. Mailorder only. www.pcconnection.com

"The Search for the Ideal Handycam." Robert Harrison, *Videography*. Feb 2001

Other sources for the "Consumer Reports on DV Cameras" section: Digital Media, Sony, Canon, Panasonic, *PCPhoto*. Nov 2000. pg 78

Video to Film

"Video for Film Release." article by Alan Stewart at www.zerocut.com

"How to Transfer Video To Film." Chris Athanas. www.digieffects.com

"Tape to Film Transfers." Greg Pak. www.filmhelp.com

DV, DVCAM and DVCPRO Formats

"DV Formats." Adam Wilt, Roger Jennings. www.videouniversity.com/dvformat.htm

"DVCPRO." http://www.panasonic.com/PBDS/dvcpro_story/index.html

Final Cut Pro vs Avid XPress DV

Article by James Monahan. www.2-pop.com/library/articles/2000-07-14.html

Frank Capria review of editing software at DV.com

SCSI information

"The PC Guide" (www.PCGuide.com). Charles M. Kozierok.
www.sparcproductdirectory.com/scsiscsi.html

Ken Seibert of ATTO Technology.

Film and Video History

The History of Film. From a screenplay by Jon Fauer, in collaboration with Volker
Bahnemann, president, ARRI USA.

Recommended Reading

iMovie 2, The Missing Manual. David Pogue. O'Reilly & Assoc

Final Cut Pro for Macintosh. Lisa Brenneis. Peachpit Press

Quicktime Pro for Macintosh & Windows. Judith Stern, Robert Lettieri. Peachpit Press.

Digital Filmmaking. Thomas A. Ohanian and Michael E. Phillips. Focal Press

Avid Editing. Sam Kauffmann. Focal Press

The Avid Handbook. Steve Bayes. Focal Press

Every Frame a Rembrandt. Andrew Laszlo, ASC. Focal Press

Photos and Illustrations

I would like to thank the many companies and people who supplied photos. I acknowledge the registered trademarks and copyrights of the individual companies. Some corporate names have been shortened in this cross-reference. They are:

Avid Technology, Inc.
Adobe Systems, Inc.
Canon USA
JVC America
JVC Professional Products Company
Panasonic Broadcast and Television Systems Co.
Sony Broadcast and Professional Company

Photos and illustrations, appearing on the pages indicated, were provided courtesy of:

Adobe 132
Apple 113, 117, 125, 126, 177
ARRI 140, 141, 144
Avid 127

Beachtek 111

Canon 15, 16, 44, 107, 202, 203, 204, 205, 206, 208
Cartoni 174
Chrosziel 165

Ewa-Marine 183, 185

Fauer 10, 48, 57, 58, 60, 61, 62, 63, 64, 65, 66, 67, 68, 69, 70, 71, 72, 73, 74, 75, 77, 80, 81, 84, 87, 88, 89, 90, 92, 94, 95, 96, 97, 98, 107, 109, 110, 154, 163, 230

JVC 209, 211, 243, 244, 245, 260

Media 100 121
Miller 175, 176

Panasonic 153, 213, 214, 215, 216, 217, 218
Panasonic BTC 247, 248, 250, 251, 252, 260

Index

About the Author

Jon Fauer attended schools in Switzerland, graduated from Collegiate School in New York, and received degrees in art and film from Dartmouth College. He studied under Andrew Laszlo, ASC, Maurice Rapf, Joseph Losey, and Arthur Mayer.

At Dartmouth he began making medical films as part of his pre-med program, discovered he enjoyed film more than medicine, and, using short-ends to shoot ski films and dramatic short subjects, decided to make a career of it.

His first major film, *Wildwater*, commissioned by U.S. Kayak Team coach Jay Evans, featured the World Whitewater Championships in Merano, Italy. That film, and the numerous awards it won, led to documentaries around the world in the jungles of Guatemala, the mountains of New Zealand, and the Altiplano of Bolivia; from the North Pole for *American Sportsman* to the Chesapeake for *National Geographic*. His work led to membership in The Explorers Club of New York.

Documentary camerawork led to feature films and TV commercials. Among other credits, Fauer was Director of Photography on *Tales from the Darkside* and the title sequence for *Bonfire of the Vanities;* camera operator on *Splash* and *St. Elmo's Fire*; 2nd Unit Director of Photography on *All the Right Moves* and *Remo Williams.*

He has directed and shot hundreds of commercials worldwide. His work includes major campaigns for Sears, Canon, US Coast Guard, Snickers, Mercedes, Buick, Pontiac, Sony, and MCI, featuring the likes of Jennifer Love Hewitt, Lee Iacocca, Naomi Campbell, Jack Nicklaus, Arnold Palmer, Luis Garcia, John McEnroe, and Jesse the Chimpanzee.

He is a member of the Explorers Club, Directors Guild of America, International Cinematographers Guild and the American Society of Cinematographers.

Fauer lives in New York City and Southampton, NY, with his wife and daughter.

About the cover

It was my daughter Marlena's first sailboat race. It was my first time with a Sony PD100A camcorder. We were both beginners. I stood on the dock with the other sailing Dads, trying to pretend I knew which button to push on the camera. Marlena was fighting back tears because everyone had told her just to follow Jake, who had been in races before. However, Jake was in irons, flapping around at the starting line, while Marlena was improbably in the lead, trying to figure out which direction the windward buoy might be. There was much screaming "right of way," and "get out of my way." There was even more commotion on the dock, as everyone wanted to try out the camera and its glorious image stabilization at high magnification.

The boats were tiny Optimists. Southampton kids were sailing against Easthampton kids in tiny boats not much larger than your bathtub, with an insidious aluminum spar taking vindictive swipes at your unprotected head. Marlena had already earned hardest head award for most encounters by an eight year old and a boom. She finished the race a few boat lengths behind Jake, and by the end of the summer, had earned an award for most improved beginner.

I think I improved as well, testing all kinds of digital camcorders and learning about the new technology. The photo on the cover is a digital image taken directly from the DVCAM tape, converted to a TIF file, and composited by graphic artist Dick Hannus.

Companion Web Site

for updates, additions, corrections and feedback, go to

www.focalpress.com/companions